Only the People
Can Save the
People

Only the People Can Save the People

Constituent Power, Revolution, and Counterrevolution in Venezuela

Donald V. Kingsbury

SUNY
PRESS

Published by State University of New York Press, Albany

© 2018 State University of New York

For information, contact State University of New York Press, Albany, NY
www.sunypress.edu

Library of Congress Cataloging-in-Publication Data

Name: Donald V. Kingsbury, author
Title: Only the People Can Save the People : Constituent Power, Revolution, and
    Counterrevolution in Venezuela / Donald V. Kingsbury, author.
Description: Albany : State University of New York Press, [2018]
Includes bibliographical references and index.
Identifiers: ISBN 9781438469638 (hardcover   ) | ISBN 9781438469652 (e-book) |
    ISBN 9781438469645 (paperback   )
Further information is available at the Library of Congress

10 9 8 7 6 5 4 3 2 1

Contents

Figures

Preface

May 2017—This book was completed before the cycles of protest and counterprotest in April and May of 2017. Theorizing in the immediacy of the moment is always a dangerous proposition. Nonetheless, a few patterns developed throughout *Only the People Can Save the People* can shed some light on more recent events in Venezuela.

In February of 1989 a series of national uprisings centered in the capital, Caracas, triggered reverberations throughout Latin America and the world. Remembered since as the Caracazo, the spontaneous rebellion against harsh market reforms was quickly quashed. As many as three thousand—the exact figure remains a matter of intense debate—were lost in the crackdown as an ostensibly consolidated liberal democratic order was shattered. In the ensuing decades, Venezuelans once shunted to the margins of politics, economy, and society began constructing modes of collective life based neither on representation within the sovereign nation-state nor the prerogatives of the market—governing logics that had increasingly become entangled during the neoliberalization of Latin America's lost decades. These energies, this egalitarian, inclusive, and transformative *constituent power* that emerged after the collapse of Venezuela's Fourth Republic, are both the foundation and sustaining force of the Bolivarian Revolution.

After the election of Hugo Chávez in 1998, the process entered a new stage, recalibrating the state to the egalitarian desires that had triggered a rupture with Venezuela's past. However, these dynamics are never unidirectional. Nor are they complete. In the years preceding Chávez's death in 2013, the collapse of the international price in oil and centralizing trends within the government saw the Bolivarian Revolution become increasingly divided between demands from the grassroots to "build the commune" and the inward-focused logic of the state apparatus. During these years the political opposition made tentative steps away from their initial putschism only to return to a path of zero-sum destabilization after the death of El Comandante. Faced with increasingly strict structural constraints, the government of Nicolás Maduro turned to the military for support. The maintenance of state power became both the ends and means of securing a future for the Bolivarian Revolution.

It was always going to be a hot year in 2017. After the Maduro government neutralized attempts to initiate a presidential recall in 2016 and then postponed regional elections indefinitely, there was no other option for the perennially divided opposition but to take to the streets. National Assembly elections in 2015 delivered a near super majority for the opposition Mesa de la Unidad Democrática (Democratic Unity Roundtable, MUD), underlining Chavismo's secular decline in the ballot boxes that began in 2007. The deteriorating economic and security situations in Venezuela offered little by way of hope for the government that these tendencies could be reversed.

However, the opposition is still seen by many in Venezuela as a collection of elites intent on returning the country to the bad old days of structural adjustment and patterned inequalities. Events in Argentina and Brazil, where right-wing presidents took power by hook or by crook and immediately implemented harsh austerity measures and rapprochement with Washington, offered little inspiration for the poor to sign on to a program of popular neoliberalism. What is more, after nearly five years of protests against the government, the opposition still had little by way of organic ties to the crucial mass of supporters that would be needed to remove the Bolivarians from power. The government seemed settled on the same strategy that allowed it to weather the protests of 2014, which left forty-three dead: wait out the opposition; allow the population to grow tired of the violence, vandalism, and disruption; watch the leadership turn on itself as appeals for foreign intervention fail to find fruit.

Leading up to 2017's intensified waves of *guarimbas* (violent anti-government street protests) and international pressure—including Venezuela first being threatened with expulsion from the Organization of American States and then, later, initiating proceedings to pull itself out of the regional body—economic and social crises worsened. Inflation was projected to pass 700%. Murder rates remained high even by Venezuelan standards. The infiltration by drug cartels of the state security apparatus—and indeed, by most accounts, of the political leadership up to and including the office of the vice president—undermined trust in the rule of law. The Maduro administration continued to forge public-private partnerships, especially in extractive industries, and especially with foreign firms, despite speaking the language of economic sovereignty and productive socialism. In the face of these challenges opposition politicians insisted regime change was the only solution, reinforcing the government's narrative that they lacked a good faith partner in the search for a response to Venezuela's overlapping crises.

In January the opposition-controlled National Assembly attempted to nullify the presidency of Nicolás Maduro. Stating he had "abandoned his post," they called for immediate elections. A vacancy in state power must be filled; balance must be restored. Maduro called the move a coup that followed a months-long show trial in absentia and proclaimed that the actions of the National Assembly amounted to its self-dissolution. The military and Supreme Court closed ranks around him.

The Venezuelan state remained at war with itself.

The year's opening hostilities faded into the next almost without punctuation, much like the iterated crises that consumed the previous three years. Tit-for-tat posturing continued as the international media intensified sensationalist coverage of shortages in medicine and food. The government continued to blame the opposition and international conspiracies. The opposition continued to demand immediate presidential, state, and local elections. Talks organized by the Vatican and former presidents from Spain and Latin America between the two sides continued to falter. Spontaneous riots and looting—unconnected to any official political bodies—occurred with increasing frequency.

On March 29, 2017, the Supreme Court assumed several powers of the National Assembly. The legislature had been found in contempt of court months before, after seating three representatives found guilty of corruption and vote manipulation. The move by the Supreme Court was described as a means to ensure the continued rule of law, though many concluded its aims were more partisan in nature. Among its first acts was to transfer significant budgetary powers—including the ability to issue debt and create public-private enterprises in key strategic sectors—to President Maduro.

The opposition referred to the measure as nothing less than an *autogolpe* (self-coup). Of course, the dramatic impact of their pronouncement was somewhat blunted by nearly eighteen years of similar accusations. Their arguments—the dictatorship carried out a coup to install a dictatorship— were tautological. Their defense of the 1999 Constitution rang hollow: they had, after all, been trying to repeal it since its passage. However, the popular response to the March Supreme Court decision went beyond the usual antigovernment repertoire. Marches were massive. Resistance was fierce and well publicized by local and international media—but these have become normal in Venezuela, where both government and opposition regularly turn out thousands of supporters, often on the same day, often in the same cities. The difference with the Supreme Court's April surprise was the unprecedented breaking of ranks that occurred at the upper reaches of Chavismo when Attorney General Luisa Ortega Díaz declared the Court's move to have posed a rupture in the constitutional order. Less than forty-eight hours after the initial ruling, Maduro convened his national security council to review the situation. The Court was ordered to return most powers to the National Assembly—except, notably, for the budgetary powers his administration argued had been used to sabotage Venezuela's attempts to recover from the ongoing economic crisis.

Protests continued on a mass scale and a near-daily basis throughout this period in the affluent sectors of Venezuela's cities. Reports also began to circulate that the poor were taking action in their own districts, including gunfights between armed gangs and state security corps. One international headline, reportedly from the Chavista bastion of 23 de Enero in the west of Caracas, quoted a protestor as saying, "I won't vote for the opposition. Even less for Maduro" (García Marco 2017). The state, in other words, was losing the passive support that allowed it to weather the crises of 2014. While the Chavista base had yet to *salta la talanquera* (jump the fence) to the opposition, the specter of active defections presented itself more forcefully than ever before in the history of the Bolivarian project.

This dynamic—the self-referential logic of state, threat of exodus by a previously perceived captive base, constant protest, and international pressure—continued into May. Henrique Capriles, former opposition presidential candidate and governor of the state of Miranda, was barred from running for office for fifteen years on charges of corruption. Julio Borges (president of the National Assembly) and Lilian Tintori (the wife of jailed opposition leader Leopoldo López) traveled to Washington for photo ops and promises of aid from the Trump administration. Every opposition figurehead called openly for a military coup. The Maduro administration announced plans to expand the national civilian militia and began charging antigovernment protestors in military tribunals. Videos on social media showing the president getting pelted by eggs and garbage at an event commemorating the battle of San Félix went viral. Progovernment accounts claimed the same footage was manipulated, and that what was actually taking place was a pueblo showing its love for the president.

Then, on May Day, Maduro announced he had decided to convoke a National Constituent Assembly (ANC, its abbreviation in Spanish). The way out of the country's latest crisis, he declared, was to restructure the governing powers of the nation and to "constitutionalize the new forms of participatory and protagonistic democracy" (Presidencia de la República 2017). The decree also contained a number of other admirable goals, many borrowed from other twenty-first-century Latin American constitutions: the recognition of the state as pluricultural, recognition of the rights of nature, the need to move to a post-extractivist economy, incorporation of the commune as a jurisdictional entity, the cementing of the state's social role through the Bolivarian Missions, among others (Presidencia de la República 2017) Maduro's declaration, in other words, referenced many objectives stated by radicals and grassroots activists who had become frustrated by the hungry, and often bloody, impasses of constituted power that characterized his administration.

And yet, concerns were immediately raised at the announcement. Unlike the process leading up to the 1999 National Constituent Assembly, Maduro's announcement was unexpected. Prior to his proclamation, the only calls for a new constitution had been issued from the opposition, who of course described the May announcement as yet another *autogolpe*. In 1999 the ANC had been carried out after mass public consultation. Delegates were chosen by universal and secret ballot. The 2017 process was from the outset much murkier. It was convoked unilaterally at the behest of the president. Over half of the allotted delegates were slotted to be chosen as representatives of state-identified sectors—communes, youth, minorities, and so forth. Finally, it was less than certain that the final document, if realized, would be subjected to a popular referendum, as had been the case in 1999. While important gestures were made toward deepening the Bolivarian Revolution, in other words, the 2017 ANC looked much more like constituted power attempting to circumnavigate obstacles of its own creation than a return to the constituent power of its founding.

Constituent power persists. It haunts, it challenges, and it creates possibilities. It cannot be neutralized, and only temporarily contained or managed. This is its virtue as much as its challenge. The events of mid-2017 illustrate the degree to which constituent power remains the most powerful legitimating myth of the modern republican age. For a time, the Bolivarian Revolution illustrated the degree to which it is also the most powerful creative force of collective life. The present conjuncture, however, is defined by reaction, crisis, and stagnation. The moment may indeed call for another constituent rupture, one beyond the promises of the government and the opposition. As ever, though, constituent power remains fickle, its egalitarian desires resisting virtuous and cynical overdeterminations in equal measure.

For its part, constituted power is entirely reactive. It can be positively or negatively so—following the lead of egalitarian desires or shoring up the defenses of the narrowly privileged—but reactive nonetheless. *Only the People Can Save the People* traces these dynamics in Venezuela between the Caracazo and the reversals of 2016. It asks how constituent power has and has not lived up to perceived wisdom on the political in the post-neoliberal age, how power flows through resistance, subjectivity, infrastructure space, and time. Foreshadowing the book's interventions, I would like to offer three interrelated and contingent observations, or perhaps three elaborations on a theme, on the events of 2017.

First, Maduro's May 2017 convoking of the ANC illustrates the unique tension between constituent and constituted power that has always driven the Bolivarian Revolution. Context matters, however, and the context of the president's unilateral attempt to potentially push Venezuela into its Sixth Republic are cause for concern. Even before the Caracazo, Chávez conceptualized Bolivarianismo as a civic-military alliance. While the coordination of grassroots movements and military discipline would always be a difficult task, if successful it promised to marshal the demographic mass of the excluded, the moral force of the pueblo, and the effectiveness of military order to transform Venezuela. This alliance was conceived as following the dynamics of constituent power unleashed by the Caracazo. It was a constitution in the sense of a noun—the Constitution of the Bolivarian Republic of Venezuela of 1999—and a verb—the constant act of constituting an institutional order capable of fulfilling Simón Bolívar's dream of a truly free and independent republic. As in Bolívar's nineteenth century, however, Bolivarianism of the twenty-first has often privileged order and stability over creation and movement. While the unconquerable tension lingers between these two poles of the political, and while this tension has driven the process forward at key moments—such as the sweeping changes that followed the coup and oil coup of 2002 and 2003—the Bolivarian Revolution forces us to ask: Can the antinomy between constituted and constituent power ever be resolved within the structures of the representative state?

In a word, no. The state needs constituent power. The reverse does not necessarily hold true. Constituted power recognizes and adapts to the egalitarian desires of constituent energies only in exceptional moments. In nearly every other moment it presents itself as the unavoidable norm, as common sense. For its part, constituent power is that which always pushes against consolidated consensuses, especially those that impose rank, exclusion, and inequality. It is this resistance to "the way things are" that sparks innovation, and it is up to constituted power to either follow its lead or to quash it in the name of the familiar.

The Bolivarian Revolution has been distinct from other statist projects in its attempts to calibrate these poles of the political as closely to one another as possible. Rather than trying to wash away antagonism through the ceremonies and commemorations of actually existing liberal democracies, it chose to highlight these contradictions, insisting its force was provided by the autonomy of its protagonists. However, at each step it has also exhibited countervailing tendencies. The attempted centralization of movements into an electoral machine like the United Socialist Party of Venezuela, the sedimentation of a political class detached from the movements of communes at the base, and the overwhelming militarization of the Maduro administration all suggest a state that has fallen prey to its own self-serving logic. The crises of 2017 should thus not only, and not even primarily, be understood as the narrowly political contest between the government and the opposition over control of the faltering petrostate. They are rather a moment—another moment—in which the state can open itself to the energies clamoring to reinvent Venezuela from below.

The convocation of the ANC certainly speaks this latter language. As I write these lines, however, it is by no means clear that Maduro's call has been carried out in good faith. Indeed, there are more reasons for pessimism than hope.

Furthermore, while constituent power is universally recognized as the originary power of republics, what happens to it after the foundation is less than certain. Both government and opposition have called for the constituent power of the pueblo in an almost messianic fashion: its time is the time of exception, of founding, of crisis. Constituent power is a savior. Only the people can save the people.

The Italian Marxist Antonio Negri talks of constituent power's absolute character, triggering the need for a rebellion as an exodus of the multitude, and a constitution for every generation. The Argentine-Mexican philosopher Enrique Dussel sees constituent power as a regenerative force, a potential that reinvigorates ossified constituted orders. Both formulations, in different ways explored in depth in the following pages, suggest the need for an approach to constituent power removed from the exceptional—a quotidian, less heroic, perhaps even quieter but no less forceful practice of common being freed from the arbitrary exclusions of contemporary liberal capitalism.

Maduro claims the ANC has become the only avenue through which his government can conquer peace in a tormented Venezuela. It is, for supporters of the government, a means to fight what they describe as the terrorism of the mobilized opposition. Proxies and allies of the administration have also insisted that while technically possible, the envisioned ANC would not necessarily rewrite the constitution in its entirety or move Venezuela into a Sixth Republic. Constituent power is here conceived, in other words, as an instrumental means to navigate the institutional impasses of a state at war with itself and the sociopolitical disintegration of Venezuelan politics in the post-Chávez era. This is certainly a less heroic understanding of constituent power. However, it also subordinates it to the prerogatives of governance— an understanding more akin to the proceduralism of liberal democracies than the autonomy and protagonism constituent power articulated in late twentieth- and early twenty-first-century Venezuela.

Usually, an ANC declares the present is neither tenable nor desirable. It is not a referendum or a legislative tweak to existing law. Paraphrasing Gramsci, an ANC occurs at a moment in which an existing order has entered an advanced state of decay, and in which a new order needs a push, an opening, an opportunity to replace it. The call to rewrite a constitution presumes state failure. It is a radical opening through which order is created, mandated, *constituted*, by constituent power. In its best light, Maduro's ANC more closely resembles a plebiscite than the precondition of a new order. It has been called to forestall rather than facilitate the dangers inherent in such radical openings, and it seems to have little interest in reconfiguring the state so as to allow for a new, less exceptional and more immanent, practice of constituent power.

Rather than the unlimited expression of collective, creative, and egalitarian energies, the 2017 call for an ANC is a moment in which constituted power attempts to call the constituent into being. It replaces biopolitical aspects of constituent power—the formation of subjects and the reproduction of modes of life—with the conventions of a legal order. Constituent power is in this light less about generation and cultivation than about participation. Recent memories of rank-and-file Chavista refusals to reduce their struggle to the vote—and especially to vote for imposed consensus candidates of the establishment—suggest such a feint has little chance for unalloyed success.

Finally, and even given the contradictions highlighted so far, the 2017 ANC illustrates the extent to which we can no longer think of constituent power as pure or untouched by the constituted powers to which it is ostensibly opposed. Constituent power is rather always entangled with the institutional situations through which it circulates. How could it be otherwise? Constituent power is perhaps above all else located and local, a formation that emerges from a particular common experience that presses for more freedom, more collaboration, less inequality, less exploitation, and less exclusion. Thinking seriously about constituent power as a quotidian rather than messianic experience means jettisoning once and for all any pretension that it exists outside the chaos of the conjuncture.

Constituent power is thus more than resistance. It creates as it fights. Better, its fight is creative. If we are to avoid the mysticism to which talk of ontology—political or otherwise—always lends itself, then we must consider constituent power as always already compromised and colored by constituted orders. Analytically and politically, then, the present calls for a politics that eschews rigid anti-statism as much as it requires a rejection of liberalism's blind faith in the sanctity and neutrality of institutions.

The 2017 ANC illustrates a deficiency in thought around constituted orders and the constituent powers that animate, sustain, and upend them. While the Maduro administration has increasingly closed in on itself, the opposition remains a non-option for anyone with progressive social, political, or economic goals. Both appeal to the constituent in a way that illustrates their own fundamental limitations. In moments like this, a return to the critical theory of constituent power places the question of institutions and ideologies—*significant, unavoidable, perhaps even necessary as may they be*—in suspicion. It becomes a vantage from which to evaluate the messy nature of power, collective life, and contestation—to choose sides, even where those sides have yet to present themselves.

Acknowledgments

⚜

This book has been longer in coming that I would have liked, and I have incurred many debts along the way. It would be impossible for me to thank everyone who has contributed to this work—let alone to my political, intellectual, and personal formation along the way—but I'll try. To anyone I've forgotten: Sorry, and thanks. Any project of this length is inevitably a collective one, even if authorship is necessarily assigned to an individual. Any mistakes or misstatements in these pages, of course, are solely my own.

Ongoing difficulties in Venezuela make me hesitant to name names here. I wish I were more optimistic about the short- and medium-term situation in Venezuela, but I remain hopeful. If I still believe the people can and will indeed save the people, it is because of my experiences working with so many dedicated and caring Venezuelans. In the subsequent pages I have anonymized the identities of interviewees and colleagues not already in the public eye, but I remain ever grateful to my extended family of friends and colleagues for their warmth, assistance, insights, and examples as fighters for a better world. I have been fortunate in the openness and comradeship of students and colleagues during my time at the Escuela Venezolana de Planificación and Misión Ribas, and in the many people with whom I've shared a meal, a story, a laugh, or an argument over the years. See you soon.

I am grateful to George and Abbey Ciccariello-Maher for facilitating my first move to Venezuela so many years ago, and for providing a roof over my head as I navigated the complexities of apartment searching in Caracas.

Though the present book carries little resemblance to my graduate work at the University of California, Santa Cruz, the guidance of my colleagues and mentors there remains central to my thinking of politics and social change. Mark Randall Paschal, David Lau, Laura Martin, Evan Calder Williams, Asad Haider, and Johana Isaacson were intellectual collaborators, coconspirators, and fellow occupiers. Alexander Hirsh, Jan Kotowski, Sarah Mak, and Katie Woolsey were and remain a second family. Special thanks are in order to the members of my dissertation committee, who not only guided my scholarship and formation as an academic but became valued friends and allies along an often-difficult path. My chair, Megan Thomas, was tireless in her guidance, support, and attention. Her commitment to socially engaged scholarship and to fighting for a better world are gifts I hope to repay by replicating. Juan Poblete is a mentor, friend, and occasional teammate on the pitch. Gopal Balakrishnan challenged me to think of politics in Latin America in a geopolitical and philosophical context that always struck to the origins of western modernity and political economy. Michael Urban's generosity of spirit and of intellect have reminded me why I chose this path at moments I've most considered leaving.

The lively community of Latin Americanistas in Toronto has provided venues for elaborating ideas and warmth through the long Canadian winter. Thanks to Susan Antebi, Berenice Villagomez, and Valentina Napolitano and students in the Latin American Studies Program for their support. Thanks also to Kevin Coleman, Luis van Ischott, and the Southern Ontario/ Northern New York State Latin American Research Group for insights and discussions on early drafts of chapter four of this book.

Victor Rivas has been an encouraging interlocutor, a close confidant, and a dear friend. Paco Beltran and Julian Campisi have been sounding boards for the frustrations associated with this project, and with life as a twenty-first-century precarious academic. *Gracias, panas.*

Part of the research for this book was conducted via grants from the Department of Political Science at the University of Toronto and the University of Toronto Faculty Association.

Thanks also to the staffs at the Caracas Metro Library, Instituto de Urbanismo at the Universidad Central de Venezuela, and CENDES for all their help in the archives.

Thanks are also in order to my editors, Michael Rinella and Ryan Morris, and the staff at State University of New York Press for guidance and patience along path from manuscript to bound book. Two anonymous reviewers also provided thoughtful and encouraging commentaries on the book's theoretical and empirical interventions.

Some of the ideas in this book have been developed in other venues, and I am grateful to previous publishers for permission to reprint portions of those texts. Elements of chapter 2 first appeared as "Between Multitude and Pueblo: Venezuela's Bolivarian Revolution and the Government of Ungovernability" in the journal *New Political Science*. Chapter 4 had its genesis in "Infrastructure and Insurrection: The Caracas Metro and the Right to the City in Venezuela" in the *Latin American Research Review*. The conclusions concerning democracy and the state of contemporary democratic theory contained in the second part of chapter 5 were first explored in

"Populism as Post-Politics? Ernesto Laclau, Hegemony, and the Limits of Democracy" in the *Radical Philosophy Review*.

Closer to home, I am grateful to my parents, Barbara and Larry Spaulding and Donald Kingsbury, Sr., for starting me on this road. Thanks to my brother, Jeremy Kingsbury, for years of late-night conversations and for always being there. Theresa Enright is a constant partner and comrade, an example of scholarship and patience, and a source of love and support. I am ever grateful for her example, her brilliance, and for sharing this life. This book was finished during Cormac Riley's first summer, and he also helped immeasurably, in his own way.

Introduction
The Challenges of Constituent Power

❧

I nitially, the neighbors were not happy with the occupation.
Mérida is situated in the Venezuelan Andes. It is a colonial city and a
college town. It is beautiful, temperate, and usually offers a merciful calm
in comparison with the capital, Caracas. Mérida is also a divided city—
politically, socially, and geographically. Its more affluent commercial and
residential zones sit above a deep ravine formed by the Rio Chama. At the
bottom of the ravine lies La Chamita, the working-class district physically
and mentally separated from the city proper until the construction of a mass
transit cable car system linked the two sides of the city. Mérida has been
a center of opposition to the Bolivarian Revolution and has seen intense
battles between government supporters—predominantly made up of the
poor and nonwhite majority of the population—and the more affluent
and whiter opposition. It was in the middle-class district of Santa Elena on
the plateau that the Casa de Costurero built its experiment in *autogestión*
(self-management).

In the 1970s the building was used for community development projects,
but it had since fallen into disuse after being sold to the municipality. By
the time the *Consejo Comunal* (communal council) "Maestro Heriberto"
started considering the building as a potential location for a community
resource and education center, it was only being used by drug dealers and
addicts. Since 2012 members of the communal council occupied, recuperated,
and transformed the abandoned building into the Casa de Costurero, a
cooperative containing a library, a computer center, a community radio
station, meeting spaces and classrooms, and a rooftop garden. The members
of the collective painted a makeshift soccer pitch on the street in front of
the Casa (a group of children will be quick to let you know if you park too
close to the goal). The plaza Miranda across the street is once again a hub
for the community—a place for neighbors to exchange gossip, for children
to run and play, or simply a place to relax in the shade after a long day of

work. The Casa, in other words, embodies the communitarian values most celebrated by Bolivarian socialism as a grassroots experiment in remaking Venezuela into a more inclusive, egalitarian, and participatory society.

In the summer of 2014 I was visiting old friends in Mérida. As we watched a rambunctious street game in front of the Casa de Costurero, we talked about the project, and about the restive politics of Venezuela since the death of Hugo Chávez. Venezuela has long been a polarized nation, even before the former lieutenant colonel's election in 1998, but events took a decisively violent and disruptive turn after El Comandante succumbed to cancer in March of 2013. Between February and May of 2014 opposition blockades and attacks on government supporters left forty-three people dead—including protesters, government supporters, police, national guard personnel, and uninvolved bystanders. Scores more were injured and terrorized by the blockades, which caused millions of dollars in private and public property damage. The political cost of destroying any hope of reconciliation between the government and the opposition was arguably even graver still.

Looking out at the neighborhood, fully impressed by the scale of the Casa de Costurero, I asked, "Could you have done this in an opposition neighborhood?"

"*Pana*," a friend active in the collective snorted, using the familiar Venezuelan term for friend, "this *is* an opposition neighborhood. They hated us at first! Now they tolerate us."

"So you haven't converted them to the revolution?" I asked, half-jokingly.

Everyone laughed at what was taken to be my gringo naïveté. Such is Venezuela: the consensus that afternoon was that the opposition neighbors of the Casa de Costurero tolerate the collective for now. Some have even expressed gratitude for the recuperated street, the cleaned-up park, and the facilities for the neighborhood's youth—but none of the collective members present were convinced their work had won over their opposition neighbors to the Bolivarian Revolution, much less to "socialism for the twenty-first century."

Members of Casa de Costurero are in an awkward position. Surrounded by an opposition zone in an opposition-dominated town, they also often find themselves isolated from erstwhile allies among the forces of order within the Bolivarian Revolution. One of the founding members said in an interview the previous year that "it is only through the occupation and democratization of space, together with popular communication, that we can build socialism" (Faddul 2013).[1] Their aim has always been to organize at the grassroots, to develop the skills necessary for what they see as a generational battle to change Venezuela, and to make "a more humane and egalitarian world" (Faddul 2013). They see themselves as a "nodal point," working with other collectives, communal councils, and the local and national government. However, the collective's emphasis on direct action, egalitarian participation, organizational autonomy, and bottom-up direct democracy has also brought tensions with elements of officialdom.

In one incident, representatives from the government's United Socialist Party of Venezuela (PSUV, its abbreviation in Spanish) came to the collective asking to rent an entire floor of their three-story building. When the PSUVistas were informed that they could use the space, but could not permanently occupy it as their own (it was already in use for a radio station and educational center), they were angered. After a protracted series of debates and arguments, the PSUV set up elsewhere. Despite the fact that the Casa de Costurero could have used the money—to say nothing of the potential for favors and state resources that likely would have accompanied proximity to the party—the collective agreed that the community-building project of the Casa was more important than the all but exclusive electoral emphasis of the PSUV.

Make no mistake about it, the collective behind the Casa de Costurero are fervent and active Chavistas—a catch-all collective identity shared, sometimes uneasily, by allies of the Bolivarian Revolution. However, in the encounter with the PSUV, we glimpse just how multifaceted Chavismo can be. For the PSUV, each electoral contest marks a new and ever more pressing 'battle' in the struggle for the future of Venezuela. To lose control of the state apparatus, they contend, would signal the end of the Bolivarian Revolution. For the collective members, the Bolivarian Revolution is about building the commune, not just winning elections. In other words, the Bolivarian Revolution is driven by a constituent energy of collectives like the Casa de Costurero that exceeds the control of constituted institutions, procedures, and bureaucracies. And yet in the present conjuncture, these two aspects of the political—constituent and constituted power—cannot be separated. They tangle in a complex dialectic that drives the process forward, even at those moments when the division within the ranks of Chavismo are as wide as those between Bolivarian Revolution and the political opposition.

The example of the Casa de Costurero illustrates the promise and contradictions of the Bolivarian Revolution, a political sequence that began with the Caracazo uprising of 1989, was institutionalized with the rewriting of the constitution in 1999, and entered a seemingly terminal series of both self-made and imposed crises by 2016. Autonomous responses to the segregation of social space, the divisions between activists and their party, and the tensions and conflicts between Chavistas and the opposition all illustrate a more fundamental driving dialectic of constituent and constituted power. This book explores this ever-unresolved dialectic through twentieth- and twenty-first century Venezuela.

Where one stands amid these tensions determines one's perspective on what, precisely, the Bolivarian Revolution is, when it began, and what it can be. For the political opposition, it is the imposition of "Castro Communism" in Venezuela, with some even suggesting that the regime in Caracas is Havana's puppet. For some in the government, the revolution begins with the election of Hugo Chávez in 1998 and the 1999 constitutional referendum. This beginning is then reaffirmed with every subsequent electoral victory, for which they mobilize with a martial discipline. For these electoral Bolivarians, triumphs in the 2004 recall and wins for the president in 2006 and 2012 highlight watershed moments along the road to "socialism for the twenty-first century." For many collectives like the Casa de Costurero, the revolution began with the rebellion against neoliberalization in 1989, the aftermath of which saw self-organized communities of the poor and excluded redefine the practice, possibility, and common sense of politics in Venezuela.

Much more than examples of a purely local phenomenon, or a flash of idealistic voluntarism butting against the sober conservatism of common sense, these later interpretations of constituent and constituted power bespeak a deeper confrontation on the meaning and organization of the political. Inspired by these interpreters, this book contributes a critical political theory of constituent power drawn from the material realities—the uneven negotiations, the emergent subjectivities, the historically entrenched lines of exclusion and common sense—of politics in Venezuela. As concepts and ways of interpreting the ebb, flow, and contradictions of collective life, neither constituent nor constituted power are unique to Venezuela. However, each takes on new meanings in the context of neoliberalization in the 1990s and the post-neoliberal and postliberal experiments of the Bolivarian Revolution in the twenty-first century. Usually, constituent power is identified with the horizontal, creative, inclusive, and transformative force of collective life. It is the democratic principle in action; it resists inequality, hierarchy, and exclusion in all forms. It does not take no for an answer. Constituted power is more vertical, routinized, and rationalized. Even in ostensibly progressive cases, it limits constituent power through institutions and procedures in order to extend it beyond its immediate expression. However, once separated from the constituent moment, constituted power becomes increasingly self-referential. It becomes invested in the "reason of state" that can, and usually does, sacrifice democracy while purporting to save it.

Viewed through the lens of this fundamental conflict, the Bolivarian government is the *effect* rather than the *cause* of a social revolution. Chávez, Maduro, and the governments they head represent forms of constituted power that must by definition rely upon the constituent forces—like the Casa de Costurero—that remain beyond their control (Beasley-Murray 2010, 127). They are apparatuses of capture—perhaps a virtuous capture, one that seeks to enhance and ally itself to constituent power, but capture nonetheless. Rather than denounce such an arrangement as unauthentically revolutionary, and against what George Ciccariello-Maher (2013) has described as the "blinkered horizontalism" of much contemporary writing on political change in Latin America that condemns the state form *tout court* (17), a more nuanced analysis of experiments in state form is called for. Such an analysis looks to the encounter, the push and pull, and the exodus and capture of constituent power in its relation to the constituted, Bolivarian, order to better grasp the changing significance of authority, citizenship, and politics.

The Bolivarian Revolution thus exceeds an accumulation of the effects of networks of autonomous practices—such as communal councils, urban land committees, collective resource management, and worker-managed enterprises (Azzellini 2015). It can be seen at a more general and intimate level in a budding political culture that explicitly seeks to close the gap between state and civil society so precious to the liberal tradition of the North Atlantic (Valencia 2015). In this, the push by autonomous actors to move beyond the conventional mediations and representations of constituted power has provided new spaces for political creation—practices of direct democracy and substantive social citizenship that have served as touchstones for activists elsewhere in the Americas and the world (Ellner 2014; Raby 2006). But these developments have also been uneven, and moments of vulnerability and manipulation by entrenched bureaucrats and elites continue to challenge attempts to recreate the state "from below" (Fernandes 2010, 234; Motta 2013). Corruption and bureaucratic intransigence should not be read as signs of failure or the folly of attempting social transformation in the developing world. They rather illustrate a more abiding aspect of the political that has for too long been obscured: politics is the result of a dialectic between constituent and constituted power, not an effect of well-designed institutions.

This is to a greater or lesser degree a truth of *all* modern republics that seek legitimacy in a rule "by, for, and of the people," popular sovereignty, or, in Anglo-American parlance, the "social contract." In the North Atlantic tradition, however, the potentially destabilizing effects of democratic excess are usually glorified at a safe distance as a part of civic identity but condemned in practice (Colón-Ríos 2012; Negri 1992; Spång 2014). The contemporary Venezuelan experience breaks from this trend, pitting the inherent tension between constituent and constituted power as the quotidian essence of the Bolivarian political experiment rather than something to be wished away by prevailing limits of common sense.

Solo el pueblo salva al pueblo—only the people can save the people—is a popular slogan, a history lesson, and a political culture in twenty-first-century Venezuela. It reminds us that power ascends from the people and that regimes, institutions, and politicians are the beneficiaries rather than sources of their constituent energies. Only the people can save the people is more than a tautology; it is both a statist valorization of the constituent and a warning that constituent power always and necessarily exceeds state power.

At its most general, this book makes three interventions. First, it contends that the contemplation of constituent power produces an unavoidable question to any democratic conceptualization or practice of the political. Constituent power asks how we will live together. It asks how we will organize shared life; it asks us how open we are to others, and to ourselves. It asks how much inequality, and what sort of limits to our boundless potential, can we force ourselves to *tolerate*. A praxis oriented by constituent power incessantly challenges the settled boundaries of our present selves; it centers on transformation and shapes the civic and social imaginary, the economy, and indeed, the concrete worlds of the cities we inhabit.

Second, the book illustrates a unique Latin American and Venezuelan approach to the question of constituent power dating back to the Independence wars of the early nineteenth century. In this tradition, constituent power is seen as linked to the constituted powers it founds in a generative and progressive dialectic. This relationship emphasizes (re)generation, experimentation, and cultivation over containment. Here constituent power is not a problem to be wished away by the consolidated apparatuses of state power. It is, rather, a constant spur to increase the scope and impact of collective democratic life. These Latin American approaches challenge North Atlantic and liberal understandings of constituent power that relegate it to the prehistory of constituted orders, or to aspects of a citizenship that has been contained in the representative organs of consolidated state and market apparatuses.

Finally, *Only the People Can Save the People* illustrates how the Bolivarian Revolution complicates this very same dialectic it uniquely recognizes. It examines the problems—either "growing pains" or contradictions—that constituent power encounters when constituted powers claim to be its ally. The book asks, to what extent are the institutions and routines of modern, state, and constituted power *inherently* opposed to the expression of constituent power? Or, is this binary only inevitable from within the contractual limits of state and civil society assumed in the liberal tradition? Even if this is only suggestively the case, how might the relationship between constituent and constituted power shift in the contemporary postliberal moment in which, according to Benjamin Arditi (2008), the conventional procedures and subject positions of modern representative democracy are complemented, challenged, and supplanted by direct, supranational, redistributionist, and more collective political experiments?

In response to these questions, this book explores the often-subterranean existence and implications of constituent power for political thought in the early twenty-first century. It asks the reader to *rethink constituent power*. That is to say, I hope not only to reconsider the assumptions, binaries, and consequences of constituent power given different historical and geopolitical coordinates, but also to initiate anew the challenge set to us by the realities of constituent power.

The red thread uniting these considerations is that constituent power should not, cannot, be read as a fixed *thing*. It is rather a capacity, and an ever-present potential of collective life. It is often easier to read in the responses it inspires among the forces of reaction, but it persists nonetheless. As such, an account of constituent power will never be a straightforward affair—perhaps nowhere more so than in contemporary Venezuela.

Venezuela's Long Twentieth Century

The modern Venezuelan state can be seen as a by-product of the discovery and extraction of petroleum in the early twentieth century. Oil provided the financial and political resources for the central state to consolidate its sovereignty over the national territory—a sovereignty that had been fragmented since independence from Spain was won in 1823. Before oil, Venezuela had an agrarian economy dominated by landed interests and local *caudillos*—strongmen who commanded large armies and, often, intense personal loyalty from their followers (Lynch 1992; Sanoja Obediente 2011).

The last in a long of string of Andean *caudillos* to seize the presidency, Juan Vicente Gómez (1857–1935) had the good fortune of ruling over Venezuela when commercial oil extraction in the Maracaibo basin began in earnest in 1914. The president used his position vis-à-vis a queue of foreign oil companies—and the national powers they represented—to secure foreign recognition of his rule and to subdue any lingering internal challenges to his all but absolute sovereignty. It also allowed him to cultivate a loyal *comprador* class of newly urbanized elites to counter the power of rural oligarchs. Under Gómez, Venezuela set out on path of managed urbanization, modernization, and economic growth and perfected a form of centralized control in an almost "magically" powerful state (Coronil 1997; DiJohn 2009; Tinker Salas 2009).

In addition to these vertical aspects of sovereignty as state power, oil also provided the opportunity for the horizontal formation of a shared identity among petroleum workers. As Miguel Tinker Salas (2009) notes, prior to the establishment of the oil industry,

> Venezuelans had no established tradition of internal migration. Not since the wars of independence in the first two decades of the nineteenth century had Venezuela witnessed a significant movement of people. Moreover, a history of civil wars during the nineteenth century had accentuated regional differences. Most early laborers arrived at the Lake of Maracaibo with much trepidation. For many the journey represented the first time they had ventured from the familiar surroundings of their homes. Thrust into large bachelors' quarters, work sites, and villages, they came into contact with people who, although Venezuelan, were not always familiar; the Maracuchos [people from Maracaibo] spoke with a different accent, the Andeans seemed more formal and reserved, and the Easterners were more direct and outspoken. The migrants did not eat all the same foods, enjoy the same music, dress the same, or even pray to the same saints . . . at one level the new encounters initiated a process of recognition, crucial to state formation and nationhood, but at another it produced frictions as regional differences emerged. (77)

From *La ruta petrolera*—the oil circuit—arose the encounters and frictions necessary for something like a Venezuelan imagined community to emerge. Venezuelans came to appreciate the geographical extent and diversity of the country to which they had been assigned by accident of birth and experienced their first encounters with human differences subordinated within this shared identity. However, emergent notions of nationhood and an increasingly mobile population also sparked concern among elites and contributed to latent racial hierarchies already established within the centralizing body politic.

Even in these early, centralizing, and top-down moments of the modern Venezuelan state one can detect a nagging anxiety around constituent power. The positivism associated with Venezuela's twentieth-century dictators started from the assumption that the "effective constitution" of Venezuelans—determined by their racial and cultural makeup, geography, and colonial history—destined the country to be forever "backward" and hence incapable of the modern representative democracy they saw in the North Atlantic (Tinoco Guerra 2010, 101; Bautista Urbaneja 2013, 77). The best form of government—arguably perfected in the midcentury dictatorship of Marcos Pérez Jiménez (1948–1958)—was thus determined to be developmentalist authoritarianism. No other form of government, it was believed, could maintain order and peace while transforming the population—via a range of measures from tutelage to substitution and eugenics—into properly modern citizens (Castillo D'Imperio 2003; Herrera Salas 2005, 75–76). Beyond the pseudosciences of developmentalism, however, these sorts of political expressions bespeak a fear of losing control on the part of elites. They also point to a perceived need to rationalize the exclusionary reality of what would be proclaimed after 1958 to be the region's only "consolidated democracy" (Ellner and Tinker Salas 2007).

Democratic Venezuela began after the fall of Pérez Jiménez in 1958 with the signing of the Puntofijo pact between center left and right political parties Democratic Action (AD, its abbreviation in Spanish) and COPEI. However, the "fourth republic" or Puntofijo years, were no less exclusionary or repressive for the population at large. Protest movements of students, peasants, and urban slum dwellers were violently repressed by the civilian governments of the Puntofijo parties, killing many, pushing some into exile, and still others into a clandestine guerrilla campaign that would last until the 1970s (Ciccariello-Maher 2013; Ellner 2008 Gómez García 2014; Velasco 2015). While oil booms, especially in the 1970s, granted the state an ability to smooth over some of the social conflicts that accompany extreme inequality, the flood of petrodollars also intensified already unfathomably high levels of corruption, government inefficiency, public scandal, and a general confidence deficit of citizens in relation to the state (Buxton 1999; Coronil 1997; Mommer 2003). By the time of Venezuela's currency devaluation on its "Black Friday" (February 18, 1983) the country had gone from one of the region's richest economies to one of its most indebted, and the Puntofijo system was already in a state of advanced decay (López Maya 2005).

Neoliberalization and the popular responses will be discussed in greater detail in the coming chapters. For now, it will suffice to say that the Caracazo uprising of February 27, 1989, blew open the Puntofijo order and began the construction of a new political rationality in Venezuela. The *partidocracia* (partyocracy—a neologism coined to describe the Puntofijo system) could not survive a government crackdown against massive anti-austerity protests that left as many as three thousand Venezuelans dead over the course of three bloody days. In the aftermath, neoliberal economic and political reforms continued in a piecemeal fashion—telecommunications were privatized in 1992 but the proposed *apertura* (opening) of the oil industry never fully materialized—and public trust in government continued to plummet. In 1992 there were two attempted coups, both of which cited the government crackdown in the Caracazo and market reforms as their proximate causes. Shockingly, both attempts were met with widespread public support, and the leader of the first, a young lieutenant colonel named Hugo Chávez, was catapulted to national fame when he made his televised surrender on February 4, 1992. In 1993 the last president of the Puntofijo system, Carlos Andrés Pérez, widely identified with economic shock therapy, violent repression, and ever-worsening, endemic corruption, was impeached on charges of corruption.

Just as importantly, the collapse at Venezuela's commanding heights in the 1990s was matched and exacerbated by spikes in protest and collective action on a scale never before seen in the country's history. Neighborhood associations, unions, and peasant networks decried the loss of subsidies, state protections, and declining services throughout the decade. Particularly among the most marginalized sectors of the population, protest transitioned into mutual aid as an ethic of self-reliance and resistance spread out of both necessity and innovation. People needed novel solutions to fight police brutality; to gain access to basic services like water, electricity, and waste removal; and to find work to support their families. In the aftermath of failed developmentalism, they increasingly sought out nonstate and nonmarket avenues to do so.

By the time Chávez was released from prison in 1994 (the newly elected president at the time, Rafael Caldera,[2] had made the release of the popular rebel leader a key promise of his campaign), a new mode of politics was already in motion. Chávez capitalized on this and staked his political future on the need for a new constitution. He named the party established for his electoral aims the Movimiento Quinta República (Fifth Republic Movement, MVR) and built on his status as a political outsider from a humble background, who had literally risked his life to pull the country out of neoliberalism, to win election in 1998. Immediately upon taking office, Chávez initiated the process of convoking a constituent assembly, which after an open process of public debate, was approved in 1999.

The next decade saw Venezuela transformed as the tensions between constituent and constituted power—and the conflict between the newly empowered majority of the population and old guard elites—intensified at every possible turn. Between 2002 and 2004 the opposition repeatedly attempted to remove the president by any extraparliamentary means at their disposal. An attempted coup was reversed by mobilizations from below in April 2002, as was a campaign of economic sabotage led by the management of the national oil industry, PDVSA, between December 2002 and February 2003. Violent street blockades known as *guarimbas* sought to create ungovernability and destabilize the government throughout 2004 and 2005. In 2004, Chávez handily won an attempt to recall him spearheaded by the United States–funded nongovernmental organization (NGO) Súmate. In 2005 the opposition boycotted National Assembly elections, citing fraud

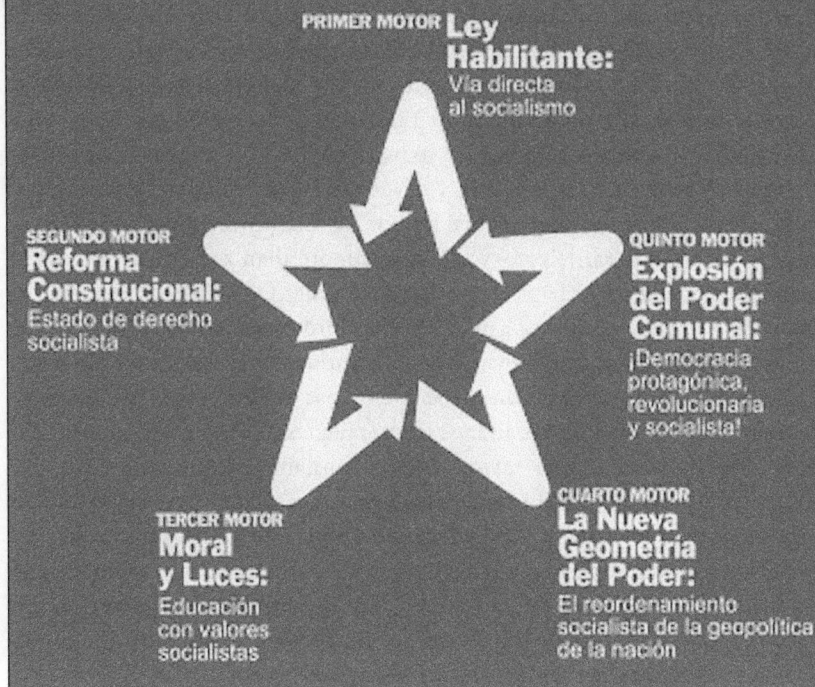

Figure 1. "All Motors at Maximum Speed to Bolivarian Socialism! First motor, The Enabling Laws: A direct path to socialism; Second Motor, Constitutional Reform: A socialist rule of law; Third Motor, Morality and Enlightenment: Education with Socialist values; Fourth Motor, The New Geometry of Power: The socialist reordering of the nation's geopolitics; Fifth Motor: Explosion of Communal Power: Protagonistic, Revolutionary, and Socialist Democracy!"[3]

before campaigning had even ended—a claim rejected by international observers. Chávez easily won reelection again in 2006 on a campaign that emphasized the need to build socialism for the twenty-first century.

At his inauguration in 2007, Chávez cited the need to "accelerate" the Revolution, and outlined five steps or "motors" toward the realization of Bolivarian socialism. The five motors were depicted as step-by-step instructions for how to achieve what the president outlined. The first motor, the enabling law, allowed Chávez to rule by decree for a set period of time (Chávez 2014, 262). The second, the constitutional reform, was intended to make the gains of the previous six years permanent, and to elevate organs like the Bolivarian Missions and the communal councils to a constitutionally mandated status. Intimately linked to the first, Chávez admitted that the 1999 Constitution had been "born in the middle of a storm" and needed to be adapted to the growing demands of constituent power (263). In this way, Chávez also suggested an understanding of the constitution that was in perpetual motion, constantly revising and reforming itself—a living and participatory document more than a social contract or a transfer of popular sovereignty to institutional order (266) (the *reforma* will be discussed in greater detail in chapter 2). The third motor, *moral y luces* sought the development of an explicitly socialist educational system that would better prepare Venezuelans for the future. The reference is to Simón Bolívar's proposed constitution as outlined in his address to the congress of Angostura in 1819. The state-citizen dynamic is here envisioned as a constant pedagogical project, one not limited to classrooms, but rather an all-encompassing and collective project of social, economic, and political education (267). The fourth motor, the new geometry of power was to be a radical overhaul of the political system, "a new way of distributing political, economic, social, and military power" across national space (268). The goal here was to decentralize power from the capital city and to displace the entropy-prone institutions of representative democracy with local and regional councils of autonomous socialist collectives. Finally, the fifth motor, the explosion of communal power was to be the realization of the new society and the definitive replacement of the old order with a more just, inclusive, and participatory state of affairs. Citing Antonio Negri, Chávez argued that constituent power circulates through space as a constantly transformative force, a "multitude in revolution" (269). This communal power, the president continued, would fundamentally reshape the nation, as the representative state would be progressively replaced by a federation of communal councils (271).

Most immediately striking in the five motors outline is how it all but completely inverts how politics had progressed to that moment in Venezuela. Rather than start from the expression of constituent power, as had been the case with the Caracazo and throughout the 1990s, the 2007 roadmap places the executive at the beginning and center of the revolutionary process.

Autonomous social networks created the political and social space into which the Chávez government moved. The five motors reverse this dynamic, asserting that it is states and institutions that create the spaces in which citizens operate.

After the failure of the second motor, the constitutional reform, in late 2007, the Bolivarian Revolution attempted to consolidate its gains rather than to follow, as it had initially promised, the call to "deepen" the revolution issued by some of its supporters that rejected the *reforma*. As some sectors of the opposition finally accepted that any challenge to Chávez would have to take place through the ballot box—eventually resulting in the Mesa de la Unidad Democrática (Democratic Unity Roundtable, MUD) still others returned to the street. During this time an emboldened student movement—again, often funded by Northern NGOs and widely celebrated in the US and European media as fighters for freedom against socialism—began to agitate for an end to the regime in both highly polished media stunts and violent confrontations with the police and government supporters.

By the time Chávez announced in mid-2011 that he had undergone multiple surgeries for cancer, the Bolivarian Revolution was actively courting the participation of the middle classes, even as it expanded its investments in the poor majority of Venezuelans through ambitious new social programs and infrastructure projects. In the presidential campaign of 2012, in which Chávez faced off with Henrique Capriles Radonski, the governor of Miranda, the latter campaigned not on a return to the Fourth Republic and market orthodoxy, but rather on a platform that criticized the government for soaring crime rates and promised to replace bombastic Chavismo with a more tempered, sober, and business-friendly social democracy of the Brazilian stripe. Capriles, that is to say, minimized any threat his administration might pose to the Misiones Bolivarianas (Bolivarian Missions) and other popular programs and effectively promised to replace Chávez with the more diplomatic Lula da Silva. Few believed him, and he lost by some eleven points to Chávez in the October 2012 ballots (he was however able to close that gap to just over 1.5% the following year when he faced Chávez's successor, Nicolás Maduro).

Chávez died in March 2013 and elections were held, as mandated in the constitution, a month later. Since then, Venezuela has been rocked by a string of violent antigovernment protests as the price of oil halved and then halved again, reaching a low of $28.50 USD per barrel in January 2016. As opposed to the recession triggered by the collapse of US mortgage-backed securities in 2008, however, Saudi Arabia's unilateral 2014 decision to flood the market with cheap crude and the corrections in the Chinese economy in 2015 put Venezuela in a uniquely precarious structural position.[4]

By 2016, these dynamics led to an all but complete economic collapse. The International Monetary Fund (IMF) estimated that Venezuela would reach 720% inflation during that calendar year. Widespread shortages in basic foodstuffs, medicine, and consumer goods triggered riots through the country. The opposition capitalized on the overlapping political, economic, and social crises and pushed for a presidential recall referendum.

The Maduro government responded to economic implosion at home, isolation from international financial networks, and deeply embedded corruption and ineptitude within the government by ceding increasing authority to the military. While Bolivarianism had always been built on a civic-military alliance (Chávez 2013; Garrido 2007) and was wary of liberalism's insistence on the separation of powers, by 2016 the situation seemed to have turned. Rather than a practical criticism and alternative to the notion that the institutions of the modern nation-state are neutral, and rather than the deepening of a protagonistic dynamic in which the state and movements coordinate efforts toward a common horizon of social transformation, the Maduro administration's moves in 2016 sought to divorce constituent from constituted power.

The post-Chávez years will be explored in greater detail in what is to come. For now, it is important to recognize that while the central concern of *Only the People Can Save the People* revolves around the dynamics of constituent and constituted power, and of the primacy of the former in relation to the latter, the impact of Chávez on politics in Venezuela cannot be overemphasized. The transition from neoliberalization to Bolivarianism to whatever follows has been punctuated by crises, struggles, advances, and setbacks. Without question, the death of Chávez was one of the most severe. However, even without such a singular force on the scene, the challenges facing the Bolivarian process and by the constituent powers that drive it remain the same: How can, should, and will collective life be organized? And, just as pressingly, what is, what can be, the role of the state in the pursuit of a better world?

Bringing the State Back in . . . but What Kind?

I first moved to Venezuela in early 2007 to study the role of the state in struggles for social and political justice. Significant parts of my generation of left-oriented scholarship and activism turned away from the state as a viable tool for pursuing social change. In Latin America, the memory of dictatorships and death squads had no time to fade before neoliberalization: the democratic state, like its authoritarian predecessor, became a tool for mass impoverishment, police repression, and the siphoning of collective wealth to local elites and Northern financial institutions (Robinson 2007). For many in the anti- or "alter-globalization" movements of the 1990s, states were seen to be as much the enemy as the multinational corporations they ostensibly served (see, for example, Hardt and Negri 2000 and Holloway 2002 for perhaps the most characteristic theorizations of anti-statist tendencies in the "alter-globalization" movements). For others, the state was too rigid, too disciplinary, too rationalized, and too attached to modernization to offer anything other than disaster (Scott 1998). Against concerns that these criticisms of the state form and of actually existing states might correspond to the wave of recalibrated liberalism being exported from its first experiments in Pinochet's Chile, Reagan's United States, and Thatcher's England (Harvey 2005), the left-wing anti-statism of the 1990s insisted on the need to press forward, and especially beyond any nostalgia for the "golden age" of postwar capitalism in the North Atlantic (Hardt and Negri 2000; Hobsbawm 1995). Theorizations and experimentations with new forms of praxis in the 1990s emphasized autonomy and dispersal, conjunctural coordination, and a creative expansion of identities and intensities rather than the state-oriented antagonisms of twentieth-century Marxist-Leninism (Colectivo Situaciones 2002).

Here Latin America was an often-influential, if spectral, presence in my and many others' political formation (Azzellini and Sitrin 2014). There was for example Fèlix Guattari and Suely Rolnik's (2008) investigation of the new unionism of the Partido dos Trabalhadores in Brazil. Unlike traditional trade unionism, the PT operated across layers of statist and non-statist mobilization during the transition from authoritarian rule in the early 1980s, traversing traditional boundaries of state, civil society, and economy. Ernesto Laclau and Chantal Mouffe's (1985) post-Marxist rereading of Gramsci in *Hegemony and Socialist Strategy* was always arguably haunted by the former's political formation in Peronist Argentina (Beasley-Murray 2012). The Zapatista rebellion of Chiapas, Mexico, with its media savvy, postmodern poetry, direct democracy, and rejection of the modern state form was a constant influence and reference for the anti-statist Marxist Left (Hardt and Negri 2000; Holloway 2002) and the Latin American philosophers of liberation (Dussel 2006). By the late 1990s, the World Social Forum—first convened in Porto Alegre, Brazil—emphasized that the future of anti-systemic agitation would have to take place through autonomous and conjuncture-dependent networks (a "movement of movements") that many hoped would replace rather than capture state power (Fisher and Ponniah 2003).

In all these cases—and this is only a very partial list, to which can be added feminist, subalternist, and postcolonial criticisms—we increasingly saw the state as irredeemably considered suspect and inextricably linked to the horrors of the nineteenth and twentieth centuries. Neoliberalization brought with it a reconfiguration of the state form: less welfare, more police; less social rights, more privatization; less national development, more financial capital; less public space, more surveillance and fences. However, against whiggish accounts of globalization and economic reforms that heralded the age of the "shrinking state," for the majority of the population, neoliberalization meant more ubiquitous forms of social control. As Wendy Brown (2003) would have it, neoliberalization entailed a mode of governance, "encompassing but not limited to the state, and one which produces subjects, forms of citizenship and behavior, and a new organization of the social." In sum, neoliberalization entailed a new regime of governmentality rather than the end of power relations first perfected by the modern state—especially for those who came to depend most on "the public" in the twentieth century. Many on the left—to say nothing of the right—were thus skeptical when the Bolivarian Revolution as a *governmental* project gave state-led developmentalism a second life in the first years of the twenty-first century.

In similar fashion, the Bolivarian Revolution's reintroduction of socialism into the lexicon of the global left seemed a dog-eared throwback for many in the post–Cold War anticapitalist and "alter-globalization" milieus. These movements were often as critical of the "actually existing" socialisms of the Soviet bloc and the failures of national liberation movements as they were antagonistic to the (neo)liberal representative democracies of the late twentieth century (Hardt and Negri 1994, 2004; Laclau and Mouffe 1985; Scott 1998). Actually existing socialism of the twentieth century had been replaced by the actually existing democracies of the twenty-first. While the cynicism of the new age and an emerging populist neoliberalism was duly noted—outsourcing state functions to a legion of enterprising NGOs, microfinanciers, and the cult of celebrity around billionaire philanthropists, for example—few had the stomach to look to the socialist traditions of Mexico in 1910, Russia in 1917, China in 1949, Algeria in 1954, or Cuba in 1959 for inspiration on where next to turn.

When Hugo Chávez announced in 2005 that Venezuela was in the process of building "socialism for the twenty-first century," and previously, when he and other officials in the government of the Bolivarian Republic of Venezuela[5] started quoting Mao Tse-tung on the role of the military in revolutionary society ("like a fish in water"), many analysts and activists— myself included—were doubtful. There were and remain concerns linking any military involvement in politics with dictatorship and human rights abuses, concerns that have preoccupied surveys of Latin American democracy since the 1980s (Hellinger 2011; Millet, Holmes, and Pérez 2009). This concern can also be seen in other, ostensibly unrelated areas of Latin American studies, such as the literature on presidentialism, decentralization, and institutional design (Eaton 2004; Mainwaring and Shugart 1997). Anxieties about any potential return to authoritarian military rule have thus far proved unfounded, even with the increasing militarization of the state apparatus by 2016. What has instead occurred in Venezuela since 1998, and which has, to varying degrees, spread throughout the South American continent, has been a rejection of the neoliberal model in favor of a renewed belief that governments have an obligation to provide for the welfare of their citizens and to intervene in and direct economies accordingly. While this rejection of neoliberalism has yet to bloom into a more coherently recognizable anticapitalism (Coronil 2011, 238; Leiva 2008), and while the price fluctuations of primary product exports to China has some worried about a new dependency (González-Vicente 2012; Jenkins 2012), the range and ambition of postliberal experimentation cannot be denied, particularly in Venezuela (Arditi 2008; Escobar 2010).

The matter at hand since the 1990s has been one of forging constituted institutions capable of responding to the challenge, example, and activity of constituent power. Among this book's other aims, I hope also to illustrate how the Bolivarian government's record has often been quite mixed in this regard. This has not always meant failure or betrayal of constituent power. Rather, I suggest that while the pursuit by constituted power to adequately reflect its constituent core will always fail—in Venezuela or anywhere else in the republican world—these failures can themselves be productive. By its nature constituent power always exceeds the constituted powers it founds. The book's wager—encapsulated in its title, *Only the People Can Save the People*—is that the only way to force good failures from bad situations is to calibrate these two core aspects of collective life as closely to one another as possible. Such a recalibration allows for constituent power to respond to "fetishized" expressions of constituted power that have become entropic, self-referential, and, at their extremes, antagonistic to the constituent powers that found them (Dussel 2006, 40–47). Finally, recognition that only the people can save the people gives the lie to modern liberal constitutionalism's pretensions toward permanence; it insists constituent power be more a daily practice than a limit case of normal political life. Constituent power requires a constituent republic, not a liberal state (Negri 1996; Virno 1996). This is what Joel Colón-Ríos (2012) has proposed as a "weak constitutionalism" that sees constituent power as an opportunity rather than a threat, in which citizens approach the constitutional order as a collective work in progress rather than monolithic and eternal institutions (155). The task for the Bolivarian Revolution as a constituent project is to remain tireless in its search for a "weak constitutionalism" that doesn't fade into a simple, uninspiring reformism or engage in the revisionist doublespeak of sculpting virtue from necessity.

Overview

The book unfolds over the course of five chapters, each exploring an encounter with constituent power in twenty-first-century Venezuela. Chapter 1 utilizes a comparative theoretical perspective to make the argument for a distinctly Venezuelan approach to the question of constituent power that dates back to the independence wars of the nineteenth century. Through a study of the Bolivarian Revolution's "three roots"—El Libertador Simón Bolívar; his teacher, Simón Rodríguez; and the mid-nineteenth-century radical peasant leader Ezequiel Zamora—the chapter traces both contemporary official renderings of these nineteenth-century figures as well as their subterranean and uncontrollable effects. Whereas North Atlantic approaches—and specifically the traditions of English and French liberalism, and later, of Carl Schmitt's consideration of the relation of constituent power to sovereignty—are all but unified in their anxiety about and their push to contain expressions of constituent power, in Venezuela we see a much more collaborative approach characterized by generation, cultivation, and experimentation. It is this tradition that is most appreciably at play in twenty-first-century Venezuela.

Chapter 2 explores the consequences for political thought of the Caracazo, an uprising and crackdown in 1989 that many contend is the year zero of the Bolivarian Revolution. Here the Caracazo is read as an event that opens into an established order (the Puntofijo system), exposes the exclusionary truth of what had been celebrated as a consolidated liberal democracy, and, most importantly, generates the new forms of political subjectivity that have since shaped Venezuela. In conversation with French philosopher Alain Badiou, I contend that the Caracazo signals an absolute rupture with a constituted ordering of politics, society, and economy. The truth of events, however, are only ever realized in their aftermath. The chapter thus traces an arc from the Caracazo, to the protagonism and *autogestión* that followed it, to the troubled attempts to capture constituent power in the party form with the creation of the Partido Socialista Unido de Venezuela (United Socialist Party of Venezuela, PSUV). Against the all-too-easy conclusion that controversies around the PSUV and its seemingly irreversible descent from a party of protagonists to a centralized electoral machine analysis of event and—I almost said against—constituent power illustrates the degree to which both categories lend themselves to unsatisfyingly mystical territories.

Chapter 3 responds to these difficulties in an analysis of collective subjectivity through a reading of two key references for Bolivarian theorizations of the concept: Italian autonomist Marxist Antonio Negri and Argentine-Mexican philosopher Enrique Dussel. The chapter argues that the experience of the Bolivarian Revolution calls for a third position somewhere between the raw ungovernability of Negri's multitude—a social force that defies any attempt to subjectivize or contain it—and Dussel's pueblo—which hews much more closely to populist conceptualizations of an organic people tied to representative institutions and leaders. In its attempts to sculpt a pueblo from a multitude, the Bolivarian Revolution presents itself as the realization or government of an original ungovernability. However, as the chapter concludes, this labor is by necessity constant; it is only from the perspective of *processes* rather than the end product of transformation that the political sequence in Venezuela since the Caracazo can be considered a *revolution* rather than a *state*.

Chapter 4 expands these social and political treatments of constituent power by examining its effects on the built environment, with special focus on the city of Caracas and urban transportation infrastructures. Through an engagement with right to the city movements and critiques, this chapter examines constituent power as having physical as well as civic and theoretical consequences. This poses a paradox, however, in terms of scale and substance: large-scale infrastructure developments require more authority and capital to execute than can usually be seen in the normal, quotidian expression of constituent power. Moreover, projects like the expansion of subway systems or the construction of housing blocks are by their very nature *concrete* to a greater extent than normally allowed for in thinking around constituent power as an effervescent and episodic expression of democratic potential. The chapter concludes by outlining the theoretical implications of this paradox for distinctly Bolivarian approaches to constituent power in the newly constrained global economic context that has prevailed since 2014.

Chapter 5 examines the relationship of the opposition to constituent power. It tracks changes in the opposition's strategy and discourse from the extraparliamentary violence of the early Chávez years to a rebranding as liberal democrats after 2010. After examining the economic and political proposals of this latter opposition, the chapter then moves to an analysis of democratic theory and its limits for thinking about politics in Venezuela. This critical look at democracy and democratic theory illustrates the extent to which the opposition can—and cannot—be considered a likely vector of constituent power against an increasingly isolated and autoreferential Bolivarian state.

In the conclusion I return to more solidly theoretical ground by considering the composition of constituent power as a force of the political in the aftermath of neoliberal restructuring. Put most bluntly, in the context of the failed promises of twentieth-century liberalism, constituent power offered a powerful critique of inequality and exclusion. As a response to neoliberal restructuring in Venezuela in the 1990s, constituent power occupied the vacuum left by a retreating and delegitimized state. Hugo Chávez was the beneficiary rather than the cause of this situation, and the Bolivarian Revolution as a statist project that began with his election in 1998 should be read as responses to the crises of neoliberalism and the expression of constituent power. But, the question remains, how will—or can—constituent power respond to the crises of the twenty-first century? If the Bolivarian state under Hugo Chávez recognized and emphasized its debt to constituent power, even going so far as to encourage its autonomous development and expression, what sort of space remains open for constituent power as a position of critique and constitution in the present, "after" Chávez, and "after" liberalism? *Only the People Can Save the People* concludes by examining the potentials of a constituent power freed from both its position as subterranean criticism of reigning liberalism and animating motor of a statist project that claims to represent it.

This then is a book about the innovations, frustrations, and challenges of power in twenty-first-century Venezuela. It is a book about constituent and constituted power, of new social subjects struggling to redefine the role and composition of states and institutions, and it is about the difficulty of building alternatives to market democracy after globalization. In other words, this book is not just about Venezuela and the Bolivarian Revolution; its questions on the nature of democracy, revolution, citizenship, and political identity can be asked of societies coping with the aftermaths of neoliberal structural adjustment throughout Latin America and the world.

CHAPTER 1

Anxiety, Containment, and Cultivation

Constituent Power in the North Atlantic and Venezuela

⚮

The natural death of a nation is always political;
but its spirit, like that of the men that comprise it, is immortal;
the spirit of society never dies—it leaves behind a body that it can longer
  retain,
in order to animate another, and reappear under a different form.
> —Simón Rodríguez, "Luces y Virtudes sociales"

"I awaken every hundred years, when the *pueblo* awakens."
> —Pablo Neruda, "Un Canto para Bolívar" (1950)

When Pablo Neruda penned the closing lines of "Un Canto para Bolívar" in 1950, in which a fictionalized Simón Bolívar responds to the narrator's existential interrogations—"Are you? Or are you not? Or Who are you?"—by saying "I awaken every hundred years, when the *pueblo* awakens," the Chilean poet illustrated a distinctly Latin American approach to constituent power. Much like the "old mole" of revolution in Marx's (1998) *Eighteenth Brumaire of Louis Bonaparte*, that "is thorough-going . . . still in its purgatory . . . do[ing]its work methodically" (121), constituent power is often elusive, effusive, and episodic, but it is always present, bringing with it the potential for new beginnings (Sader 2011). In Neruda's poem Bolívar is not an individual; he is historical and collective potential, a recurrence, a hiding moment. Rather than a millenarian or messianic dream of rescue from beyond, then, this promise of Bolívar-as-constituent-power is profoundly immanent—always already here, a potential waiting to be activated.

There are of course other responses to questions of constituent power in Venezuelan and North Atlantic political thought. South American elites have just as much fear and anxiety of constituent power as their North Atlantic counterparts. Elite concerns at democracy's fragile balance between tyranny and anarchy have most consistently sided with the former rather than risk the latter, and despite powerful countercurrents, the colonial era bequeathed "no operative concept of political equality" to the fledgling republics of South America (Drake 2009, 57). There are, furthermore, significant subterranean currents of constituent power in European thought and politics that run against the demobilizing fears of modern liberalism. Most importantly, for our purposes, the red Spinozist thread that runs throughout the modern project and emerges in the 1970s with the Italian autonomist and French aleatory Marxist schools undermines the unity of a North Atlantic "tradition" (Althusser 2001b, 2006; Hardt and Virno 1996; Negri 1991, 2007; Wright 2002).

In nineteenth-century Latin America constituent power was most often glimpsed in the tumult and rupture of civil war or peasant uprising. However, given the generally fragmented sovereignties of the postcolonial continent— arguably in Venezuela more than anywhere else, where the period from 1830 to 1848 saw an estimated 139 uprisings and peasant revolts (López Calero 2017, 33)—the episodic appearance of constituent power was more a military than theoretical matter. In Venezuela as elsewhere, any attempted expression or exodus of constituent power was hunted down by the modernizing state when it finally emerged, as in the case of the Venezuelan Federal War of 1859– 1863 (Araujo 2010, 49; López Calero 2017; Müller 2001). Constituent power is in other words most recognized in the reactions it engenders: military pacification campaigns and elite anxieties that the unwashed masses and lawless hinterlands might damage their carefully constructed and protected worlds. Subsequent calls for the systematic (re)colonization of the region by ostensibly more civilized racial stock from Europe are but one expression of the problem constituent power always poses for its constituted counterparts.

When formal, liberal, democracy finally came to Venezuela in the mid-twentieth century, the prevailing approach was similar to that dominant in the North Atlantic, celebrating "the constituted while pretending to exalt the constituent" (Negri 1992, 31). The *pueblo*,[1] popular sovereignty, and democracy were piously referenced but systematically silenced elements of an elitist order (Araujo 2010). Constituent power, then, was at best a museum piece—admired but only visited under carefully guarded circumstances. Despite this, the mole of constituent power—either in or beyond its Bolivarian guise—persisted and persists.

After a discussion of dominant approaches and flashpoints in the North Atlantic, this chapter examines Bolivarian understandings of constituent power in Venezuela. Against modern liberalism's anxiety and suppression of constituent power, this Venezuelan approach follows that of Neruda's Bolívar. Here constituent power is a potential to be cultivated. It is the generation of previously excluded, subordinated, or silenced political subjects and an ever-present potential of collective life that haunts any attempt to enforce hierarchy, exclusion, and inequality. As the generation of new forms of political subjectivity, constituent power forces a practice of governance based in contingency and experimentation. The challenge facing any democratic governmental practice, Bolivarian or otherwise, is to rise to the challenges posed by potential expressions of constituent power, in all their motion, creation, and incessant experimentation.

Anxieties and Limit Cases:
Constituent Power in the North Atlantic

Constituent power's long and tortuous history in the North Atlantic spans a number of concepts and locally situated conflicts. Andreas Kalyvas (2005) has suggested that whereas thinkers as diverse as Jean Bodin, Hans Kelsen, Hannah Arendt, and Michel Foucault speak of sovereignty as a commanding and repressive power imposed upon subjects, a no less modern (or Eurocentric) tradition spanning John Locke, Thomas Paine, the Abbé Sieyès, and Carl Schmitt considers sovereignty and constituent power to be synonymous. Here, "the concept of sovereignty as the creative, founding act of the constituent subject departs from the traditional notion of sovereignty as the higher and final instance of command" (226). In this regard, it might be helpful to think of constituent power's place in North Atlantic political thought as part of a constellation of concepts and experiences that emerge in the context of the secularization and massification of political power—most obviously constituent power's ostensible other, constituted power, but also, for example, democratic legitimacy and popular sovereignty.

Scrubbing History to Make Politics Safe from Constituent Power

The interactions of constituted and constituent power in modern political thought and practice can be characterized as the former's attempts to subordinate or silence the latter. North Atlantic constitutional and democratic theory prefers to relegate constituent power to an inactive and symbolic role (Colón-Ríos 2012, 8; Spång 2014, 5). In England it emerged as a foundational principle of democratic political legitimacy and was elaborated by factions such as the Levellers in the revolutionary tumult of the mid-seventeenth century. However, the restoration of the (parliamentary) monarchy scrubbed the idea of constituent power from political discourse entirely (Loughlin 2007, 47). The liberal tradition only allowed for democratic forms of governance once elites "found reasons for believing that 'one man, one vote' would not be dangerous to property, or to the continuance of class divided societies" (Macpherson 1977, 10)—that is, after they have been denuded of constituent power's disruptive, transformative, and egalitarian potentials. By the twentieth century, Albert Venn Dicey would conclude that the concept was foreign to Britain, that the constituent power of law making—what he termed its "legal sovereignty," against the "political sovereignty" of "the people"—rested with the Crown-in-parliament (quoted in Colón-Ríos 2012, 90). In revolutionary France, almost immediately after its elaboration by the Abbé Sieyès (2003), constituent power was deemed dangerous and destabilizing. Even though it has since been invoked at moments to strengthen the state—for example, in the changes to the constitution under Charles De Gaulle in 1958—constituent power has by and large been subsumed in a "quasi-mystical identification between the people and the Assembly" (Jaume 2007, 84). In Germany, the development of the idea of constituent power has been tempered by its deployments in the Kaiserreich, Weimar, and Nazi eras in which "the reference to the popular will has served . . . as an argument against egalitarian procedures and in favor of the charismatic leadership of an executive" (Möllers 2007, 104). It is thus perhaps less than surprising that in the federal and post-reunification moments, German constitutionalism has had a "thoroughly formalist approach to the question of constituent power" (104). Rounding out this rough historical sketch, in the United States, Bruce Ackerman (1998) sees constituent power as dangerous and destabilizing, taking place where "law ends, and pure politics (or war) beings" (11). Constituent power is by nature extraconstitutional—it establishes rules but is not subject to them. In other words, with constituent power the guarantees, stability, and protections of liberal orders are thrown into question. Anything is possible. Indeed, the modern history of mainstream constitutional thought in the North Atlantic can in many ways be read as an attempt to contain constituent power and to ensure the permanence of institutions, even if this means constricting the meaning and practice of the democracy these very institutions are meant to safeguard (Colón-Ríos 2012, 17; Negri 1992, 25).

In spite—or perhaps *because*—of the silencing and displacement of constituent power, related concepts like democracy, popular sovereignty, and rule by the people remain some of the most powerful legitimating myths of modern politics. A foundational ambivalence animates dominant approaches to the concept: democratic republics base their claims to legitimacy in the ostensible realization of popular sovereignty in spirit if not in practice. These very republics claim at the same time, however, that limits must be put on the exercise of power—popular, constituent, or constituted—through institutions and the rule of law (Schweber 2007). Whether viewed cynically as a means by which elites protect and reinforce their privileged status (Wolin 2004, 554) or as necessary for shoring up and protecting freedoms (Arendt 1991, 133), constitutionalism asks constituent power to adapt itself to the rule of law, not vice versa (Colón-Ríos 2012, 18). The resulting paradox—in which constituent power founds and legitimates constitutional orders by its extralegal nature, and yet by this very extralegality poses a threat to stability that must be contained or defined away—is a foundational contradiction of the North Atlantic liberal tradition. While a radical democratic current has from the beginning worked to undermine this resolution—both in the streets and in theory (Azzellini and Sitrin 2014; Lummis 1997)—liberalism's stultifying hold on the political imaginary and institutions of the republic remains secure.

The mechanism maintaining this hold has been to replace expression with representation. Jason Frank (2010) characterizes the aporia of constituent power and popular sovereignty in the United States thusly: "the people have been at once enacted through representation—how could it be otherwise?—and in excess of any particular representation . . . the authority of *vox populi* derives from its continually reiterated but never fully realized reference to the sovereign people beyond representation and beyond the law, the spirit beyond the letter, the word behind the words—the mystical foundations of authority" (3). The constituent power of the people is in other words a sacralized element of democratic identity rather than an actual, direct, and quotidian practice.

Constituent Power as the Limit of the Political

Most often constituent power is considered a "boundary or limit concept" (Loughlin 2014, 218) in which the "normal" breaks down into crisis, opening a political space for founding and constitution. It is the basis of political power rather than its procedural unfolding. "Power thus resides neither in "the people" nor in the constituted authorities; it exists in the relation established between constitutional imagination and governmental action" (231). Here, constituent power corresponds with Claude Lefort's (1986) conceptualization of democracy as that which emerges after the "decapitation" of political power in the *ancien régime*. Power is in other words an "empty space" occupied only temporarily by finite, mortal beings, and in which the only constant is a questioning, challenging, openness (303). Democracy, and the constituent power that propels it, is thus not defined by the rule of law, but rather by insisting that the question of who legitimately represents the people remain unanswered (Loughlin 2014, 234). This conceptualization of authority as "empty" inches closer to a governance attuned to the inherent contingency of constituent power. However, as a critical enterprise tied to the formation of legitimate representation, constituent power's conceptual imaginary, and the scope of its potential expression, remains ancillary to constituted power.

Democracy, in other words, is transmogrified into a procedure for legitimating rule rather than a primary, constant, and creative practice.

Democracy, popular sovereignty, and constituent power in the North Atlantic tradition form a conceptual cluster that establishes the grounds for legitimate, representative, government. They determine the boundaries of political practice rather than its substance. For example, the "right to revolt," with which John Locke (1998) closed his Second Treatise on Government (412), or the limits of the social contract, reached for Thomas Hobbes (2000) at the moment in which the sovereign can no longer protect the citizen (153), are the sorts of limit experiences that only come into effect *after* a "government dissolves itself by acting against the people's trust" (Colón-Ríos 2012, 8). Constituent power, even in these founding articulations, is thus relegated to moments of crisis, exception, and breach of contract.[2]

Later, the Jacobin and Jeffersonian thread of North Atlantic republicanism elevated this right to rebel to a duty intended to guarantee the fusion of freedom and equality. Thomas Jefferson (2007) famously argued that this duty to rebel ought to be exercised every generation, and even went so far as to suggest that rebellion with dubious causes and aims was better than no rebellion at all for the life of the nation (30). However, the maturing republics quickly neutralized any threat of a more continual and iterated practice of constituent power. In France this took the form first of an institution of passive and active citizenship—divided along lines of gender, property ownership, education, and race (Wallerstein 2003; Wollstonecraft 1995). In the United States the end of the Federalist debates and the suppression of Shay's Rebellion in 1787 effectively ended any possibility for an institutional design open to interventions by constituent power.

More disconcertingly, human slavery, settler colonialism, and their socio-institutional legacies have had the perverse effect of inserting a certain form of constituent power and popular sovereignty into a colonial discourse. Especially in North America, a racialized popular sovereignty has been a key trope deployed to justify territorial expansion and the conquest of indigenous lands (Goldstein 2014). Something like a perverse constituent rejection of the institutions of formal equality by constituted powers in the twentieth century can also be seen at play as whites moved to shore up informal and legal realities of white supremacy as an imagined and exclusionary community of racial equals (Roediger 1999). This then, is a marred constituent power afraid of itself—one that willingly flees into the embrace of constituted power to protect itself from a demonized other.

In the North Atlantic tradition we can thus trace a troubled trajectory of constituent power. Unleashed by the revolutions against monarchy and the aristocracy in the eighteenth century, continental and new world (white) elites moved swiftly to domesticate or deny its emancipatory drive before it could threaten the consolidation of their newly won social and political dominance. Since this original contradiction and capture, it has been relegated to a quiet aspect of civic identity, safely removed from actual practice. In the most perverse expressions of this new dynamic, constituent power, popular sovereignty, and democratic equality have been turned against each other. Constituent power in the United States, in the context of settler colonialism, Manifest Destiny, and racialized slavery and segregation, becomes an attribute of constituted power as exclusionary, antidemocratic, and murderous.

Constituent Power, Procedure, and Popular Sovereignty: Kelsen versus Schmitt

To put the stakes of these approaches into greater relief, it is worthwhile to revisit the twentieth-century debate between Carl Schmitt and Hans Kelsen on the making and remaking of constitutions and their competing understandings of the nature of political power. The argument—and its considerable aftermath—illustrates modern constitutionalism's ambivalence toward constituent power. It also exposes the degree to which debates on constituent power in both the North Atlantic and Latin America have been dominated—positively or negatively—by questions of constitution making and legality.

There is, however, an undercurrent to this genealogy, one that can also be glimpsed in key aspects of the Bolivarian Revolution in Venezuela. Here, constituent power has more to do with processes of subject formation and a cultivation of its potential than with the adoption of a legal code. It is, in other words, an ontological *process* that exceeds the symbolic formation of a "collective singular—*we the people*" (Loughlin 2014, 231). It is a mode of constituent power that "does not presuppose the modern state form" or assume that the trajectory of constituent power always points toward a constitution, but rather problematizes each of these positions and their assumed natural relationships (Spång 2014, 78). Indeed, from this perspective, by the time a "we the people" statement has been uttered, the wave of constituent power has already passed.

Enter two thinkers of interwar Weimar Germany: a Nazi jurist and a legal positivist. Whereas Schmitt considered constituent power anterior to, and hence beyond and above, any constitutional order (Schmitt 2004, 2008; Spång 2014, 3), Kelsen only very late in his life recognized it as a "noble lie" of constitutional thinkers (Kalyvas 2005, 232). For the normativist school of legal scholarship with which Kelsen is associated, the question of constituent power is an irrelevance in regard to the positive and scientific function of the rule of law (Dyzenhaus 2012, 257; Loughlin 2014, 222). For Kelsen (1945), a legal order is a self-referential moment in the "infinite chain of causes and effects . . . within natural reality," and as such, the search for a "first cause" or "sovereignty" is an ideological rather than a juridical matter (384). Questions of democracy, of citizenship, and of legitimacy are issues of procedure, not ontology. In this light, "the people"—or any other marker of collective identity, for that matter—is not a law-giving, nor authoritative, entity. Rather, people and state—constituted—power exist in a mutually defining but subordinated relationship in which "the people of the State are the individuals whose behavior is regulated by the national legal order; that is, by the personal sphere of validity of this order" (241). Thus, the "'source' of law is always itself law" (132), which is to say, the force of law is legible, present, and neutral.

There is an admirably immanent but nonetheless proceduralist bent to this line of analysis that borders on solipsism. The position that the ultimate source of legitimacy for a given legal order arises from the system of legal norms itself effectively removes the "head from the king" in our political theorizing. However, the notion that "legal order and law itself are best understood from the inside, from a participant perspective that argues that legal order has intrinsic qualities that help to sustain an attractive and viable conception of political community. . . [These] intrinsic qualities . . . give law its authority . . . without [them] there is neither law nor authority" (Dyzenhaus 2012, 233) does little to help explain for change in constitutional regimes. Nor does normativism explain how unequal power relations invest themselves in the reproduction of constitutional orders as an autonomous, closed, and self-sufficient regulatory universe. Even less satisfying is the way in which normative-positivist accounts of law dismiss matters of "justice" as subjective and ideological moralism (Kelsen 1945, 49). In a properly understood liberal order, according to David Dyzenhaus (2007), the question of constituent power simply never arises, and especially not in any practical sense (129). Constituent power as the capacity of the people to remake constituted orders is dangerous and subversive (Dyzenhaus 2012, 257). In this line of constitutionalist thinking constituent power is either defined away by normally functioning liberal democracies, or it is a threat to the very stability and order of public life.

For Carl Schmitt, such a position is politically, philosophically, and juridically untenable. Schmitt's critique of liberalism and neo-Kantianism held that "the grounds of a constitution are existential. A constitution can only rest on a concrete sovereign will and not on an abstract norm" (Cristi 1998, 188). Constituent power is sovereign, which is to say, both anterior to and above the constitutions it founds (189). Like Sieyès, he identifies constituent power as an expression of "the people"—*das Volk* for Schmitt, *nation* for Sieyès—which for Schmitt (2008) "denotes in a clear sense a people brought to political consciousness and capable of action" (101). He continues: "the constitution-making power [of the people] is unified and indivisible. It is not a coordinate, additional authority (legal, executive, judicial) alongside other 'powers' that are distinguished from one another. It is the comprehensive foundation of all other 'powers' and 'divisions of powers'" (126). Explicitly opposing Kelsen's normative emphasis on the continuity of positive law and procedure, Schmitt concludes, "the legitimacy of a constitution does not mean that a constitution originated according to previously valid constitutional laws. Such an idea would be thoroughly nonsensical" (136) in that such an act of submission would amount to the surrendering of a state's sovereignty and capacity for autonomous, self-generated, action. For Schmitt, the constituent power of the people is what gives constitutions their force, "guarantee[ing] the terms of their existence" in a way that the prevailing normative-positivist accounts of his day and our own—in which the law is free-standing and autoreferential—logically, politically, and conceptually simply cannot (Loughlin 2014, 219).

Schmitt was of course no democrat, which returns us to the fundamental ambivalence surrounding constituent power in the North Atlantic. Even in one of the most forceful articulations of its range, reality, and potential, Schmitt "comes to accept and recognize the *pouvoir constituent* of the people only because he had found a way to disarm it" (Cristi 1998, 192—French in the original). Or so he hoped. As one of the twentieth century's most compelling conservative thinkers, his goal was not to press forward and maximize constituent power. Quite the contrary, Schmitt was in search of a defensible position against what he considered to be an incoherent and unsustainable bourgeois liberalism and the more threatening specter of rampant Bolshevism (Balakrishnan 2002). He opens his 1929 essay "The Age of Neutralizations and Depoliticization" ominously: "we in Central Europe live 'sous l'oeil des Russes'" (Schmitt 2007, 80—French in the original). More than just alarm bells from an anticommunist, Schmitt points to an internal threat to the European order in the passage from French Republicanism to Soviet Communism. That is, in a dialectical turn, the contemporary Russian threat is one in which the enemy—whose "intent[ion is] to negate his opponent's way of life and [who] therefore must be repulsed or fought in order to preserve one's own form of existence" (1996, 27)—emerges from the "core of modern European history" (2007, 81). The task of the conservative is, of course, to find a way for constituted power to neutralize this danger.

The threat posed by Bolshevism is so profoundly existential for Schmitt in that it expresses and then deploys a fundamental truth of the modern

European order against itself, pressing reason, politics, and technology to their most logical, radical, and revolutionary conclusions. The secularization and diffusion of sovereignty presses toward an immanent state of soviets, the consequent flattening of distinction within the political amounting for Schmitt to an inhuman negation of life itself. In other words, Schmitt only makes the transition from the decisionism of his early work to constituent power in the late Weimar period when faced with the terminal crisis of the bourgeois order—one pushed forward by a subterranean constituent power he in turn sought to disarm by turning it against itself. Ever averse to democratic instability, he only comes to embrace constituent power when he thought he had discovered a response to the threat of "absolute democracy" in the form of state representation and the juridical separation of its "positive doctrine" from its "metaphysical" or "political theological" potentials (Cristi 1998, 192). In sum, when Schmitt talks of constituent power, he is really talking about a sovereignty that—against the general wishy-washiness of Weimar liberalism—is capable of foreshortening the radically open and dynamic force of constituent power into the singular oppositions of his larger theory of the political (Negri 1992, 8).

With this understanding of constituent power as boundless and constituted powers as contingent, we can now turn to Venezuela's Bolivarian Revolution. A majority of mainstream thought in the North Atlantic sees constituent power as a dangerous and destabilizing force. They have, in turn, sought ways to contain, negate, and otherwise neutralize it. However, every attempt to neutralize constituent power can only in reality ever hope to displace it, or force it underground, and then only temporarily—"well grubbed, old mole!" (Marx 1988, 121). Even Schmitt recognized this. Indeed, the constitutionalist tradition's subordination of constituent power to the technical-functionalist stability of the liberal state appeals to popular sovereignty in the name of democratic legitimacy but limits both experiences to the petty party politics of electioneering and the maintenance of the status quo. In this situation, the very tools of constitutionalism, meant to secure the permanence of a regime where modern freedom can be finally realized and, importantly, protected from its own excesses "contribute[s] to the sharpening, not the prevention, of civil strife" (Schmitt 2004, 93). In other words, the North Atlantic tradition has sought, at all costs, to avoid the difficult pursuit of political forms suitable to the *inevitability* of constituent power. As such, liberalism guarantees future conflict.

Ignoring this inevitability, and the resulting need to enforce the fiction of the permanence of constituted orders, all but guarantees that constituent power will be expressed in violent episodes of the return of the repressed. In the next chapter I argue that this was forcefully illustrated in Venezuela with the Caracazo of 1989. What distinguishes the twenty-first-century Bolivarian

Revolution from other political sequences, however, its explicit attempt to adapt the state form to the constituent energies that exploded with the announcement of structural adjustment in the late twentieth century. That is to say, rather than move to stifle or neutralize constituent power, Bolivarian thought seeks to follow it, to cultivate it, to move into the political spaces opened by autonomous actors, and in so doing, to press the state itself increasingly toward functioning as a nonstate (Ciccariello-Maher 2014, 803). In this, today's Bolivarian process has drawn from Venezuela's own endogenous histories of constituent power and revolutionary republicanism. It is to this genealogy that I now turn, after a short detour.

Incompleteness as Transition: Two Statues

I used to live in the center of Caracas near a confluence of monuments and competing political and architectural visions for the city. In my neighborhood, the modernist campus of the Universidad Central de Venezuela lay a short walk south from the massive roundabout and fountain at the Plaza Venezuela. To the east, the Bulevar Sabana Grande offered an open-air pedestrian mall and a hub of cultural and consumer life. To the west, the sprawling greenery of the Botanical Gardens and the Parque los Caobos.

Nearby, in the median of the Autopista Francisco Fajardo, which bisects the city, rises Alejandro Colina's (1951) statue of the syncretic deity María Lionza. There are many versions of the *diosa*. The last dictatorship, for example, attempted to Christianize her, decking her out in the robes, crowns, and female chastity of Catholicism's *marianismo* (Coronil 1997, 170). Michael Taussig's (1997) *The Magic of the State* introduced her to English-speaking academic audiences as the entrancing and terrifying Spirit Queen of the Monte Sorte. The statue wading between the lanes of the Fajardo is an unapologetically powerful assertion of both feminine power and indigeneity. In Colina's rendering, she is naked, sitting astride a tapir, her muscles flexed and arms overhead holding a female pelvis as a sign of fertility.

Every day devotees—*lionceros*—crossed the highway to make offerings to the *diosa*. Without fail, fresh flowers, candles, and fruits could be seen about the statue by cars speeding—or, more likely, crawling—by on the freeway. I was increasingly interested in the *marialeonceros*, but I could never get a straight answer to who they were, where they lived, how they made their way to the statue. My (middle-class) commuting companion was at the very least certain they were poor people. They faded into and out of the *ciudad espiritista* (the spiritualist city), the quotidian and informal spaces created by practitioners that crisscrossed the official organization of urban space (Ferrándiz Martín 1999, 45). In their wake, the residents of the spiritualist city left traces that faded like the flowers draped around the statue, which by the time of our commute were slowly wilting in the afternoon sun and the freeway's smog.

A second monument had already been turned into a memory by the time I first moved to Caracas in 2007. Just off the fountain at the Plaza Venezuela, Rafael de la Cova's *Colón en el Golfo Triste* (Columbus in the Gulf of Sadness) was removed by indigenous rights activists on October 10, 2004, whose direct action took the government by surprise. Traditionally known as the *día de la raza* (day of the race—Columbus Day in the United States), the official holiday had been renamed the *día de la resistencia indígena* (Day of Indigenous Resistance) by a presidential decree two years earlier. However, a recognition of indigeneity on the official calendar was not enough: the physical world had to correspond to the new values being forged by constituent power.

The column on which the toppled statue remained, guarded by less than convincing fencing. By the time I made it to the neighborhood it was covered in political and more immediately visceral graffiti—an empty space or canvas of representational power. In 2015 the statue of Columbus the conqueror was replaced by an aggressively muscular rendition of the cacique Guaicaipuro, a leader of the anti-Spanish indigenous resistance.

People I met were divided on the toppling of de la Cova's *Colón*. Most Chavistas felt Columbus was responsible for genocide. Any state commemoration of the murder could only ever be grotesque. Others I spoke to were more ambivalent in their responses.

"It isn't about Columbus, it's about history, and the Chavistas want to rewrite our history" was a common sentiment among opposition supporters I interviewed. Even those that agreed Columbus was a killer insisted the monument itself told part of the city's story, though not a few also emphasized the heroic aspects of the myth of "discovery." Another acquaintance, a reader of Dussel, Mariátegui, and other figures of Latin American decolonial thought simply shook his head and spit when I asked if there was anything worth salvaging from the *día de la raza*.

In either case, these two statues illustrate the inevitably incomplete relationship between constituent and constituted power. Both monuments performed a sort of civic training, localizing spaces for commemoration and signs of national identity in the case of *Colón en el Golfo Triste* or attempting to isolate and contain a goddess of nature's raw fecundity by surrounding her with the ostensibly insurmountable concrete barriers of the modernizing city and the busy freeway. These are cases in which the developmentalist state of the mid-twentieth century attempted to freeze the perpetual motion of constituent creativity.

They failed.

The degree to which the no less developmentalist—but more symbolically inclusive and polyglot—Bolivarian Republic of the early twenty-first century can succeed where the Fourth Republic couldn't is less than certain. Official discourse sets constituent power as fundamental and inalienable. However, as a statist project, its capacity to emphasize and cultivate constituent power collides with the centralizing tendencies that became increasingly prominent in the Bolivarian government since 2007.

Either We Invent or We Fail!
Constituent Power in Venezuela

Joel Colón-Ríos (2011) argues that whereas the North Atlantic tradition has, at best, relegated constituent power to a symbolic role in the storied past of national mythology, in Latin America, the concept has substantive weight in juridical praxis and the political imaginaries of social movements (365). In Venezuela in 1999 and in Ecuador and Bolivia in 2007, constituent power moved quickly from rebellion to foundation in the form of constituent assemblies and rewritten constitutions. While constituent power is by no means exhausted in legal documents, demands for new beginnings in a moment otherwise defined by the postpolitical condition of compromise and consensus after the "end of history" are striking in their boldness (Brown 2006; Rancière 2001, 2004; Swyngedouw 2009; Žižek 2008). In the case of Venezuela, Chávez made good on his campaign promise to convoke a constituent assembly after being elected. Legislators immediately launched a legal challenge to the move. They objected the existing constitution (like most other actually existing liberal constitutions) only allows for amendment by the legislature itself. For Colón-Ríos (and the Venezuelan Supreme Court, all of whom at the time were pre-Chávez appointees), while legally sound, this argument is philosophically flawed. It places constitutional procedure over constituent power, an untenable position in a democracy. The Court concluded "constituent power point[s] to an *unlimited* popular power, an unbound people who could rewrite the established constitutional forms without being subject to the constitution's amendment rule" (268). Put differently, if—as is proclaimed in all modern liberal republican charters—all power rests in the people, the Venezuelan courts declared this power to be inalienable (371). Replacing constituent power with constitutionalism equates democracy with the rule of law—a dangerously slippery slope at a time when law and order concerns are deployed against even formal democratic equality.

In this section, I outline a Venezuelan approach to constituent power, one that recognizes, cultivates, and intensifies its inalienability while pressing toward ever greater expressions of creativity and class antagonism. After a brief overview of constituent power as read through the "three roots" of twenty-first-century Bolivarianismo—Simón Bolívar, Simón Rodríguez, and Ezequiel Zamora—I emphasize the degree to which constituent power in this tradition has not just been concerned with political authority but also, and perhaps primarily, about the generation of new collective subjectivities. While this tradition is as complex and contradictory as that of the North Atlantic—*how could it be otherwise?*—by exploring enduring ways in which it served as a revolutionary thrust to break with constituted impasses, we can better appreciate how constituent power is generative for thought and action in Venezuela and beyond.

Above all else, Venezuela's relationship to constituent power is Venezuelan. Beyond nationalist idiosyncrasies, however, the Venezuelan development of the idea of constituent power complements juridical practice with ontological explorations into collective subjectivity, critiques of the global division of power and nature, and demands for social justice. It has been a living and malleable concept, defying orthodoxy. For example, in his wide-ranging and frequent public addresses, it was not uncommon for Hugo Chávez to discuss the idea of *poder constituyente y poder constituido*—constituent and constituted power—through readings of the Gramscian theory of hegemony, Maoist approaches to the military's role in society, liberation theology, world-systems analysis, and the politics of the Popular Unity government of Salvador Allende in Chile—all anchored by quotations, rereadings, and interpretations of Venezuelan history and letters.[3] Undisputedly, the most frequently cited figure in these speeches was Simón Bolívar, arguably *the* most important symbol of Venezuelan identity since the nineteenth century (Carrera Damas 2008; Lombardi 2008).[4]

Chávez cites "three roots" of philosophical inspiration for the Bolivarian Revolution. As Javier Biardeau (2009), a left-wing critic of the "myth of a progressive Caesarism" (88) around Chávez notes, in Bolivarian discourse "there are always references to certain central figures that interpellate and constitute subjects from the discursive fields of education (Teacher—Simón Rodríguez), politics (Leader—Simón Bolívar), and war (General—Ezequiel Zamora)." However, as he adds in a footnote, if these "archetypal images" do not provide a roadmap for the Bolivarian project for Venezuela, "one can still derive the attributes of a *political style* necessary for the construction of a revolution adequate to our times" (74; emphasis in the original, translation modified). I hasten to add that these historical referents are not steady signifiers. In drawing from Bolívar, Rodríguez, and Zamora, government discourse opens the past for reinterpretation, reconfiguration, and what Emilios Christodoulidis (2007) describes in a different context as "constituent self-definition" beyond the control of any official discourse (204). That is to say, the histories sanctioned by the state invite subterranean currents:

Bolívar the leader is accompanied by Bolívar the skeptic. Rodríguez the educator opens the door for Rodríguez the antiauthoritarian, antinationalist, and autonomist cosmopolitan. Zamora the general of the Federal Wars raises the specter of Zamora the proto-communist *llanero*[5] leader of a total war that refuses to recognize any boundaries or timelines in the pursuit of equality. What is more, in addition to these potential accompanying readings of key figures, other examples, referents, and interpellations enter the fray: the syncretistic cult of María Lionza, the insurrection *against Bolívar* led by Manuel Piar, and the ostensibly royalist *caudillo* José Tomás Boves being perhaps the most prominent in a country in which anxiety around constituent power has been linked to anxieties around race since the colonial era. In each of these cases we see both an instantiation of the ungovernability of constituent power—its creative instability extends to the terrain of the symbolic—as well as theoretical contributions to the contested field from which the Bolivarian Revolution, in its official as well as unintentional manifestations, draws.

Before turning to their theoretical contributions, a few biographical notes of the figures under consideration will be of use to readers unfamiliar with Venezuelan history.

Of the "three roots" Simón Bolívar is the most likely to be known outside of his country of origin. Born wealthy in Caracas and orphaned in his youth, he was briefly under the tutelage of the second "root," Simón Rodríguez, whose iconoclasm and idiosyncrasies were "a channel of independent thinking" in Bolívar's formative years (Lynch 2006, 25). After several failed insurrections and exiles in Jamaica, the United States, and Haiti—where Alexandre Pétion offered him moral, material, and technical support in exchange for a promise to end slavery in Spanish America (97)—Bolívar would lead the armies that liberated present-day Venezuela, Colombia, Ecuador, Peru, and Bolivia. Well-tutored in European history and philosophy, he nonetheless insisted thought, revolution, and statecraft in the Americas set their own courses (29). Among his heterodox proposals for a postcolonial pedagogical republic that might train away the "permanent infancy" in which Spain kept its subjects, Bolívar envisioned a "Gran Colombia" that would unify South America and protect it from the predations of a United States he saw late in life as "destined by Providence to plague America with miseries in the name of Freedom" (Bolívar 2003, 173). Bolívar's proposals for continental unity and enlightened progress were unqualified failures. By the time of his death in 1830—at which point he was all but penniless and on his way to exile—the sort of factionalism and conservative retrenchment he most feared was already the norm in South America.

Simón Rodríguez outlived his most famous pupil, and his path is similarly marked more by a stubborn refusal to surrender than success. He left

Venezuela in 1797 shortly after becoming Bolívar's tutor amid allegations of having participated in an anti-monarchist plot (Uslar-Pietri 1954, xvii). During his more than quarter century in exile—during which he changed his name to Samuel Robinson in a nod to Daniel Defoe's novel and Jean-Jacques Rousseau's pedagogical tract, *Émile* (xvii)—Rodríguez traveled to Jamaica, the United States, England, and multiple locations in mainland Europe, studying and opening experimental schools along each step of the way.

When he returned to the Americas in 1823, it was with the explicit aim of "inventing a new system of schooling for newly liberated peoples" without imitating the "corrupted educational models, philosophies, and practices of the past" (Kohan 2015, xiii). This emphasis on newness, an intense rejection of imitation, and a recognition of the need to experiment is characteristic of a relationship to constituent power shared by Bolívar and Rodríguez. Bolívar gave his old tutor tremendous material and political resources to build student- and inquiry-centered schools in newly liberated Colombia, Bolivia, and Peru. Bolívar and Rodríguez considered the school to be the central ground for social, economic, and political transformation in the postcolony, which is perhaps why they were closed by local elites in short order. Rodríguez lived out the rest of his life rather unknown in his native Venezuela—it was only with the resuscitated Bolívarophilia of the late nineteenth and early twentieth century that he would be rescued from obscurity (Borges 2005, 17–23). After years of traveling throughout Pacific South America working in various industries and establishing still more pedagogical socialist communities, he died in Peru in 1854. In 1954 his remains were moved to the Panteón Nacional in Caracas. It was the first time he returned to Venezuela since his departure in the late eighteenth century.

Ezequiel Zamora is in many ways a result of the failure of the republican projects of Bolívar and Rodríguez. For most Venezuelans, independence changed the composition but not the nature of power; conditions were, if anything, worse and exploitation even more acute after the official transfer to a Creole ruling elite. In much of the country, isolation, anarchy, and illiteracy reigned (Müller 2001, 31; Sanoja Obediente 2011, 323). By 1859 civil war broke out between conservative oligarchs and liberal reformers over questions of land ownership, effective citizenship, and socioeconomic equality (Müller 2001, 32). Zamora—already a radical peasant leader—entered this conflict as an outspoken opponent of elite privilege but was killed in battle in 1860. In Chávez's (2005) telling, when Zamora died, "the hope of a people died. The revolution turned to anarchy, retreated, failed, and the ruling class and the oligarchy held on to power and spread their hegemony over all the mechanisms of power" (54).

Bolívar, Rodríguez, and Zamora make up the "three roots" of official Bolivarian discourse in the twenty-first century, representing the political, educational, and civic-military fronts in the project for social transformation and serving as indigenous sources for thinking about the political in Venezuela. As such, they are most often articulated into a postliberal theoretical universe that emphasizes social change through the congruence of citizen and state, a skepticism toward the free market and any attempt to naturalize inequality, and the potential for a civic-military alliance in the fight against social ills (Chávez 2005; Gott 2008a; Maduro Moros 2013; Rojas 2008). In what follows, I emphasize how these figures contribute to a distinctly Venezuelan response to the challenge of constituent power—both in their day and in the present—that replaces the anxiety and reaction of the North Atlantic with generation, experimentation, and cultivation.

Bolívar and the Foundation of Political Freedom

On February 15, 1819, Simón Bolívar (2003) convoked the Congress of Angostura in which he relinquished dictatorial powers and proposed a constitution for the Venezuelan Republic. In the speech, delivered on the eve of his third attempt to liberate the Americas from Spanish rule, Bolívar both extolled the virtues of republican government and argued that the federalism of the last insurrectionary attempts brought on their own failure. "Many ancient and modern nations have shaken off oppression," he observed, "but rare are those that have succeeded in enjoying even a few precious moments of freedom; almost at once they have fallen back into their former political vices, because it is the people, not their governments, who drag tyranny in tow" (35). He concludes, "The habit of domination makes [the people] oblivious to the charms of honor and national prosperity, and they are indifferent to the glory of experiencing true freedom, under the tutelage of laws dictated by their own will" (35). Bolívar's thinking here both exposes his debt to thinkers of the French Enlightenment such as Montesquieu and Constant as well as his own distinct approach to the modern and republican thought (Urueña Cervera 2007). He starts from Montesquieu's (1989) maxim that the laws of any given state need to reflect the character and disposition of its people and their surroundings but then follows this observation to its rational conclusion: that any republican statecraft in the Americas will have to draw from its own experiences, not the annals of European philosophy.

For Bolívar, building an American practice of governance oriented toward freedom in the aftermath of Spanish colonialism—to link freedom and liberty—hinges on a series of unprecedented challenges. The first concerns the practical matter of waging a war for independence and the military discipline such an endeavor requires. Secondly and concurrently comes the organization of democratic-republican institutions. Martial discipline and democratic free association rarely amplify one another. All subsequent challenges derive from the distance between political independence and sovereignty from the exercise of liberty.

The resonance here with his teacher Simón Rodríguez (1990), who concluded war with Spain resulted "not with Independence, but an armistice" (19), is no doubt not accidental. Both Bolívar and Rodríguez emphasized that full freedom lay somewhere beyond victory on the battlefield. Put differently, the realization of freedom—always a collective act—rests upon the cultivation and expression of constituent power; political independence and sovereignty were for Bolívar and Rodríguez necessary but by no means sufficient prerequisites for such a project.

The case of the Americas in the early nineteenth century poses an inter-esting challenge in this regard. The war for independence did not come about as the result of a popular movement against foreign oppression. Even among the Creole population, who were most concerned with protecting and augmenting their economic and racial status, there was little in the way of consensus about independence (Drake 2009, 54; Serrera 1994). Indeed, by some accounts, the wars for independence were less a struggle for sovereignty and autonomy than a transatlantic civil war between elites, initially less about independence than equal status with the Iberian kingdoms of the Spanish Empire (Rodríguez O 1998). This reading is borne out by the fact that independence first arrived as a *fait accompli* when Napoleon's armies invaded the Iberian Peninsula in 1808 and deposed the Spanish monarchy. The first *cabildos abiertos* (open councils) summoned to respond to the sudden vacuum in imperial authority pronounced themselves loyal to the king—illustrating the less-than-revolutionary aims of Bolívar's contemporaries (Chasteen 2008; Silva and Uribe 2014).

For elites, independence was less about the generation of new subjectivity than shifting rank and title. Rather than an uprising of constituent power, these early moves for regional autonomy were not aimed at the formation of a new political order. Much less were they attempts to fully replace the strict racial and caste hierarchies of the Empire with egalitarian institutions. Even after the war effort took on a decidedly anti-Spanish and republican character, these colonial and postcolonial elites—much like their cousins in North America—would move to shore up their privilege in the face of a potential redistribution of wealth and power by whatever political, philosophical, or ideological means at their disposal (Mignolo 2005). It was precisely this sort of conservative factionalism that Bolívar sought to counter.

Bolívar's (1985) approach starts from a sobering series of observations. At Carúpano, in 1814, he lamented, "to destroy a government, whose origins have been lost in the obscurity of time; to subvert established principles; to transform custom; the upheaval of opinion and, finally, the establishment of liberty in a country of slaves is a work almost impossible to execute spontaneously" (52). Elites were divided or opposed to independence, let alone to forming a republic, and his armies were horribly, incomparably, and utterly outgunned. And yet, throughout his writings during the wars and then in their aftermath, Bolívar insists on the need to cultivate the behaviors, customs, and practices of a new republicanism among the freed peoples of the Americas. This ethos of cultivation can be seen most characteristically in Bolívar's constitutional proposals at the Congress of Angostura in 1819. Here Bolívar adds to the traditional liberal trio of legislative, executive, and judicial branches of government a *poder moral*, or Moral Power,

> whose dominion is childhood and the hearts of men, public spirit, wholesome customs, and republican morality. Let us so constitute this Areopagus that it will keep vigil over the education of our children, over our national system of education, and purify the corrupted aspects of our republic, denouncing ingratitude, selfishness, coldness of affection for the country, idleness and negligence on the part of citizens, and condemn the causes of corruption and pernicious examples, correcting our customs with moral castigation, not only against those who attack them but also those who undermine them, not only against whatever violates the constitution but also what violates public respect. (Bolívar 2003, 49)[6]

The parallels with Rodríguez, for whom it was necessary to define a *neocracía*—a new order—in the Americas, and who saw government not just as the administrator of politico-military sovereignty but first and foremost of the promotion and distribution of knowledge, are again not accidental (Jorge 2005, 184). The *poder moral* sees republican governance as having a productive and pedagogical relationship with constituent power. It aims to "correct" what three centuries of Spanish rule had produced at the level of political subjects—to make citizens of peasants, slaves, and subjects. Colonial life, he reckoned, left both the virtue and know-how of independence lacking in the Americas and caused the first attempts to establish independent republics to fail.

Bolívar's *poder moral* was thus a project of political constitution both in its sense as noun—*the Venezuelan Constitution*—and verb—the act of *constituting* the Venezuelan citizenry. In this way, the nineteenth-century Bolivarian project in many ways predicts what Michel Foucault (1991) would later describe in terms of governmentality, or, the means by which political power invests itself at the level of individuals and populations. Rather than the sovereign command, Bolívar can be seen here as recognizing that the unity he considered an absolute prerequisite for republican governance must come before any attempt at institutional design might be possible.

Earlier political statements, the *Cartagena Manifesto* (1812) and the *Carta de Jamaica* (1815), for example, are exercises in reflection and recomposition in the aftermath of political and military failure and in preparation for the next campaign. In these statements and elsewhere, Bolívar (2003) concludes failure was penned by those "worthy visionaries" who saw in the first independent Venezuelan state an "ethereal republic" based on the "perfectibility of human beings" rather than on their actually existing condition (11). Midway through the text of the *Cartagena Manifesto*, Bolívar—here drawing from Machiavelli—states that the virtues of a true citizen are "impossible to attain in absolutist governments," and what is worse, they are even harder to practice *ex nihilo* in times of war. Again echoing Machiavelli, Bolívar insists, "government must necessarily adjust itself . . . to the context of the times, men, and circumstances in which it operates" (6). The resulting Bolivarian theory of the subject demands attention to the condition of the present. The "citizen," in other words, cannot be found in nature but is rather the result of a series of interventions, cultivations, inscriptions, and recognitions.

Perhaps the most forceful attempt to *constitute* a constituting power of a people while the war can be seen in Bolívar's 1813 declaration of War to the Death against the Spanish occupation. Bolívar begins by addressing "Venezuelans," announcing that his "army of brothers" has been sent by the "sovereign congress of New Granada" to "Destroy the Spaniards, protect Americans, and establish republican governments which will form the Confederation of Venezuela." He goes on to list the inhumanity of the Spanish and the justness of the cause of independence and liberty before ending with a direct appeal to "Spaniards and Canarians," in which he declares amnesty for those who join the republican cause and promises death for any who fail to actively fight for an independent Venezuela.

Bolívar's declaration recognizes the conceptual demand of a constituent power that dwells beyond the temporal and spatial limits imposed by the Spanish Empire. The declaration does not stand in for or subsume constituent power; it illuminates a new truth of the political and an axiom that would come to guide the republican project in Venezuela. The amnesty, for all who transformed themselves through collective action into Venezuelans, outlines a ground on which a singularly *Venezuelan* history was to begin. From that point a proliferating series of identifications tied to this new territorial-juridical reality of—variously signified—América, Venezuela, and Gran Colombia could be formed, expanded, and cultivated. While the political and social composition of this new collective entity had yet to be determined by 1813, neutrality in relation to its construction was, for Bolívar, not an option (Bolívar 1985, 18–19).[7]

We have then an opening of constituent power as a raw, new, and creative force. Bolívar's declaration attempts to give name and direction to this force, but there are of course very real limits to the reach of these events. First, the singularity of Bolívar's statement obscures the collective nature of the project of nation building. Second, and more damningly, the historical context of the *decreto* and the independence wars illustrate internal limits of the republican project in relation to the realization of constituent power. There are, furthermore, concerns that must be raised around the martial trappings of Bolivar's republicanism. While Diego von Vocano's (2012) Hegelian reading of the military's dual role in multiracial national and subjective liberation—both country and subject being given over to their own consciousness in the act of choosing to subordinate themselves to the command of another (69)—the resulting emphasis on discipline and order are nonetheless inimical to the unfettered expression of constituent power. The civic-military alliance of twenty-first-century Bolivarianism has, furthermore, repeated Bolívar's tendency to respond to challenges by centralizing power in the executive, a move that Paul Drake (2009) and others have suggested is a result of his often racialized concerns about democracy's viability among the newly independent *Americanos* (64).

The case of José Tomás Boves, a royalist caudillo who died in 1814 after complications from a wound suffered in battle, offers a particularly striking historical example of nineteenth-century Bolivarianism's inability to fully grapple with the excessive potentials of the constituent moment. Although Boves was depicted at the time (and for much of posterity) as an example of Royalist barbarity, he was rather something more of an independent vector pushing Venezuela beyond the intra-elite struggle for a transfer of political control and into an actual social revolution (Rodríguez Rojas 2014). Indeed, his *llanero* "legion of hell," made up of over ten thousand runaway slaves, mestizo peasants, and indigenous peoples, recognized no higher authority— royal or republican—than Boves, illustrating a more fundamental demand for autonomy than the simple royalism with which the rebellion has been labeled (Ciccariello-Maher 2014, 795). His allegiance to the crown has barred him from the official pantheon of heroes in Venezuela. However, Boves has recently been revisited as a powerful example of historical and actually existing racisms and as an illustration of the limits of early republicanism in Venezuela. More recently, radical Bolivarians have characterized Boves's armies as an unconquerable popular force of commoners pitted against a political sequence that had from its beginning been dominated by racially preoccupied and economically powerful elites more intent on furthering their class interests than founding a republic (Ciccariello-Maher 2014, 796). Boves, and more concretely, the threat of an army of freed slaves, forced a radicalization of the revolution. Against elite pressures to the contrary, Bolívar had little choice but to make good on earlier promises to abolish slavery. Put differently, the emergence of newly empowered political subjects—slaves, peasants, and the Legion of Hell—shaped an emerging constituted order through the articulation of their constituent and violently egalitarian force.

Or, as Chávez himself argued in 2012, the years of the "legion of hell" were

terrible years, those. But . . . from my point of view it defined the path
of the revolution for independence. Simón Bolívar, among others, but
primarily him, understood that the Venezuelan people wanted a real
revolution and not the pantomime of one. The rich in Caracas and the
landlords in Aragua didn't want to liberate the slaves. They didn't want
social equality for *pardos* [mixed-peoples], for blacks, or for Indians: even
Bolívar had not understood this. And what happened then? Well, blacks,
pardos, the poor, and the extremely poor joined up with whoever offered
freedom, and that was José Tomás Boves. Boves wasn't a royalist. He was a
leader of the poor . . . of the poor against the rich and the white. (Quoted
in Rodríguez Rojas 2014)

Boves, then, marks a limit to Bolívar's early republican project, but also
pushes it toward a more radical path. With Boves, the self-organization and
activity—the constituent power—of the excluded comes to shape the path
of Venezuelan politics and history.

These encounters with Bolívar highlight political—if fraught and
internally inconsistent—aspects of constituent power as generation and
creation. For Bolívar, constituent power requires cultivation, and it can
never be found in a vacuum. It is, rather, forever beset by enemies: the
vested interests of elites, the institutions of constituted power, or even the
impatience of underdeveloped constituent power itself. Perhaps above all else,
Bolívar's thinking on constituent power is realist: it is unavoidable, a matter
not only of governance and freedom, but of humanity itself. Constituent
power perpetually encounters limits; it is how those limits are negotiated
that defines the republican project.

Simón Rodríguez: Invention, Experimentation, and Cultivation

Bolívar offers a political expression of the pedagogical principles outlined
by Simón Rodríguez. Rodríguez's entire *oeuvre*—including the provocative
eccentricities of his prose, style, and approach to the essay form itself (Briggs
2010; Kohan 2015)—can in many ways be seen as articulations of constituent
power rooted in contingency, creativity, and experimentation. For Rodríguez (1990), revolutionary ruptures provide openings and opportunities;
they are, in his words, the "products of circumstances, not of projects" (19),
and while he considers himself above all else a republican dedicated to the
intertwined causes of freedom and liberty (7), he nonetheless also recognized
that governments reflect the internal composition of a people (114). As such,
a properly Rodríguezian revolutionary project must be tireless in its work to

eradicate traditions that allow political and social irrationalities of the past to persist into the present. In place of these limits internalized by social subjects, his approach to pedagogy fosters the shared cultures necessary for a freer future (185).

In a Platonic tone, Rodríguez insisted on government's role in contributing to the development of the citizenry, seeing education as—a "profound socializing instrument . . . a weapon of liberty, that, in the first instance, is an internal liberty" (Jorge 2005, 15)—as key in the passage from circumstance to (collective) project. In other words, Rodríguez (1990) envisioned a pedagogical apparatus oriented toward direct self-governance, of subjects capable of a politics "without kings and without congresses" (69). However, quite apart from the sort of rugged individualism that would emerge in North America, for Rodríguez such an endpoint could only be reached via the social, which in turn had to be inculcated through a project of popular education (79; Robinson 2005, 262).

Readers in the twenty-first century will likely raise alarm bells at the dystopian, even totalitarian, potential of such a proposition. With the state so intimately involved in the production of knowledge, what guarantees prevent it from abusing its power to manipulate the truth? Oughtn't we to expect the state to act as the proverbial "thought police" over a body politic that has now transitioned from colonial servitude to the postcolonial illusion of self-governance and freedom? Rodríguez was keenly aware of these concerns, especially in the aftermath of the independence wars, as Creole elites quickly moved to replace colonial exclusion and inequality with their own, "national," regime. Indeed, he argued that any sort of "idleness, vice, [or] criminality" was the result of a collective ignorance that was wholly and completely the fault of society rather than nature (Rodríguez 1990, 215). The threat of thought policing and social control is in part avoided by the flattening of state-citizen relations. Put differently, Rodríguez refuses to separate governed from governing, as became the norm within modern liberalism. *Citizens are the state*, in a constantly evolving social whole.

This dynamic requires absolute equality and questions the compatibility of democratic freedoms with the representation and procedure already being posited as necessary by the liberalism of his lifetime (Rodríguez 2004, 187; Robinson 2005, 261–264). Unlike later formations that relegated a majority of the population to subordinated tutelage, the pedagogical communities he founded were relentless in their drive to break with preexisting hierarchies, challenging the exclusions of race, class, and gender that underpin colonial and postcolonial societies in Latin America (Miller 2006). Cultivation is, in other words, for Rodríguez a profoundly immanent process. While it is true that his political vision prioritized the construction of an all-inclusive *pueblo*—in other words, one that would not only be inclusive of the poor and excluded by economic and political elites as well—he also prioritized the participation, empowerment, *and self-direction* of the poor and excluded and was an outspoken critic of the miseries enacted on humans in the name of economic profit (Kohan 2015, 48–49; Rodríguez 2004, 193). If equality and inclusion applies to actually existing elites as well as to the historically excluded, it is with the latter that the agenda for social transformation must be set.

A final aspect of Rodríguez's thought on constituent power complements his insistence on equality and cultivation. Rodríguez's (2015) insistence on the openness of the educational process, on his radically "bottom-up" understanding of a pedagogy committed to living, testing, experimenting, and learning "without fear of committing errors" (167), are key to elements of his thought that can be seen in the Bolivarian Revolution of the twenty-first century. For Rodríguez, pedagogy was less a practice of imposing ideas than of encouraging inquiry and experimentation (Kohan 2015, xiv). It was less a matter of mastering data than of finding, producing, and sharing knowledge. Any hope for a republican project rest in the progressive elimination of ignorance. However, his understanding of education and human nature also depicted learning as an inherently social activity driven by the curiosity of learners themselves (Rodríguez 1990, 194). The process would above all else be an open encounter with the new, appropriate to the novelty of the postcolonial American reality (Rodríguez 2004, 190).

The openness of Rodríguez's system is encapsulated most pressingly in contemporary Bolivarian discourse in one of his most famous formulations: "Inventamos o erramos!"—we invent or we fail! Here he calls for a continuous process of reinvention in the pursuit of forms of collective life adequate to the postcolonial American situation, but also in the processes of self-creation and discovery as constant experimentation. For Rodríguez, the response to the question and challenge of constituent power lies neither with mimicry nor the establishment of new orthodoxies, but rather in contingency, creation, and the reflexive education of equals.

The Bolívar and Rodríguez "roots" of the twenty-first-century Bolivarian Revolution emphasize the cultivation of creative and contingent constituent power in step with the autonomous generation of political subjectivities. Rodríguez, for example, speaks less of "states" in the political sense than of government (Jorge 2005, 97), which is to suggest an interest less in forms and organization than in practices and relationships. Even in those moments in which Bolívar might be said to be at his most constitutionalist—in the Angostura address of 1819, for example—it is clear that he shares his teacher's primary focus on the production of new subjectivities. That is to say, while both Bolívar and Rodríguez owe undeniable debts to the European Enlightenment and while both bear traces of a liberalism that was still at the time a heterodox mix of anti-monarchism, republican egalitarianism, and liberal individualism (Kalyvas and Katznelson 2008), both also insist on the pressing need to push beyond any mere imitation or repetition of the North Atlantic tradition.

The insistence on the Americanness of the American revolutions are carried through in the Bolivarianism of the twenty-first century. Nicolás Maduro (2013), writing in the preface to a reprinting of Chávez's *Libro Azul* shortly after El Comandante's death, suggests "in many and diverse respects, [Rodríguez] is more important for us than Karl Marx, and that is because he thought from our reality, he rooted his thought [in our reality], assimilating what ideas he had to from Europe, but thinking from the presuppositions of our America" (24). Rodríguez is an important vector of liberation, but he is also for contemporary Bolivarians a decolonizing force in both thought and action. Rodríguezian thought is the generative basis for new forms of American identity, rooted in the post-independence struggle to build a free republic in Latin America.

A final concern must be raised that arises from thinking Bolívar through Rodríguez, especially in the troubled context of post-Chávez Venezuela. The teacher was much more of a democrat than the pupil, whose military approach to most questions colored his republicanism in aristocratic hues. However, both of their projects were centered squarely on the formation of human freedom—which in their time had yet to be confined by liberal democracy to the private sphere or the ballot box. Constituent power demands we appreciate democracy as something more than elections. Even still, the Maduro government's willingness in 2016 and 2017 to suspend elections when it was apparent they would lose are disturbing occurrences for the protagonists of constituent power as much as for liberals. It suggests a distancing of constituted order from the forces that made it possible, and a creeping autoreferentiality that sees the maintenance of state power as an end in itself. One potential theoretical warning to draw here is that the intersection of Bolivarian civic-military, pedagogical republicanism, Chavista centralization of power, and Rodríguez's comparatively anarchic and directly democratic egalitarianism is perhaps always a fraught one. Rodríguez's "inventamos o erramos" in this light is less a practical conclusion than an ontological one. We are in constant motion, or else we *are not*. Prioritizing one aspect of the Bolivarian constellation over the others leads quickly to that constellation's disintegration.

Ezequiel Zamora: Tremble, Oligarchs!

Ezequiel Zamora's relationship to constituent power is both more and less direct. A radical general in the Federal War of the nineteenth century killed in the heat of battle, Zamora is most often associated in contemporary Bolivarianism with a benevolent, progressive, military force for the civic-military alliance of the twenty-first century (Maduro 2013, 26). His slogans—"Tremble, Oligarchs!" and "Liberty or Death!"—correspond to the high tide of the federalist cause and its most radical moments of peasant mobilizations against the agricultural elites of postcolonial Venezuela (Müller 2001, 68). His federalism draws a geography of power in which networks of autonomous communities collaborate under principles of solidarity and mutual aid (Chávez 2013, 66). Despite the centralizing tendencies that accelerated in twenty-first-century Bolivarianism after the 2006 elections, this model of confederation and solidarity remains an orienting principle for many in the movement, particularly those organizing under the banner of the *estado comunal* (communal state) (Angulo 2017, 99; Ciccariello-Maher 2016). As a militant of the liberal party in its ascendency, Zamora also anticipates the degree to which contemporary liberal states neither fully realize nor contain constituent power. His is a push for equality and solidarity, a pursuit for which he gave his life (Chávez 2013, 84). He also symbolizes constituent power's necessary violence in the face of hierarchy and exclusion. We see in Zamora, in other words, an illustration of constituent power as perpetual and relentless motion—even, in the case of the Federal Wars, against the very institutions that it ostensibly created.

The example of Zamora also resonates with Rodríguez's insistence that social transformation emerge from the self-organized initiative of the excluded, the critique of private property, and a skepticism toward centralized state power. He operated in the "wild west" of the Venezuelan *llanos*, at a time when bands of indigenous people, former fugitive slaves, and landless peasants took the "social question" into their own hands through the expropriation of property and land. The general himself gave tacit approval of these actions in the logic and the target of his armies: "everyone is equal, down with the *godos* [oligarchs], property is of the commons, we shall make a homeland for the indigenous" (quoted in Müller 2001, 39). Importantly, Zamora's pronouncements also echo the constituting capacities of constituent power. His armies are made up of a founding communal authority that both abolishes the economic basis of the prevailing order, while the enemy is identified not only as competitor in battle, but a partisan of an invasive, revanchist force—he refers to the conservative side of the Federal War as *godos*, a term usually reserved for Spaniards and Royalists, some three decades after the wars for independence.

Like the other two "roots" of the Bolivarian tree, then, Zamora's contribution to the Venezuelan conceptualization of constituent power emphasizes the necessary violence—legal, epistemic, and physical—of political foundings. But even more to the point, while he offered plenty of the sort of martial, hypermasculine, and weaponized slogans useful in mobilizing masses for political ends, he also insisted on holding his forces to democratic and civilian control and insisted on the convocation of elections and a constituent assembly—even as conservative soldiers marched on his positions (Müller 2001, 66). Zamora is in other words more than just a symbol of an uncontainable class antagonism; he is also and just as potently posed as an example of the positive coexistence of revolutionary struggle, direct democratic praxis, and the realization of constituent power.

Concluding Remarks

This examination of the historical and philosophical roots of Bolivarian discourse points to a conceptualization of constituent power distinct from that of the North Atlantic. Although it would be a stretch to suggest either of the various approaches in Venezuela or Europe and North America form something as internally consistent as a school or a tradition, and while both are challenged by persistently unruly expressions of constituent desires, we can nonetheless point to a divergent set of assumptions, desires, and understandings—especially in consideration of twenty-first-century attempts to reconfigure state and constituent power in the Bolivarian Revolution. First and arguably most important among these is the emphasis—found especially in Simón Rodríguez, Ezequiel Zamora, and the challenges mounted by Boves to early Bolivarianism itself—of constituent power as a "commoning" practice. As Silvia Federici provocatively suggests, commoning presents us with a mode of collective life beyond the market and beyond the modern state form, with an emphasis on appropriating the means of social *reproduction*, and in which "the production of ourselves as a common subject" is the priority of political struggle (Federici 2011). Constituent power is, in other words, a radically egalitarian project involving an intense degree of participation, self-direction, and intersubjective development— *protagonismo*, in twenty-first-century Venezuelan argot.

Against this, the North Atlantic tradition, in the long process of secularization that has resulted in actually existing democracy, has since the sixteenth century sought to contain constituent power. Even in those cases where constituent power is celebrated—as it and its proxies necessarily are in an era that avers liberal democracy to be the only possible and desirable way of organizing collective life—it is only allowed to be visible insofar as it results in a constituted order. It can only ever be felt in its full force in moments of crisis, and even then only in those unimaginable crises that exceed the procedural capabilities of actually existing liberal democracy.

Rodríguez's and Bolívar's attention to the uniqueness of the postcolonial condition and what they both saw as a pressing need in turn to create similar unique political institutions all point to the second aspect of constituent power in the Americas: experimentation. For them, independence in many ways "happened to" South America when the Spanish Empire fell to Napoleon. The task of the postcolonial republic was to cultivate a civic culture capable of self-governance and focused on the common good (Rodríguez 1999, 246). For Rodríguez this entailed an intense degree of creativity and flexibility on the part of institutions—first and foremost the school. If both Bolívar and Rodríguez saw the need for a pedagogical state actively involved in the production of knowledge and citizens, they also held that education occurred not through programming and imitation, but rather through inquiry, interaction with the world, and collaboration with fellow citizens on an equal terrain (Rodríguez 2004, 206).

Finally, constituent power in the Bolivarian key has been keenly focused on the emergence and strength of new subjectivities. Quite simply put, if the experience with Boves showed Bolívar anything, it was that would-be designers of public institutions ignored mobilizations of previously unrecognizable bodies at their own peril. This means—perhaps in line with Schmitt's insight, and reflected in the 1999 decision by the Venezuelan Supreme Court—that while constituent power shapes, constrains, and orders constituted powers, the reverse can hold true only temporarily. With constituent power, then, we can glimpse a form of political (that is to say, collective) ontology that is always potentially in the process of becoming. In so doing, constituent power holds the promise—I almost typed threat—of rendering an existing order obsolete, of breaking with the present. It is, in Mikael Spång's (2014) estimation, "an act of dissolving society as it is and in the process being courageous enough to say good-by to what we are" (177).

This appreciation of constituent power leads to further tensions, confusions, and conflicts more than to anything we might consider close to a recognizable state form. This has been the case for contemporary Bolivarianism as much as it was for the various failures of Bolívar, Rodríguez, and Zamora. The constituted powers of the twenty-first-century Bolivarian state forget their debt to constituent power as often as other actually existing democracies, if in different ways; Bolívar the general, who insisted on unity and discipline, is often cited more than Bolívar the radical republican. The remaining chapters of this book are tasked with outlining moments and emergences in which, against all odds, constituent power asserts itself to reshape the political, the physical, and the subjective substance of daily life.

CHAPTER 2

Rupture, Protagonism, Party

The Caracazo as Event

❧

The Caracazo of February 27, 1989, was a cataclysmic return of the repressed that abruptly ended illusions of a Venezuelan social peace. During a week of uprising and bloody state reprisal, hidden class and racial divisions of the Puntofijo years and the Fourth Republic (1958–1993) asserted their undeniable existence. Against prevailing notions of a social peace, an exceptional democracy, or of a Gran Venezuela, the Caracazo exposed the extreme social violence that always accompanied the normal functioning of the country's representative democratic and rentier capitalist systems (Fariñas 2009). The preferred benevolent self-image of the developmentalist state dealt itself a near-fatal blow with the Caracazo, setting off a series of political and social transformations that rewrote Venezuela's past, present, and future.

The Caracazo marks the beginning of a process of unbinding and emergence. Bruno Bosteels, in his work on the politics of French philosopher Alain Badiou, contends that all politics are punctuated by moments in which "the state's excessive power becomes visible . . . as the result of an emergent political subject." With the result that political sequences like those initiated by the Caracazo do not "start out from a previously given bond or group, not even when this social bond is defined in terms of the class struggle, but precisely from a local unbinding of the common bond" (Bosteels 2011, 30). Badiou calls these moments events, or points in time from which all previous and future politics are defined (Badiou 2005, 176).

The Caracazo is an event. In the words of Venezuelan intellectual and former minister of communes Reinaldo Iturriza, with the event of the Caracazo "new forms appear, extraordinarily modifying the political context, provoking a reexamination of the conditions in which the future will take place" (Iturriza 2006, 38). The event is a subjective and temporal opening. It rewrites the relationship to the past, present, and future, becoming a new benchmark or reference against which to measure fears, aspirations, and potentialities. Indeed, for Badiou, political subjects *qua* subjects are only possible in relation to an event (Badiou 2009, 277). Events initiate a sequence in which subjects are produced through their pronounced fidelity to the possibility of a new ordering of society, one glimpsed in moments of egalitarian rupture.

Three procedures mark the Caracazo as an event. Pushed by subjects once relegated to the nonbeing of social marginalization and political representation in an economically, racially, and geographically segregated system, the Caracazo *opened* the political terrain of twentieth-century Venezuela. In the second procedure, it *exposed* the scene into which it intervened, illustrating the constant violence and exclusions of an order that presented itself as democratic, peaceful, and affluent. Events force constituted power to express its always present potential for repression. In the third procedure, the Caracazo is a moment of subjective, social, and political *generation*. In its aftermath, new ways of doing politics, new individual and collective bodies, and new social relations were more than just a mere possibility; they were necessary. The Caracazo, as event, thus signaled an absolute and previously unthinkable rupture with a constituted ordering of being.

However, in rendering legible what was once previously unthinkable, the Caracazo also problematizes the relationship between event and constituent power. Events are only retroactively recognizable as founding moments. Constituent power is an always present excess or possibility of the relations that define a given political sequence, but are not wholly preconfigured by the previous order. Indeed, in their aftermath events shift the very meaning and legibility of that previous order. They mark a transvaluation of values, to borrow Nietzsche's turn of phrase, and their truths are carried forward by the subjects they engender. Events thus also tend to lend themselves to secondary processes of sacralization and neutralization, relegating the constituent powers that created them to the extremes of political experience at the birth and death of regimes.

Bosteels insists that Badiou—the thinker most associated with the idea of the event—is well aware of this. "Badiou's own philosophy," he writes, "does not pretend to save the purity of the event by haughtily withdrawing from all immanence and situatedness. The point is to study the consequences of an event within the situation, not to elevate the event into a wholly other dimension beyond being" (Bosteels 2011, 285). Thinking about the event requires reconciling newness and beginning with structures, procedures, and subjects that make this newness recognizable. Events, like constituent power, require carriers for the truths they expose to have any material significance. Both need, produce, and are produced by collective subjects. In other words, with the Caracazo we can see the passage of the new to the normal or of an emancipatory potential's capture by constituted power—a capture that can move toward more or less egalitarian horizons.

This chapter moves across three conceptual fields and three historical moments: the Puntofijo era and the rupture of the Caracazo, the neoliberalizing 1990s, and the Bolivarian Revolution in the twenty-first century. The Bolivarian Revolution describes the Caracazo as the foundation of a liberatory political sequence, passing from event as rupture, to the consolidation of subjects in practice, and finally to the party form—and specifically, to the Partido Socialista Unido de Venezuela (United Socialist Party of Venezuela, PSUV)—as the projected carrier of egalitarian forces. In attending to this sequence, however, this chapter raises concerns around the inadequacy of any dialectical thinking that relies on binary oppositions and deterministic resolutions rather than dialectics as the contingent and internal relations of complex systems. These concerns then move to a sustained consideration of Jodi Dean's 2016 *Crowds and Party*, as one of the most compelling (but in the case of Venezuela, lacking) accounts of the party in twenty-first-century liberatory politics. Far from the realization of constituent power, or from the constant extension and recalibration of the latent power of the crowd to its potentials, the party in the case of the PSUV attempts to replace egalitarian desires with electoral contexts and the identification of the revolution with the state, replacing the former with the later.

Event: *El Caracazo*

The Caracazo "is an event of a political nature; with it, 'something distinct' appears on the scene; that is, the *turba*" (Iturriza 2006, 41). Here, Iturriza makes explicit reference to Deleuze and Guattari's *A Thousand Plateaus*, using the term interchangeably with "the masses," "the many," and "the multitude" (Iturriza 2006, 14).[1] *La turba* can also imply a combustible biomass like peat moss, lending a potential force of nature to the term, despite the fact that he later insists there is "no place" for "metaphors that align [the Caracazo and the *turba* that emerged with it] with natural phenomena." All the same, the *turba* is flammable, combustible. He continues: "The *turba* doesn't function *like*, nor does it act similar to nor imitate anything. Better, it comes as an undetainable upsurge, an uncontrollable oceanity" (Iturriza 2006, 43). The *turba*, like the Caracazo, is something unprecedented that forces a complete reconfiguration of a political situation. Its force realigns society, changes the rules of the game.

But what, precisely, did the Caracazo break with? What was the situation from which it emerged? How has this past been rewritten with the recognition of the Caracazo *as event*? Was it as unforeseen as has been claimed? And what are the stakes involved with the various ways in which it has been narrated by observers, supporters, and detractors of the Bolivarian Revolution in the twenty-first century? This section does not aim to tick all the boxes that mark Caracazo as an event. Doing so would only serve to reify the event as a category of pure beginnings. Our aim is rather to consider how thinking of events like the Caracazo *as events* can be seen as symptomatic of particular desires and relations—both among specific political subjects (*la turba*, Bolivarians, opposition, Chavistas, and so forth) as well as to the collective projects of past and future in Venezuela.

The Puntofijo pact was an institutional arrangement that defined Venezuelan politics for the thirty-five years bookended by the fall of Marcos Pérez Jiménez and the Caracazo. Signed by the leaders of Acción Democrática (Democratic Action, AD), the Comité de Organización Política Electoral Independiente (Committee of Independent Political Organizations, COPEI), and the Unión Republicana Democrática (Radical Democratic Union, URD), the pact sought to ensure the stability of representative democracy in oil-rich Venezuela. The pact amounts to a common minimum program for the liberal-democratic state and an agreement to hold and respect elections (Levine 1973, 43). In practice, writes Fernando Coronil, Puntofijo was an "an agreement to make pacts. This underlying accord entailed a commitment to avoid political conflict as well as structural change. The pacts therefore served to control the transformation of political identities during a transitional period; they sought to reform, but also to preserve, the existing social structure of economic and social relations" (Coronil 1997, 229). The Puntofijo system, in sum, preserved and developed the lucrative petrostate for those who controlled it while making enough concessions to democracy to prevent a more radical reconfiguration of Venezuelan society.

While the signatory parties agreed to share power with one another, they jealously protected their arrangement from outside interference and internally were so rigidly centralized that each invited future conflict. The early years of the pact were turbulent, as the first AD governments of Rómulo Betancourt quashed rebellions by students and junior officers, some of whom explicitly saw Puntofijo as a betrayal of the anti-dictatorship uprisings of 1958 (Ellner 2008, 57; Linárez 2006; Ojeda 1970). Shrewd electoral and institutional manipulation between AD and COPEI, furthermore, allowed them to increasingly marginalize the URD—whose popularity in Caracas outstripped that of AD, its closest ideological competitor—from the benefits of the agreement. Cold War anticommunism and Betancourt's preferred iron-fist response to subversion led to an official prohibition of the Partido Comunista de Venezuela (Venezuelan Communist Party, PCV) and provided an ideological smokescreen when necessary to deal with party dissidents and upstarts from the base and youth leagues.

Steve Ellner and Miguel Tinker Salas describe the degree to which AD was successful in its capture of civil society and trade union organizations throughout the Puntofijo years, operating these ostensibly autonomous spaces as its own exclusive territory (Ellner and Tinker Salas, 2007, 9). Indeed, so complete was AD's control of the Confederación de Trabajadores de Venezuela (Venezuelan Confederation of Workers, CTV—the national umbrella trade union organization) that the union became a key source of elite reaction to the early Chávez administration (Ellner 2008, 115). AD also controlled key university administration posts, faculties, and student organizations, the latter of which it expected to accept strict party discipline and highly circumscribed, usually *ex post facto*, participation in the policy-making process (Campbell 2003, 49). These exclusionary and often violent conditions of Venezuela's "exceptional democracy" immediately inspired a short-lived but nonetheless influential guerrilla campaign to violently overthrow the *partidocracia* (partyocracy—a popular portmanteau that sarcastically places a question mark over Puntofijo's preferred self-image as an "exceptional democracy" in an otherwise troubled region).

By the time the regional economic crisis reached Venezuela in early 1983, calls were already mounting to overhaul Puntofijo's constrained democracy and Venezuela's rentier capitalism. Midway through the 1980s, the government acceded to decentralizing reforms. By the 1984 administration of Jaime Lusinchi (AD) even created a presidential commission for the reform of the state. The proposed reforms from the commission would be partially implemented throughout the late 1980s and 1990s. They included, for example, the direct election of governors for the first time in the country's history, curbing AD and COPEI's ability to control municipal elections through closed list systems, and the partial delinking of state and local funding from executive mandate. Rather than moves toward participatory or a more inclusive democratic practice, however, they were widely interpreted as intended to "resuscitate [the] political legitimacy" of a Puntofijo system all but universally seen as a corrupt and inefficient governing edifice freed of any responsibility to the population at large (Campbell 2003, 49).

The system was broken. Or worse, it was functioning as intended, but was now straining in the face of growing resistance at home and the challenges of globalizing neoliberalism. Between 1978 and 1994, per capita gross domestic product fell by over 15 percent. At the height of the crisis—just after the Caracazo—foreign observers found 80 percent of the population living at or just above the poverty line, and over half of the working-age population was employed in precarious and informal work (Días, Rodríguez, Villegas 1996, 109). As the regional downturn of the 1980s deepened and resistance to Venezuela's initially piecemeal and heterodox neoliberalization grew, these timid gestures toward constitutional reforms quite literally exploded on February 27, 1989. After the explosion, calls for administrative and electoral decentralization were overtaken by demands to convene a national constituent assembly and to refound the republic (López Maya 2011, 22).

In the uprisings that began on February 27, 1989, the poor explicitly pitted themselves not only against the second government of Carlos Andrés Pérez but also against the neoliberal structural adjustment policies of the International Monetary Fund (IMF). Pérez had recently been reelected president on a platform explicitly antagonistic to the IMF—on the stump he referred to the international lending body as "la bomba-sola-mata-gente"— "nothing but a bomb that kills people" (quoted in Coronil 1997, 375).[2] Once in office, however, Pérez enacted one of the most orthodox Structural Adjustment Programs the continent had yet seen (Karl 1997; López Maya 2005.

The response from below was immediate. Though initially centered in suburbs of the capital where the shock first took form in an overnight jump—in some cases well over 100 percent—in the cost of transportation, the rebellion soon spread throughout the nation. A high degree of coordination was exhibited as the revolt grew. In some cases neighborhood committees were formed in order to better distribute the labor and the spoils of looting. As protests turned to grocery stores and markets, people "found to their outrage that stored deposits of subsidized basic food stuffs that had disappeared from the market were waiting to be sold at marked-up prices. Cases of powdered milk, cornmeal, pasta, and coffee were passed to the street and distributed, as the outnumbered police looked on. Some policemen, themselves poorly paid, helped looting take place in an orderly fashion or took part in it as well" (Coronil and Skurski 1999, 315). Surprised by the scale and ferocity of the uprisings, Pérez called in the military while insisting on national television that the situation was under control. The resulting pitched street battles eventually pushed protesters away from the affluent cores of cities like Caracas to poor and historically politicized barrios like Petare and 23 de Enero. The military treated these poor fringes as free-fire zones. After five days of looting, street battles, and state reprisals in which anti-aircraft cannon were deployed on densely populated super block apartment complexes, as many as three thousand people were left dead.[3]

Riots mark important transitions throughout the twentieth century in Venezuela. With each perforation of an established order, new collective subjects emerged, giving name to itself while also—and this is key— renaming the order against which the riot, insurrection, or uprising rebelled. "The people took to the streets," writes Iturriza, "in 1936, as the *vulgo* (masses, commoners) at the death of a dictator; as the plebeians, in 1958, overthrowing a dictator; as the poor, in 1989, this time opposing democracy" (Iturriza 2006, 15). In 1936—with the death of Juan Vicente Gómez—and

1958—the overthrow of Marcos Pérez Jiménez—the unrest was temporary and immediately folded back, respectively, into a caretaker dictatorship or to a highly circumscribed, pacted representative democracy. In 1962, military and civilian attempts to overthrow Rómulo Betancourt left hundreds dead in the (unconnected) Porteñazo and Carupanazo. In all cases, the disruptions were immediately relegated to the status of threatening memories, their popular content neutralized and replaced in dominant narratives by a story of democratic consolidation and elite-led transitions.

The Caracazo differs from this long history of riots, *jacqueries*, and insurrections, according to Iturriza, not because of the quantity nor the identities of participants, nor for the methods used in the uprising or reprisals. Each moment was the result of expressions by previously disempowered or otherwise frustrated groups, even if each moment also saw these subjects folded back into a more or less rigidly hierarchical order. Rather, he insists, the difference rests with the relations engendered among participants, connections that result in an utterly unpredictable mass and force (Iturriza 2006, 42). Whereas previous uprisings were quickly extinguished by the violent force of the consolidating liberal democratic state, the Caracazo occurred in a conjuncture where the state was weakened by corruption and the neoliberalizing global economy. In its aftermath, it became an event, exposing the lies that had sustained Puntofijo democracy, opening space for new forms of political organization, and generating the subjects that have defined Venezuelan politics since.

After the Caracazo it was no longer possible to consider the Puntofijo era a benign epoch of social cohesion and national development. That is to say, the *Caracazo as event* not only marked the emergence of a previously unrecognized *or unrecognizable* political subject—according to Iturriza, *la turba*, the multitude, the masses—but also and just as importantly reshaped the familiar, revoked the commonsense, recast the very nature of the prevailing order. The Caracazo was temporally multidirectional; it rewrote history even as it shaped the present and future.

This revision of the Venezuelan political imaginary was as immediate as it was complete. For example, in the accounts appearing in *El día que bajaron los cerros* (The day the hills came down), the widely distributed and cited collection of accounts of the Caracazo published in 1989 by the newspaper *El Nacional*, the journalists repeatedly editorialize on Venezuela's shattered self-perception. "Yesterday [the February 27, 1989] Caracas was Beirut. No one thought the situation could come to this. Very few could have seen something like this ever happening in this valley, considered only a month ago as the center of democracy in the world" (Araujo et al. 1989, 33). "Lines of people queueing for food are no longer the sole patrimony of socialist

countries, they have become daily figures in our much maligned democracy
. . ." (43). "It was a repetition of a phenomenon that had already happened
in Brazil and in the Dominican Republic, in which measures put in place
by the International Monetary Fund produced popular responses of looting
and pillaging" (37). The comparisons to other Latin American countries
don't stop there, nor are they any more favorable for Venezuela's preferred
identity. Comparisons to Colombia's civil war (49) and to Pinochet's coup
in Chile (75) are particularly telling. Venezuela, the reporters note, in a few
short hours has moved itself from a tourist destination to a "location" for
war reporters from the Associated Press, veterans of conflicts in Nicaragua,
El Salvador, and Angola (75).

In a very real way Venezuela not only changed politically and socially, it
also *changed rank*. The country could no longer hold itself above the rest of
the developing world, according to the reporters in *El día que bajaron los
cerros*. Indeed, in the accounts of the different ways in which the Caracazo
was experienced—a sense of siege and paranoia among the rich, an initial
carnival followed in short order by battle and massacre for the poor—one
gets the sense of an awakening that Venezuela had never *really* arisen from the
developing world in the first place. With the Caracazo, the country's entire
recent history of democracy and social peace were thrown into question.

The result was a fecundity of rebellious subjectivity, opening what Roland
Denis describes as a "labyrinthine diversity of spaces in rebellion whose
unity in action in the first moments was [no easy or foreseeable matter]"
(Denis 2001, 24). In the decade following the Caracazo, spaces had to be
liberated or created to address the needs of the growing numbers of those
impoverished or displaced by neoliberalization. Subversion took a constant,
dispersed, and creative character both of necessity—to avoid the heightened
security and surveillance of the neoliberalizing 1990s—as well as a reflection
of the growing desire for a form of politics suited to the new reality. Such
was the egalitarian ultimatum levied upon—and, in turn, by—the subjects
engendered by the Caracazo.

The Caracazo signals the collapse of an old order and the difficult first
steps of something distinct—if not entirely metaphysically "new." It is the
desire for newness that animates the thinking of the event, even as the new
comes via a dialectically fused rewriting of the past. Thinking about the
event in this way sustains a collective, egalitarian, desire—the event enables
the continued expression of constituent power.

Men with Guns outside la Escuelita

By the time I first moved to Caracas in 2007 the revolution had entered
into a dynamic that George Ciccariello-Maher (2007a) described in terms
of a revised "dual power." The state apparatus under Chávez continued to

dominate the politics, civil society, and economy of Venezuela. However, at the same time, the momentum of autonomous social movements, activated in the aftermath of the Caracazo, continued along a different logical path. Allied to but not ultimately reliant on the constituted power of the state, the end goal of the Bolivarian Revolution's protagonists was to replace representative liberal institutions with the direct and participatory exercise of communal councils. For Ciccariello-Maher and others (see, for example, Azzellini 2010 and 2015), the distinction at this point had to do with the newly forged complementarity of forces. In this moment of the Bolivarian Revolution, the state worked to protect and encourage the incommensurable constituent power that had been reshaping Venezuelan politics since the eruption of the Caracazo.

There have, however, always been endogenous and exogenously imposed conflicts causing detours in the process, even in the most politically advantageous conjunctures. In 2007 the Chávez government had consolidated its control over the national oil company and international prices for crude were nearing their peak of over $140 USD per barrel. Social spending was at an all-time high as were social indicators. The opposition was in a state of disarray. Some voices on the Venezuelan right were finally (if temporarily) acknowledging that the political terrain had shifted definitively, and elements of the business class were very publicly joining ranks with the government. While debates around the PSUV and the Five Motors simmered within Chavismo, these were as often as not treated as tactical matters rather than ideological conflict: socialism for the twenty-first century was the goal and the path. Debate centered on how, and how fast, to progress along it.

At the time I was volunteering in Misión Ribas, the Misión Bolivariana targeting secondary education. My class of fifteen was comprised entirely of women—all mothers, and all workers in the center of the city. We met evenings in the living rooms of their *ranchitos*, illegally and self-built cinderblock homes that ceased being temporary at least a generation ago. After a few meetings, we were able to move to a permanent classroom space the community had attached to the coordinator's home, a few hundred meters away from a Misión Barrio Adentro clinic. Despite being visibly exhausted from the day's duties, they were all without exception eager for class and for the opportunities the diploma would offer them.

This was a tightly knit group. Many of the *vecinas* (neighbors) grew up together. All had worked together to navigate the lean and mean years, and they were also all ardent Chavistas. Reasons varied by individual, but few aligned with the Bolivarian Revolution out of doctrinal conviction or a personal affinity for El Comandante—though the consensus around the room was that he was one of the only good men in government, and that he was surrounded by *alacranes* (scorpions). All emphasized, instead, that the revolution worked with them, aiding them as they tackled the practical necessities of their lives.

"We have always had our dignity. Now we have a school too," was a common sentiment. That these communities climbing up the hills surrounding Caracas existed in the first place was testament to collaboration, mutual aid, and creativity. These were not planned neighborhoods. Water, electricity, stairs, sewage—all aspects of infrastructure from houses to roads were created or acquired by neighbors long before Hugo Chávez. While previous politicians inevitably engaged with the *ranchitos*, either for populist campaigns or criminalization, all insisted the Bolivarian Revolution was different, that it not only offered them more resources, but that it was *theirs* in a more substantive and deeper-reaching way. For the *vecinas* in Misión Ribas, the Bolivarian Revolution was a government that recognized them not merely as votes, nor primarily as the threat they posed should they again descend from the hills. It was, rather, a project they constructed *and defended* as they did their own hillside community.

They were protagonists of a process of their own making. Chávez was less a politician than a collective creation. They saw the classes in Misión Ribas not only as means to better themselves, but as part of the struggle.

"Against whom?" I asked, on an awkward but not altogether uncommon occasion. Our classes wrapped up around 9 pm, and as I had to work first thing in the morning, one of my students' teenaged children would normally guide me down the maze of informal streets, stairs, and pathways to a bus that would take me to the subway station and eventually home. On this particular evening, however, Carlos* shook his head solemnly, "You're going to stay with us tonight."

When I asked why, he answered, "Stupid guys with guns." His matter-of-fact, almost dismissive, tone was strangely calming, despite the soaring murder rates in Caracas. "You're fine here." There was no immediate threat, apparently—this was just a precaution, and that was that.

After a few rounds of conversation among the students, we were sitting on Yessica's* stoop, sipping coffee as we wound down the day. In the ebb and flow of the ensuing conversation that touched on anarchism and the World Social Forum, taxis (safer to call one than to flag one down on the street, they warned), and soccer, the "stupid guys with guns" never came up. When I pressed the matter—this was after all the first time in my life a commute had been interrupted by armed civilians—the response was both personal and sociological. Yes, the *malandros* (thugs) were frightening; everyone had been touched by the atmosphere of generalized social violence that has only intensified in the years since. Of course they were a problem.

---

*Names have been anonymized.

But they were the result of years of underdevelopment, of neoliberalism, of the Fourth Republic. The *malandros* were an obstacle and a symptom of what the women were working against, but not necessarily a primary one.

So who was the problem?

"Them," replied Emilio,* gesturing to the city center below. "The ones with the money."

"Ah, the opposition," I replied.

"Some wear red now too," chimed in Yessica.

"Like the *boliburguesía*?" I asked, using the neologism for members of the bourgeoisie that had opportunistically joined the ranks of the Bolivarian Revolution.

Laughter. "Yes, of course, but not always. There have always been sons of bitches in the government. Always. They have always had [the money] for themselves. . . . They aren't going to just give up all that wealth, that luxury. . . . They're selfish; they don't care about us, the *pueblo*. We have to fight for what is ours."

While the government of the Bolivarian Revolution provided materials and support for the students of Misión Ribas, this dynamic of *cogestión* (comanagement) required the *autogestión* (self-management) of these communities for its original and sustaining initiative. Organization, mutual aid, and creative thinking and action were normal on the urban periphery, a fact of life that was increasingly the only option with the austerity after the Caracazo. Antagonism and protagonism against inequality and toward a more inclusive, participatory, and just future were not abstract concepts. They were rather a means for negotiating daily life, even when stupid guys with guns, corrupt officials, or the many other difficulties of life in the Bolivarian Republic, made that negotiation seem impossible.

Protagonism: From Riot to (Bolivarian) Revolution

One of the more striking aspects of the Bolivarian project as government has been the degree to which its dynamism has been divided between the executive branch and autonomous movements. In this, it follows and attempts to challenge dynamics that were first established in the aftermath of the Caracazo. While it cannot be denied that institutional and symbolic authority were increasingly centered on the president, the 2000s also saw the proliferation of autonomous movements demanding land reform and democratic workplaces, local governing bodies like the communal councils, and social welfare programs organized according to principles of *cogestión* like the Bolivarian Missions. Thus, while liberal observers sounded alarms over the potential reversal of administrative decentralizing reforms of the 1980s and 1990s by a strengthened executive (Banko 2008), such concerns miss the substantive and direct devolution of powers to the citizenry that were taking place at the same time. Put in other words, regardless of the degree to which Chávez indulged in the penchant to rule by decree that inevitably accompanies the military mind, the Bolivarian era also saw the cultivation of a directly democratic, inclusive, and collectively oriented political sensibility among populations that have historically been among the poorest and most marginalized in Venezuela's history.

These egalitarian desires are key to the Venezuelan concept of protagonistic citizenship (Kingsbury 2016b). Whereas notions of participatory democracy emphasize active engagement within established decision-making regimes, protagonism seeks a deeper and more foundational role, determining the shape, scope, and values that inform the work of the commons; it is constituent power as civic identity and political action. It both defines and defies, maintaining a critical distance from the state institutions that depend on it. The analytical shift may be one of degree rather than kind, but it still suggests that protagonism recognizes the capture of constituent power will always either be incomplete or, more maximally, impossible.

In the decade between the rupture of the Caracazo, the election of Chávez, and the rewriting of the constitution, the norms of Venezuelan political order crumbled. Venezuelans took to the streets in greater numbers and with greater frequency than in any other period in the country's history (López Maya 2005). Two attempted coups were widely celebrated in 1992 by a public that felt betrayed not only by the regime of Carlos Andrés Pérez but by the Puntofijo in its entirety. In 1993 Pérez was impeached and, in 1994, for the first time in the history of Venezuelan democracy, a candidate was elected to the presidency from a party other than AD or COPEI.[4]

These were also moments of what Roland Denis describes as the *buhoneroización* of Venezuelan society.[5] Precarity became ever more generalized as public-sector employment and the social safety net suffered wave after wave of attack by the neoliberalizing state. What is more, with these erosions, the informalization of daily existence, and the deepening of austerity, levels of crime and fears of insecurity reshaped the physical geography and national imaginary in ways that define Venezuela well into the twenty-first century.[6]

Two general tendencies characterize the moment between the Caracazo and the election of Chávez. The first is the concurrent neoliberalization of state, society, and economy and the emergence of new modes of political organization and activism. In this sense, Venezuela is increasingly defined not only by increased incidences of insecurity and localized protest, but also by experiments in *autogestión* and *cogestión*, in which "people manag[e] collective

decisions themselves rather than surrendering them to a cadre of state officials" (Purcell 2014, 147). In the context of social and political reconfiguration, borrowing from Marina Sitrin's (2006) work on Argentina, the emphasis
"is based not in the *what* but in the *how*"—in the relationships that press
into uncharted territory, an experimental decentralization from below (vii).

Throughout the 1990s, Venezuelans politicized new aspects of daily life
and forged modes of engagement beyond the established boundaries of liberal
and representative democracy. For example, Sujatha Fernandes notes that
in the face of economic austerity and the discrediting of traditional power
brokers like electoral parties and trade unions, women in the urban periphery
formed new roles for themselves. In the face of a traditionally hierarchical,
clientelist, and *machista* political culture women created gendered spaces—
such as soup kitchens and the *círculos femininos* (women's circles, which
often emerged as schisms or offshoots from movements and neighborhood
associations otherwise dominated by men)—that increased their ability
to negotiate effectively with state and non-state actors. In other words, as
the state increasingly withdrew from its welfare provisions and as previous
regimes of political legitimacy and behavior collapsed, women challenged
their place and status, emerging as powerful actors in the coming phases of
Venezuelan politics (Fernandes 2007; see also Motta 2013).

Coordination by neighborhood groups changed the nature of local
governance and reconfigured expected dynamics of command and obedience
between citizens and officials. Electoral reforms in the late 1980s were meant
to salvage Puntofijo's hold on institutional power rather than reform it
(Campbell 2003, 49). However, and especially after the Caracazo, they allowed
for progressive candidates like Aristóbulo Istúriz to gain the mayor's chair in
Caracas with new mass, union, and popular parties like La Causa R (Radical
Cause). Once in office, Istúriz attempted to support and institutionalize
the position of neighborhood assemblies, *mesas técnicas* (working groups),
and social businesses as recognized players in the increasingly de facto if
not de jure directly democratic governing of the city (López Maya 2011,
14). For example, the *mesas técnicas de agua* (Water Working Groups, MTA)
were formed during the Istúriz administration and were active from 1993 to
1996. These bodies (dismantled shortly after Istúriz was replaced by Antonio
Ledezma in 1995) coordinated between community assemblies, government
officials, and the city-owned water provider, Hidrocapital, to plan and
provide potable water to the neediest parts of the city—often on the informal
urban periphery, where inhabitants lacked legal title to their land and their
homes. The memory of the MTAs as a project in "upcycling" *autogestión* into
cogestión would eventually be resurrected in 2001. They have since spread
throughout the country as the preferred model for the management and

development for water infrastructure. By 2007 there were over 2,700 MTAs across Venezuela (López Maya 2011, 29).

These movements were by their nature intensely local—experiments in self-help and mutual aid born of the necessity of structural adjustment—and often only tangentially unified, especially prior to the coagulating effects of Chavismo. In a contrapuntal motion to these instances of *autogestión* and *cogestión*, a liberatory, revolutionary, militaristic, and charismatic Bolivarianism also circulated in Puntofijo's aftermath. In this current, Chávez increasingly played the role of an "egalitarian caudillo" (Denis 2001, 115). That is, Chávez functioned by the end of the 1990s in much the same way that Ernesto Laclau describes a populist empty signifier that emerges as a unifying subject and trajectory from a crowded ideological field and comes to define a varied and heterogeneous political movement (Laclau 2005, 2006). However, despite the effects—and affects—of this early Chavismo, the limits of an inevitably electoral populist were already on display.

Chavismo coagulates in two senses. It brings together several disparate tendencies, social functions, myths, ideologies, and positions into a sustained counterattack on neoliberal common sense. But it also uses the unquestionable charisma and political acumen of El Comandante to channel the novel potentials that circulated in the wake of the Caracazo into a disciplined, hierarchical, and seemingly eternal campaign. In other words, it seeks to press a transition from *autogestión* to *cogestión* and in turn to channel the latter into a statist project of electoral democracy.

In other words, protagonism in the Bolivarian Revolution operates in a dual register. It emphatically insists that political experience exceeds the boundaries set by liberal democracy without falling into doctrinaire anti-statism, and it inserts the force of *autogestión* into an evolving relationship with state power. With protagonism, politics is meant to remain expressive and generative; it moves within but also beyond the state. Protagonism is meant to be that which keeps constituent power and its egalitarian ruptures open, active, and present.

In an intervention published after Chávez's death, Roland Denis insists that the Venezuelan state once again became a vector of undiluted constituted power—it had lost its reference and its roots in constituent power, revolutionary rhetoric aside. While constituent and constituted power in the Bolivarian process always interacted in a tense dialectic, the conjuncture once again demanded a break with institutionalized forms that had outlived their usefulness. Protagonism, as self-generated activity and relationships rooted in a relentless egalitarianism, for Denis, provided the only path beyond the inevitable institutional and opposition reaction that followed Chávez's death.

In short, Denis poses the expression and expansion of counterpower as protagonism beyond the liberal and even Bolivarian state as the solution to the recurring limits of constituted power, even when the latter attempts to ally itself to the egalitarian desires of the people. His is an attempt to reopen the debates Chavismo keeps trying to close: to what extent is constituted power—as the state form—an irredeemable capture and foreclosure of the liberatory potential opened by the Caracazo? To what extent are elections inimical to the subjects that carry the potential of the event? Finally, in terms more directly attuned to the controversies of Bolivarian politics before, during, and after Chávez: What is the relation of the party form to the subject? *Can parties be subjects?*

The Party: On Revolutionary Openings. And Closings.

The entangled challenges of liberation, development, and individual and collective freedoms are tied to the production and reproduction of subjects. The question, then, is how best to produce, foster, maintain, and extend the individual and collective subject forms that are most honestly oriented by an egalitarian desire. The preceding discussion of events and protagonism have suggested that subjects emerge in the aftermath of ruptures with a constituted present, pressing from their appearance to rewrite the world, its rationalities, and its hierarchies. But these emergent subject forms require something—a prolongation of the encounter, a mythical supplement, an affective drive—to sustain and expand the egalitarian gaps opened in events like the Caracazo. A brief examination of previous experiments with collective forms helps illustrate the centrality—indeed, the mutual implication—of questions of subject, structure, and liberation in Venezuela.

In his *Letter from Jamaica*, Simón Bolívar lamented that centuries of Spanish colonial rule founded an American race somewhere "between the legitimate owners of the land and their Spanish usurpers," that was ill-prepared for the challenges of self-government (Bolívar 1985, 73). The colony produces the colonized as a subject locked into a subservient position, excluded from the practices of the self—education, commerce, and government—so central to modern notions of the individual. Bolívar, in other words, anticipates the interventions that dependency theory would make a century and a half later: underdevelopment is a condition created and enforced by the developed world. It is not a "natural" state or the consequence of one's progress along the universal, progressive, and linear trajectories of civilization. His response to the situation came in 1817, with his Address to the Congress at Angostura, in which he drew the outlines of an *estado docente* (pedagogical state) capable of transforming postcolonial subjects into agents of an independent and free Venezuela. While both Bolívar's diagnoses and prognoses betray the philosophies of the Enlightenment era that produced him—prejudices, overstatements, willful exclusions, and all—they nonetheless also illustrated a more enduring need of politics. Subjects are not only produced by structures and events, they are also prone to entropy and thus in need of supplements, adjuncts, supports, sustained encounters of the sort that can maintain and augment moments of voluntaristic creativity into the approaching horizons of a different world.

Later, the successful Cuban Revolution of 1959 provided a powerful alternative to the economistic stagism Orthodox Marxism or the *partidocracia* of Puntofijo (Marín 2011, 147). Castro's 26th of July Movement proved that mass, popular, revolutionary action directed by small vanguards of dedicated militants could topple a dictator with powerful allies in the North (see also Gómez García 2014; Zamora 2006). The reaction from the United States and its allies, particularly AD president Rómulo Betancourt, illustrated the lengths to which liberal consensus would go to derail any movements for independence from the Cold War division of powers in the Americas. The repressions of the early Puntofijo years "recalled the worst years of Pérez Jiménez" as Betancourt "declared war on the left" to consolidate his control of now-democratic Venezuela (Gott 2008b, 101).

In Venezuela, Fabricio Ojeda would have heard Che Guevara's call to build a "new man" for the socialism being built in contemporaneous Cuba. Ojeda was a leader of the "patriotic junta" that overthrew Pérez Jiménez and representative in the National Assembly with the URD until it was pushed out of Puntofijo in 1960, at which point he and others founded the guerrilla Fuerzas Armadas de Liberación Nacional (Armed Forces of National Liberation, FALN). Like Guevara, he insisted that new societies required new subjects to build them, and that this new subject would by necessity exceed the bounded individual of the prevailing order. The collective was central, inculcating an ethics of shared responsibility and overcoming the fatalistic sense of "invincibility" the Empire projected onto and into the developing world (Ojeda 1970, 47). This new guerrilla subject needed to be adaptable to circumstances, a proper militant capable of using every political and military tool to her advantage. She would have to be, in short, an individual creative nexus of theory and practice that only ever gained meaning and identity as part of a struggle for collective liberation (Ojeda 1970, 128). For Ojeda, Venezuela had all of the resources—and grievances—necessary for success revolution; it only lacked the leadership and initiative of a vanguard revolutionary party.

The collapse of the Puntofijo system was triggered by the mobilization of subjects once covered over by the representative democracy that suppressed Ojeda's revolutionary hope in Venezuela in the 1960s. Throughout the 1990s and into the early Chávez years, these subjects persisted in their protagonism, insisting that a Venezuela founded on principles of solidarity, equality, and participation was not only possible, but that it already existed in the breathing networks resisting neoliberalization. This then, is the subjective truth lurking beneath the official pronouncements of the Bolivarian government: the revolution taking place in Venezuela since the Caracazo has been fundamentally a question of the formation and persistence of modes of subjectivity opposed to the common sense imposed by late capitalism on the developing world.

As Venezuelan intellectual Franco Vielma has put it:

> Chavista intersubjectivity has been able to implant universal values on political, economic, social, and cultural reality . . . after 17 years in political power, [these values] have created profound conditions, altering the nature of language, codes, symbols, and visions of social life. . . . the real enemy of economic elites is Chavista subjectivity and its interpretation of a democratic and popular solidarity economy. . . . the existence of this economic subjectivity blocks the installation of a neoliberal agenda of the sort [the opposition] seeks to install once it recaptures power. (Vielma 2016)

Using the language of Chavismo, Vielma highlights the degree to which conflicts about the political are always bounded by the lifeworlds of the subjects that inhabit it. Chavismo, for Vielma, is a form of intersubjectivity—an interpretive universe or imaginary through which subjects assess, code, and construct their world in relation to others. The key to the Bolivarian conjuncture after the death of Chávez is, for Vielma, the degree to which Chavismo has become the hegemonic ground of the national imaginary. Vielma insists that Chavismo will endure the crises of 2013–2016 because it has established itself as the ground on which social reproduction takes place in twenty-first-century Venezuela.

All these attempts to build and foster particular modes of political subjectivity—the *estado docente*, the New Socialist Man, and Chavista intersubjectivity—have run into similar practical difficulties. The modern and modernizing state was Bolívar's solution. This failed due to the factionalism and self-interest of the elites to whom that state was entrusted. Postcolonial Venezuela looked socially and economically much the same as it had before independence. The singular tyranny of the king was multiplied a hundredfold by local Creole despots and caudillos.

Ojeda and the FALN's doomed guerrilla campaign provided key examples and militants for the Bolivarianism to come at the end of the century. They couldn't overthrow Puntofijo, however, because conditions on the ground in Venezuela could not sustain a guerrilla campaign of the Cuban variety. Puntofijo democracy—while constrained, exclusionary, and repressive—proved more adept at responding to subversion than the outmoded dictatorships of recent memory, offering, for example, land reforms beneficial to peasants in the regions with guerrilla activity. Indeed, when Rafael Caldera (then the sitting president and leader of COPEI) issued a blanket amnesty for the guerrillas in 1969, the guerrillas had already become isolated from the peoples for whom they ostensibly fought. Many of the peasants for whom they were fighting in the countryside saw the heterodox cells of students, dissident politicos, and former military as more a "nuisance" than liberators (Wright 2001, 78).

Chavismo aims to transfer the autonomous energies of post-Caracazo subjects into the mechanics of the Bolivarian state. This final approach to the politics of subject formation and to politics *as* subject formation means to deploy institutional forms—first and foremost the communal state and the PSUV—capable of maintaining the constituent energies that produced, and later, have been produced by, the rupture that was the Caracazo. In this pursuit, the PSUV was meant to play a crucial, defining, and coordinating role, but the nagging question remains: Can the party form advance where statist development and revolutionary vanguardism have failed? The answer, of course, depends on the praxis and composition of the party.

Jodi Dean offers a compelling reconsideration of the much-maligned party form as an instrument of liberatory struggle. Dean argues for a party freed from the mechanisms of a given state. The party is, rather, a "carrier" that maintains the rupture opened by what she calls a "crowd." It is, properly speaking, a revolutionary rather than electoral organization: transformative, more a relation than an institution. It amplifies the energies and desires unleashed in moments—events—of egalitarian possibility. Dean's arguments concerning crowds and the party form never touch directly on Venezuela. This is, I think, a missed opportunity, as Venezuela offers a living contemporary example of precisely the sorts of processes she describes. Dean's observations are nonetheless instructive as critical and theoretical positions from which to consider the PSUV as an actually existing party within the larger liberatory sequence since the Caracazo. As such, it will be worthwhile to spend significant space reconstructing her argument before moving into a more detailed analysis of the PSUV.

Dean begins by inverting liberal mythology, contending that crowds rather than individuals are the basic units of politics. Whereas the liberal tradition posits a presocial state of nature inhabited by autonomous individuals, Dean insists that the formation of the individual is in fact a recurring act of enclosure, a *desubjectivization* aimed at rendering the common unthinkable, that captures and alienates the creative potential of collectivity (Dean 2016, 73–76). In the early twenty-first century, the crowd is less an alternative to the liberal individual than a "rupture" with a now fully consolidated global capitalism. "The crowd," she writes, "is a necessary but incomplete component of political subjectivity, the opening cut by the concentrated push of the many, the disruptive power of number. Whether this push will have been an emancipatory egalitarian expression of the people as a collective political subject depends on the party" (Dean 2016, 115). Crowds are fundamental to any emancipatory politics in that they punctuate a given order. In the case of the Caracazo, the function of the crowd exceeds the confrontations with authority, the looting, and the marches. The crowd, rather, exposes the previous liberal order as anything but its projected self-image of democratic inclusivity and shared development while insisting through concrete action that alternatives are both viable and necessary.

However, as Dean insists, ruptures and uprisings alone are not sufficient to sustain an emancipatory sequence. A people needs more than an event to form and free itself:

> The party is the bearer of the lessons of the uprising. It is both the perspective from which the uprising is assessed and is itself, as an organization capable of learning and responding, an effect of the uprising. The party learns from the subject it supports—and that it is the support of this subject is clear insofar as the subject necessarily exceeds it. (Dean 2016, 155)

Neither crowd nor party, then, is the subject of a liberatory sequence. But rather,

> [t]he crowd event is the Real that incites the people as a collective, partisan subject. The party is the body that renders the subjectivizing crowd event into a moment in the subjective process of the politicized people. The people as subject is neither crowd nor party but between them, in the overlap of anticipation and retroactive determination with respect to a political process. (Dean 2016, 157)

The party holds open the gap first created by the crowd event, the uprising, the Caracazo. It both reflects the desires and potentials of the crowd back onto itself and supports the crowd against entropy, opening a third space wherein a properly partisan subject—the people—can emerge. "More than a body focused on the state," then, "the party is a form for the expression and direction of a political will. It concentrates disruption in a process in order to produce political power: *these acts are connected; they demonstrate the strength of the collective*" (Dean 2016, 158; emphasis in original). The party, according to Dean, is thus carrier, subjectivizing structure, and an example of the power of the many.

Dean's theorization of crowds and party is not a mere idealization of the relationship of rupture to the new structures created in its spirit. She is rather attempting to wrestle through the same questions of subjects and political processes outlined by Roland Denis and Reinaldo Iturriza: how to translate the liberatory potential of an event like the Caracazo into a sustained assault on the inequalities, exclusions, and violences that make up the fabric of this world. The party form illustrates strength in numbers, but it also amplifies and echoes the questions the crowd asks of itself in the moments it breaks with a constituted order. She continues:

> that the subject of politics is collective means that its actions cannot be reduced to those associated with individual agency, actions like choice or decision. The punctuality of the subject could suggest that it is only evental, only disruptive, utterly disconnected from anybody, creation, institution, or advance and thus without substance or content. But this would ignore the persistence of the subject in the press of the unrealized. This persistence needs a body, a carrier. Without a carrier, it dissipates into the manifold of potentiality. *Nevertheless, with a carrier some potentiality is diminished. Some possibility is eliminated. Some closure is effected. This loss is the subject's condition of possibility, the division constitutive of subjectivity.* Political forms—parties, states, guerrilla armies, even leaders—situate themselves within this division. (Dean 2016, 183; emphasis added)

The party is an expression of a particular political will, one born in the course of a break with constituted power. However, as a structure necessarily exterior to the subjects that make it up and lend it a reason for existence, a logic and a trajectory, the party itself is in turn also an expression of a type of constituted power. The party carries with it a necessary and unavoidable diminution of collective potential, but without it, something like effective collective capacity would be unthinkable.

Dean's party form thus maintains the gap opened by the crowd, but it extracts a toll. It reflects the energy of the crowd back onto itself to stretch moments and ruptures so that it can reconfigure itself into an enduring political—that is, collective, but not uniform—entity. The event, the crowd, the party, and the people thus interact with one another in a tense and potentially liberatory sequence in a way that, even though Dean never entertains any sustained interaction with Venezuela, could well have been taken directly from Bolivarian discourse. This all begs the question: How do self-declared revolutionary parties in Venezuela measure up to the party as carrier of an unrelenting and collective desire for emancipation as theorized by Jodi Dean?

The immediate precursor to the PSUV, the Movimento Quinta República (Fifth Republic Movement, MVR), was always only an electoral vehicle for the Chavista project. It simply was never going to live up to Dean's vision of the party form's revolutionary role and potential. Of much more interest to the present discussion of the degree that the party form can—or cannot—be thought to gather, amplify, and prolong the egalitarian potentials glimpsed in evental ruptures like the Caracazo is the formation of the PSUV in 2007. The PSUV was created after Chávez's reelection in 2006, after a heady four years of coordination between the autonomous movements and the government. However, with the formation of the PSUV, the Chávez government made significant centralizing moves that altered the shape and trajectory of the Bolivarian process.

Starting in mid-2006, Chávez called for the dissolution of the MVR and all allied parties and their inscription into a coherent, disciplined, and united political party (Chávez 2007). The president insisted that to be effective, the PSUV would need to rid itself of the "alphabet soup" of political parties and personalities that had previously made a morass of Venezuelan politics (Lugo-Galicia 2006). The PSUV was to be a "party not of cadres, nor a party of masses, but a party of bases," and, insisted Chávez, "the popular bases, the communities, they will give life, birth, and form to this party; nothing will be imposed from above. Everything will come from the bases" (quoted in Lugo-Galicia 2007b). More than a political party, then, the PSUV aimed to be an "organic body" that would unify and give ground to revolutionary forces (Lugo-Galicia 2007a). In the debates surrounding its formation, militants emphasized over and again that, in the words of former youth minister Mary Pili Hernández, "this party cannot be an end in itself," that it needs to be an instrument of social transformation, not its stand-in (Pili Hernández 2007). In short, the PSUV promised at its moment of inception to be less an electoral vehicle than a tool at the service of social movements looking to transform Venezuela—a revolutionary organization.

In the end, while many smaller and local electoral groups dissolved into the PSUV, larger parties and those with longer histories—notably the Communist Party of Venezuela as well as the left of center Patria Para Todos (Fatherland for All—PPT) and the more centrist social democratic Podemos (a play on the Spanish verb "we can" and a portmanteau of *Por Democracia Social*—For Social Democracy)—remained outside the new *oficialista* grouping. The PCV and PPT remained allied but outside of the PSUV—a position for which they each lost no small part of their militants to the new party of Chavismo (Azcargota and Hernández 2007, 21; Lander

2007). In the case of Podemos, the president made good on his promise to consider all parties outside of the PSUV as members of the opposition, especially after its leader Ismael García opposed the ultimately failed 2007 Constitutional Reform.

Despite the promise of offering a new way to pursue politics in Venezuela, and despite the inspiring sign of presenting Venezuelans with the first internally democratic political party in the country's history, the PSUV, it must be concluded, has been a disappointment. Indeed, some erstwhile allies have alleged the party is now recreating many of the same sins of the Puntofijo system—nepotism, proliferating corruption, lack of political vision, willful isolation from the population at large, and a lack of space for dissent or effective rank-and-file participation (González 2014). In the words of Roland Denis, "the creation of the PSUV has been the starkest expression of the general impoverishment of popular capacities that began in 2005. . . . The party is an apparatus with neither logic nor political efficiency. It is totally lacking in ideological organizational, and mobilizational coherence. . . . it is simply an electoral machine, in which there are internal battles for access to power within the bureaucratic-corporatist state" (in Spronk and Webber 2011, 253). Denis goes on to describe the PSUV's attempts to either subsume or neutralize the autonomous spaces that have been constructed in Venezuela since the 1990s, moving to close the gap between *autogestión* and *cogestión* so completely as to identify it all with the state.

Many contend with Denis, however, that the actions of the PSUV either catalyzed or are symptoms of a troubling cooling or even betrayal of the revolutionary project in Venezuela opened in the aftermath of the Caracazo. The problem, as expressed by militant and longtime minister in the Chávez and Maduro governments Hector Navarro, concerns the confusing of the government with the revolution (Navarro 2015). That is to say, in the hope of salvaging the party form, which Dean avows is the necessary starting point for any politics of radical transformation, the PSUV seemed to at first offer a material instantiation of revolutionary possibility. By 2016, that hope was all but completely extinguished. While it might be possible to explain away this outcome to the particularities of Venezuela, there are nonetheless key aspects seemingly hardwired into the party form that lend themselves to closing rather than intensifying revolutionary openings. A few examples help illustrate these concerns.

After months of violent antigovernment protests and a series of troubling developments within the party itself, the PSUV held its first congress since the death of Hugo Chávez on July 26–31, 2014. Militants came to the party with concerns not only pertaining to the renewed aggression of the opposition, but to the internal dynamics of the party and its relation to the

Bolivarian Revolution more generally. They did not leave the event with their fears allayed. The Congress put the growing autoreferentiality of the PSUV on full display. Of the 900 delegates in attendance at the proceedings, only 537 were elected from the rank and file. The rest were a mix of appointed functionaries, state officials, and stalwarts of the Bolivarian Revolution (María 2014). While this suggests a growing bureaucratization of the party or, at the very least, of a distance between the party's decision-making bodies and the seven million Venezuelans it claims as members, a year later, small but significant tendencies within the PSUV—for example, the Trotskyist collective Marea Socialista (Socialist Tide), which had been involved since its inception—broke ranks with the official party of the Bolivarian Revolution and ran their own candidates in elections for the National Assembly.

Shortly after the 2014 protests underlined the stark political divide in Venezuela, President Nicolás Maduro announced a shuffle of his government. In a move that had been long called for by the left in Venezuela, Rafael Ramirez, the powerful head of PDVSA, whose portfolio also included a long list of other government ministries and a seat on the directorship of the PSUV, was removed from his position with the state oil company and moved to the foreign service. During his tenure, many complaints had been launched about corruption and mismanagement of the company, and in the years immediately leading up to Chávez's death, even government officials recognized that PDVSA's ability to modernize production and maintain facilities at existing capacity had weakened significantly. Promises to double national production from 2.5 to 5 million barrels annually by 2015 never materialized—indeed, some sources suggest output in 2014 failed to live up to rates from a decade earlier (González 2014). PDVSA's debt ballooned to $78.5 billion by 2012, and marquee investments like the infamous FondoChino (Chinese Fund) ended in scandal as $5 billion USD simply vanished. In failed attempts to address PDVSA's infrastructural and production woes, where the company couldn't work out deals with the Chinese, it entered into "associations" with "external investors which often carr[ied] conditions even more onerous than the 'operating agreements' with oil majors during the 1970s" (González 2014). Ramirez, as the head of PDVSA and several key energy related ministries, has widely been blamed for the deterioration of the state entity. However, he was until 2014 too powerful to dislodge from positions of power and, even after his displacement from PDVSA, remained on the national political directorate of the PSUV. His reappointment to Venezuela's delegation at the United Nations can thus in many ways be seen as something of a privileged exile.

However, his *membership*, if not his leadership in the PSUV was never questioned. Nor was the issue of Ramirez's vision of the role of oil in

Venezuela debated at the party congress in 2014. These were (perhaps rightly) seen as matters of state, even if the congress made moves to close the gap between party and state when it named Maduro party president. This latter move, dissidents have suggested, closes already scarce ground within the PSUV for internal debate and hampers the party's ability to offer policy alternatives and analysis to the government (Gómez 2014a, 2014b; Navarro 2014).

The 2014 Congress offers other examples that speak both to the general concerns around the party form as well as the specific problems of the PSUV. Among the declarations, platforms, and discussions at the event—a thirty-two-point summary of which was made public after the proceedings and which included naming Hugo Chávez the "Supreme Commander" and the "Eternal Leader" of the party—there was all but no room for self-criticism (PSUV 2014). "No time was allotted to considering whether the practices of the PSUV through the Chávez years matched the socialist rhetoric of its leadership or took account of the government's concessions to the bourgeoisie since Chávez's death" (María 2014). Indeed, the left in Venezuela has increasingly raised concerns not just that the Maduro administration conceded too much ground to an opposition and entrenched business class that have proved time and again will stop at nothing to unseat his government, but that they have been doing so with an air of secrecy completely antithetical to the principles of democracy and socialism, as well as to their commitment to the Bolivarian Revolution (Gómez 2014b). The PSUV, rather than a collective body capable of pressing the government further down the path toward socialism, has become an instrument used by the state to retroactively validate the decisions it makes without consulting its base, members of the party, or of the citizenry at large.

A series of expulsions, also not debated at the Party Congress, were even more disconcerting, especially for those who envision the party form as an apparatus capable of reflecting and amplifying egalitarian desires. In the same cabinet shuffle that saw Ramirez removed from PDVSA, long-standing planning minister Jorge Giordani was unceremoniously retired from government. Giordani is considered by many as a key architect of the Bolivarian state and economy since the 1990s. When he was removed from his post in June of 2014, he published an open letter in which he aired the government's dirty laundry. Among other crimes against the Venezuelan people, Giordani accuses his former colleagues of moral and economic corruption, reintroducing dangerous elements of capitalism back into the Venezuelan state, and of straying from the legacy of Chávez (Giordani 2014).

In the wake of his rendering of accounts, Giordani was expelled from the PSUV. When Hector Navarro, another architect of the Bolivarian process and long-standing minister under Chávez, published a letter saying some of Giordani's accusations had merit and at a minimum should be publicly debated, he too was expelled from the party.[7] Similar expulsions have taken place when militants—often founding members of the party from the radical base of the Bolivarian Revolution—have criticized the party leadership.

According to Roland Denis, Giordani's exit—and the expulsions surrounding it—is evidence of a "leadership in conflict with itself," and despite Giordani's criticisms of Maduro, remains "a typical example of the moral and political bankruptcy of a state leadership that knows very well the mess it is currently in" but refuses to listen to the grassroots in addressing the crises (Denis 2014). Giordani's letter is perhaps predictably rather short in terms of the author's own failings during his nearly fourteen years as planning minister. The letter says nothing of the labyrinthine exchange controls that have incentivized corruption and only benefited currency speculators. It is silent on the perennial failure of "endogenous development" and economic diversification, slogans the Bolivarian Revolution has failed to live up to as much as any previous government. Despite its references to socialism—mentioned only a fraction of the times Chávez is invoked—Giordani's letter does not address the government's failure to escape the well-worn dynamics of rentier capitalism and, even more damningly, of the systematic closure, capture, and neutralization of any autonomous expressions of constituent power. Indeed, Denis concludes, the exercise reeks more of a failed minister attempting to "exonerate himself" than an actual, substantive critique of the derailing of the Bolivarian process that has been taking place since the electoral-institutional phase of the revolution began in 1998.

Despite the fact that the party claims over seven million members—no mean feat in a country of thirty million souls—it was dealt a crushing blow in the December 2015 legislative elections, where the opposition coalition MUD won 115 of 167 seats in the National Assembly. The PSUV won fifty-five. With this majority, the opposition stepped up its efforts to derail the Bolivarian Revolution through both legal and illegal means, further amplifying a pattern of destabilization that had already been picking up pace and intensity since Chávez's death in 2013.

If we consider the Bolivarian Process as a sequence full of contradictory drives and desires—revolutionary autonomy versus military centralism, postcapitalist economics and the hard realities of the petrostate, protagonism and the overshadowing figure of Chávez—any party formed within this milieu would have found navigating these competing tendencies a difficult task. As much as the Giordani affair and the 2014 Party Congress are significant for the substantive issues they raise, they also highlight the degree to which the party form lends itself to closure in the name of revolutionary discipline.

The years following the Caracazo and the first moments of the Chávez government were marked by a proliferation of novel and radical experiments in alternative politics, economics, and living. During these moments, the egalitarian gap or rupture of social upheavals not only remained open, they were expanded by the energies of subjects refusing to live in any other type of world than the one they were in the process of constructing. While the party doesn't close this gap, *because nothing can*, it attempts to freeze it, to lock in its meaning, to insert it into a narrative and a timeline in which the PSUV and the Bolivarian state with which it is increasingly identified is the *realization* of the Caracazo's truth.

In the confrontation between the PSUV and MUD that took up much of 2016, as the latter attempted to recall Nicolás Maduro and the former became an ever more closed apparatus meant to support the state, Marea Socialista militant Nicmer Evans noted acerbically that the government and opposition had "electorally kidnapped" Venezuela (Evans 2016). That is to say, the government and opposition have effectively colluded with each other to limit the space for debate and participation in Venezuela. Each has presented itself as representative of a country divided in two, and presents the electoral choice between them as the only way to advance Venezuela's overlapping social, economic, and political crises. Such a foreclosure of possibility is inimical to both constituent power and to the promise of the Bolivarian Revolution's earliest days. Far from a party of revolutionary mobilization and transformation, the PSUV has become a party of the establishment, more concerned with its own longevity than the egalitarian desires that made it possible in the first place. By 2016, Marea Socialista positioned itself as a party of the Left opposition to Nicolás Maduro, campaigning on issues willfully ignored by both the Bolivarian government as well as the Washington-backed opposition, such as the announcement in early 2016 to open 11 percent of national territory to foreign mining concerns.

The question of the PSUV, the way it was announced rather than formed, the degree to which it has since prioritized elections over direct action, and its tendency to favor discipline over debate and internal democracy illuminates differing prioritizations of constituent and constituted power within the larger Bolivarian process. The PSUV has become an instrument for those who propose the constituted power of the state can unilaterally create the conditions upon which constituent power can be effectively expressed. Less maximally, they insist that the state is indispensable for social transformation, forgetting that the most powerful moments in the Bolivarian Revolution— the Caracazo, the 2002 counter coup, the communes—have occurred despite rather than due to the machinations of state power. Commentators like Denis, collectives like the Casa de Costurero, and the protagonists of Misión

Ribas illustrate the limits of such thinking. While they remain allied to the social vision of the Bolivarian Revolution, they also insist that any proposition to subordinate constituent to constituted power is inherently upside down. Constituent and constituted power can work together, but the former must always have precedence over the latter. The party can augment protagonism, as Dean illustrates. However, as the short life of the PSUV has already made clear, it can only do so contingently, and then only as a tool of the constituent powers and crowd events from which it emerged.

Self-Criticism as Conclusion and Transition: *El Golpe de Timón*

One of Chávez's final major speeches offered self-criticism and recognition that the Bolivarian Revolution had reached an impasse of its own making. Two weeks before the speech, Chávez had won reelection by one of his slimmest margin, capturing only 55 percent of the vote. While many pundits speculated the dip in the polls had to do with his ongoing battles with cancer, his comments in the *Golpe de Timón* (change of course) speech to his newly formed cabinet highlighted the tension between constituent and constituted power. The *Golpe de Timón*, and the seeming lack of any willingness by the Maduro government to take up its spirit, have since become key references for left critics of the government, the PSUV, and the current state of the Bolivarian Revolution.

"Where is the commune, better, where are the communes?" he repeatedly asked. "We keep building homes, but we can't see communes anywhere, nor the spirit of the commune, which is much more important in this moment than the commune itself: communal culture" (Chávez 2012, 20). In another self-critique of his government and the larger revolutionary process, he added, "I believe we have new codes; I believe we have a new legal architecture that comes from the Constitution; we have laws of communes, of the communal economy, laws of economic development zones; but we have done almost nothing with them; we are the ones who are responsible for their success and execution" (Chávez 2012, 37). In the speech, which was broadcast, printed, and widely circulated and debated, Chávez took ministers to task for reinforcing a political culture of personalism around his figure, and of doing too little to establish the groundwork for the *estado comunal* (communal state) that was by that time the orienting slogan and goal of the Bolivarian Revolution (Chávez 2012, 22–23). He even went so far as to critique the government's tendency to affix a *socialismo* on every public works project undertaken by his government, warning against "falling into the illusion" that changing a thing's name can stand in for concrete action (Chávez 2012, 27). Above all else, the revolution needed to relaunch itself, again. And for that, the state and party would have to recognize their complicity in either leading the process astray or actively subverting its liberatory potential.

There is something of a return to the potential opened by the event of the Caracazo in the *Golpe de Timón*. In the speech the president recognizes that the protagonism that made his government possible cannot be subsumed entirely by the normal functioning of constituted power, even when that constituted power in its state and party forms claims to represent the realization and extension of constituent power's egalitarian desires. Thinking of the Caracazo as event, and the *Golpe de Timón* as a coda, conclusion, or more hopefully, as a relaunching of a liberatory sequence allows us to recognize the *longue durée* of the Bolivarian Revolution in all of its tangled and dialectical potential. Events can be retroactively seen as opening, exposing, and generating moments of the political, but without particular forms of individual and collective subjectivity, they face the likelihood of dissipating into political memory.

Empirically, while Chávez's words may be striking for their depth, honesty, and publicity, there is nonetheless an irony that cannot be ignored when a *very* strong president at the helm of a *very* strongly presidentialist system laments the lack of "communal culture." The self-criticisms in *Golpe de Timón* neatly illustrate the theoretical tension between constituent and constituted power, and the degree to which the former depends on the latter. Without the event, the "explosions of communal power" (the "fifth" sequential "motor" of the Bolivarian Revolution explored in the introduction) that created and have driven the Bolivarian process, that process will stagnate, founder, and ultimately collapse. When Chávez chastises himself and his ministers for failing to fulfill their tasks, he only gets part of the equation correct. While he correctly recognizes that without constituent power, institutions become autoreferential and, at best, inefficient and stagnant, at worst, repressive and reactionary, he nonetheless mistakenly implies that constituted power can create or stand in for constituent power. This is also the self-sufficient illusion into which the PSUV has fallen.

Put most directly, in *Golpe de Timón* Chávez recognized the damage post-2006 recentralization had wrought on the revolutionary process, a reversal in which the PSUV had played no small part, and the limits of constituted power. While he set himself and his government the task of rectifying these errors, he also, if only implicitly, recognized that such a rectification cannot be issued from above. This is both the nature and the challenge of constituent power.

CHAPTER 3

Multitude, *Pueblo*, and the Ungovernability of Constituent Power

✧

Part of the power of social classifications lies in the way they are often presented as natural—ahistorical and apolitical. Yet, as several scholars working in critical, Marxist, world systems, feminist, and postcolonial critical theories (among others) have illustrated, the identities taken for granted today are themselves constructs of particular class and state projects within North Atlantic modernity (Appadurai 1996, 146; Balibar and Wallerstein 2011; Foucault 2009; Quijano 2014, 289; Stoler 1995). Even still, discourses of race and nation remain powerful mobilizing tools. Some have even argued that the successes of left of center governments throughout Latin America in the early twenty-first century obligates us to consider a "relegitimization and reterritorialization of the nation-state" (Beverley 2011, 42). However, such revisionist attempts carry with them volumes of qualifications. When not tied to an even deeper inter- and transnationalism, the most likely outcomes of cultivating a nationalistic sentiment remain a potentially brutal and parochial division—far from the promise of harmonious unity offered by the mythical national community.

Especially during the Chávez years, the Bolivarian Revolution sought to avoid these familiar dangers by tempering its nationalism with emphases on South-South collaboration, regional integration, humanist transnationalism, and its preferred understanding of constituent power as the cornerstone of collective identity. Any sense of national pride was tied to a mythology of a borderless egalitarian future. Bolívar himself, after all, was a practical internationalist. He insisted on continental unity and cooperation at the Panama congress in 1826 as the only path forward for successful postcolonial reconstruction. He was also, furthermore, an incipient anti-imperialist, warning that the United States seemed "destined by Providence to plague America with miseries in the name of Freedom" (Bolívar 2003, 173). Bolivarian Venezuela, the government of Hugo Chávez insisted, has only been following the lead of El Libertador as it forged international ties among its neighbors, and the global south more generally.

Within the Bolivarian project itself understandings of collective identity often shuttle between poles of the cohesive national community and the ungovernable forces of constituent power. By triangulating a geohistorical people, celebrations of constituent power, and the discursive linking of the government to ungovernability and protagonism beyond its control, the Bolivarian Revolution attempted to distance itself from essential notions of the nation while also declaring itself a tool of the people. By ungovernability I mean something quite distinct from the "overload thesis" in urban studies of the 1970s and 1980s that argued too many conflicting social demands crippled states and signaled a need to both diminish social expectations of upward mobility and equality as well as the capacities of the welfare state (see, for a review and contemporary consideration, Hager 2012). I instead mean ungovernability as the breakdown or refusal of constituted political authority and the failure of the formal politics of the nation and its hegemony over the political imagination (Kingsbury 2013). It can result from constituted power's implosion or from the open revolt or exodus of the populace. It should not be conflated with law breaking, even if one can certainly be a symptom of the other. Ungovernability hews much more closely to the protagonism explored in chapter 2, in which the refusal to abide by a constituted order is accompanied by the positive construction of alternatives to the status quo.

This is of course an often-clumsy dance that all democratic and republican regimes must join, as modern political legitimacy is premised on the assumption that authority is secular and at least nominally inclusive or at least voluntary and contractually based. But the Bolivarian Revolution's awareness and celebration of a constituent and ungovernable expansiveness—the *turba*, the multitude, the *pueblo*—has been both more incessant and more internally complicated than standard expressions found in populist sequences or mass democracy more generally.

Venezuela, like all modern nation-states, must find ways to redirect ungovernability, to sublimate the chaotic, unpredictable, and raw constituent power of human community into the consent and obedience of the citizen-state relation. While most carry out this labor by rooting authority in a shared historical or biological origin (hence the couplet nation-state), and while the Bolivarian Revolution is nothing if not nationalistic, this chapter explores the degree to which Bolivarian discourse has successfully forged a collective subjectivity as common ground rather than as enforceable identity: a plane on which subjects combine and emerge rather than a mystical essence against which they can be measured, judged, and included or excluded. Put differently, this chapter explores the extent to which the notion of *Venezolanidad* has been reconfigured in the course of the Bolivarian

Revolution from an exclusive sense of selfhood to ideals of democratic participation, social justice, and egalitarian desires. It asks what sociological forms arise in the course of this (attempted) reconfiguration.

As the Bolivarian Revolution maneuvers between representation and ungovernability, it moves between constituted and constituent power, a fluidity that reflects an unsettled political and social ontology between multitude (or *turba*) and *pueblo*. The tension between these exercises of political power can be seen most clearly in the government's discursive celebration of events like the Caracazo of 1989, the 2002 countercoup that returned Chávez to office after a forty-eight-hour counterrevolution, and the reversal of the 2002–2003 Golpe Petrolera (Oil Coup)—but also in moments of failure, such as the 2007 Reforma Constitucional (Constitutional Reform). That is to say, the Bolivarian Revolution bases its legitimacy not on legality, nor on biological notions of race or nation, but rather on the subjective force of egalitarian ruptures and, more importantly, its ability to substantiate these events and give them institutional force. In so doing, it also renders itself vulnerable, inviting criticism, reforms, and unexpected turns. This is—or can be—a virtue; when it fails in this openness, it has failed in its attempt to be a *revolution rather than a state*.

Across the rest of the chapter I argue that the notions multitude and *pueblo* characterize different but not necessarily mutually exclusive expressions of egalitarian desire and constituent power in Venezuela. They are both attempts to find a "we" up to the challenges of collective life and egalitarian desire. In their strongest iterations, these positions push a statist project like the Bolivarian Revolution toward more liberatory horizons. I begin with a consideration of Enrique Dussel and Antonio Negri—the most compelling theorists, respectively, of *pueblo* and multitude whose ideas have been operationalized and experimented with in twenty-first-century Venezuela. I then move to three moments in which multitude *and pueblo* have reshaped history in a way similar to the Caracazo: the 2002 countercoup, the Golpe Petrolera, and the 2007 Reforma. The chapter closes with a consideration of constituent power's excessiveness beyond even the classifications of multitude and *pueblo*.

On the Antinomies of Politics: Multitude and *Pueblo*

In actually existing liberal democracies autonomous action by the citizenry is channeled into the private sphere and civil society or is converted into the faux-civic exercises of party politics. This dynamic characterized Latin America during the 1980s and 1990s, resulting both in the "lost decades" of growing inequality and technocratic rule by experts. Democratization led to a paradoxical de-democratizing of key aspects of collective life (Robinson 2007). While it is true that the twenty-first century saw this (neo)liberal consensus replaced across the region by a strong regional agreement "on the importance of redistributive and interventionist role of states" (Cheresky 2012, 109), it is also true that this new convergence of opinion has not signaled the end of liberalism, modernization, developmentalism, or much less of capitalism in Latin America. It has, rather, further hybridized and entangled with an already heterodox sociopolitical and economic milieu (Arditi 2008; Coronil 2011; Escobar 2010). Multitude and *pueblo*, as attempts to think new forms of praxis and collective subjectivity, operate within this unsettled time and space, rejecting both the foreclosure of the political toward which neoliberalism aspires and the demobilizing tendencies of constituted power.

Multitude and *pueblo* offer alternative approaches to social ontology and revolutionary change to classical Marxist emphases on the industrial working class. Whereas multitude is posed as a response to the global challenges of post-Fordism (Hardt and Negri 1994, 2000; Negri 1992; Virno 2004, 2006), *pueblo* reflects more specifically Latin America's place in the capitalist world system (Dussel 2007; Ojeda 1970). The dislocation of factory labor to networked sites in the global south, the prominence of the so-called knowledge economy and finance capital, and the dismantling of the welfare state and its disciplinary institutions mean both that the industrial working class no longer exists as a spatially concentrated and developed unit and that new opportunities have arisen for both exploitation and resistance (Virno 2004). The multitude is the collective subject that is capable of responding to the new openings and enclosures of the post–Cold War era because it is not, strictly speaking, a subject. It is, drawing from the seventeenth-century Jewish philosopher Baruch Spinoza, "a *plurality which persists as such* in the public sense, in collective action, in the handling of communal affairs, without converging into a One" (Virno 2004, 21; emphasis in original). Multitude, in other words, preexists the formation of the modern nation-state with its need for order and stability. It is also that which persists and troubles modernity's margins from within, a diffuse vector of constituent power. Multitude is, finally, a form for collective collaboration and encounter capable of navigating the ruthless rootlessness of the present. It is precarious, but at home in precarity as a state of constant motion, creation, and combination.

Latin American capitalism never developed an industrial powerhouse, and its class composition has as a result always been much more mixed than economistic Marxisms could account for (Quijano 1981, 64). Indeed, throughout the twentieth century, local communist parties backed by Moscow were often cool on the prospects of revolution, arguing that Latin

American societies needed to pass progressively through the stages of liberal bourgeois democracy and industrial production before a communist seizure of power could be entertained (Gott 2008b, xxxiii). This changed with the Cuban Revolution, which Enrique Dussel recognizes as a watershed moment for the political encounter with the *pueblo* (Dussel 2007, 483). Rather than searching—or waiting—for the ideal moment, as defined by European Marxisms' predictions, Che Guevara insisted that in Latin America, "the proletariat was a small, insignificant and historically conservative 'labor aristocracy,' subservient to US-led programs. Taking his cue from Mariátegui, he saw the only path to revolution as through an alliance of three revolutionary classes—workers, peasants, and (most unusually) students—and through the actions of the guerrilla unit, the *foco*." Guevara argued that this sort of coalition was made possible due to the fact that it was consciousness rather than one's position in the economic mode of production that most contributed to one's potential for revolutionary subjectivity and action (Kapcia 2008, 98). With the elaboration of the *pueblo* as a distinctly Latin American concept, social positions were increasingly privileged over narrowly economic and structural approaches in Latin American understandings of revolutionary transformations, all while maintaining an anticapitalist emphasis on inequality and exploitation.

Both multitude and *pueblo* are vectors of egalitarian desire. Both refuse any and all justifications of separation and inequality. Both demand equal participation in the decision-making processes that determine daily life. They differ on matters of concreteness and representation, or, on ontology and on political forms. Whereas multitude refers to a persistently diffuse and mobile force, the *pueblo* is a more organic and representable understanding of community. The *pueblo* is a local expression of the production and reproduction of human life in common (Dussel 2007, 491). Multitude is that reproduction delinked from the confines of place, nation, and state.

Dominant strains of the North Atlantic tradition consider both multitude and *pueblo*, and constituent power more generally, as threats to order and progress. One can read historical processes of democratization as attempts to stifle, contain, neutralize, or redirect multitude and *pueblo* into more captive, obedient, and governable expressions of collective life. Hence their frequent expression as ungovernability. For twentieth-century democratic theorists such as Hannah Arendt and Sheldon Wolin, this long-term trend of actually existing democracies has resulted in a stifling of the political and an emaciation of the rejuvenating power of participatory culture and praxis (Arendt 1991, 207–223; Wolin 2004, 315–390, 581–606). Enrique Dussel sees this separation of the political from what citizens consider most relevant in their lives as a situation of "double corruption" that enables governments to consider themselves the sources of political power (he calls this power "fetishized") and in which the population becomes servile, apathetic, and passive (Dussel 2006, 14). For Dussel, this double corruption can also be see in the anti-statism of, for example, the alter-globalization movements of the turn of the twenty-first century, as well as in the social fragmentation and voter apathy often associated with "the postmodern condition." Reformulations of politics that call for a disengagement with the state as project, characterized by Michael Hardt and Antonio Negri and John Holloway are thus for Dussel dangerously off the mark. By presenting constituent and constituted power as mutually exclusive, Hardt, Negri, Holloway, and the tendencies they represent accept without contest the self-serving lie of a fetishized power that has become autoreferential and domineering (Dussel 2006, 43). In Dussel's estimation, this acceptance and subsequent exodus from institutional and statist policies—against the best intentions of its protagonists—facilitated rather than rejected neoliberalization in the 1980s and 1990s (Dussel 2006, 14).

Dussel differentiates between the latent constituent power of the multitude and its rationalization as an ethical and institutional force through the figure of the *pueblo* (Dussel 2006, 27). The *pueblo*, as a people of and for itself, is the sovereign force of democratic politics, but only when it has a coherent structure. For Antonio Negri, Dussel's system risks contributing to the long-standing neutralization of constituent power by modern juridical thought and the state-form (Hardt and Negri 1994, 7). Both Dussel and Negri valorize constituent power over fixed notions like nationality or liberal citizenship. Their next theoretical steps after this shared rejection, however, take them in opposition directions that also illuminate the constitutive gap in which the Bolivarian process experiments with collective subjectivity and agency. Multitude and *pueblo* mark ideal cases of ungovernability and governability, highlighting dynamics of inclusion and exclusion that haunt any discussions of citizenship, civil society, belonging, and the modern nation-state.

For Negri, the multitude is neither unity nor chaos and resists such binary distinctions. It is, rather, a contingent collectivity, an "almost infinite set of singularities" (Casarino and Negri 2008, 93). Singularities, in their turn, stand in contrast to the transcendental and sovereign individual of liberal social contract theory in that whereas the former assumes a selfsame identity, the notion of singularity emphasizes flux, change, interaction, and movement (Deleuze 1988, 111). Whereas the notion of individuality projects a sameness, equivalence, or essence, singularity implies the perpetual and collective activity of creation. The multitude is thus *neither* unitary *nor* chaotically heterogeneous, neither nation nor mob. It is, rather, a becoming-common of the various singularities of which it is comprised.

As theorized by Dussel, the *pueblo* also resides in the space between chaos and unity, navigating between latent possibility and political actualization. For Dussel, the *pueblo* is a vector of what he calls a *hiperpotentia* that extends the raw potential of constituent power into a rejuvenating and animating force of the political.[1] While recognizing that constituted power always preys upon constituent power, for Dussel there is no alternative. Constituted power has no animating force of its own. It requires a constituent power that is always outside and in excess of its established form. As such, constituted power is inherently prone to entropy and tyranny. *Hiperpotentia* is the *pueblo* revolting against this inevitable development. It is a liberating essence akin to but wholly differing from the multitude's relentless antagonism to the state. *Pueblo* reinvigorates constituted power; multitude flees it. Dussel in other words adds a third category to Negri's antinomy constituent-constituted power, which for the former makes all the difference between virtuous and vicious cycles of the political.

Dussel's understanding of *pueblo* retains a core anticolonial inflection and admits influences of dependency theory (Dussel 1995). In many iterations, *pueblo* bears a striking resemblance to the Marxian distinction of the proletariat as a class both in itself and for itself (Dussel 2006, 64). Here Dussel writes of the *pueblo* as "an organic historical collective—not only a mass or a multitude, but a historical subject with memory, identity, and its own structures. It is also the totality of the oppressed of any given system . . . the *pueblo* is exteriority" (quoted in Salas 2005, 882). Dussel also speaks of the *pueblo* in language that, while more immediately Levinasian in its emphasis on alterity and ethics, retains its core Gramscian inflection of "the popular." He writes, "'class' is a social condition of the oppressed subsumed by capital in its totality; the 'pueblo' is the communal condition of the oppressed as exteriority" (quoted in Salas 2005, 882). Thus, the *pueblo* is for Dussel both the systemic product of social marginality and exclusion as well as a deeper relation to alterity and otherness.

For Negri, the *pueblo* is a captured and domesticated constituent power. The multitude's inherent creativity and power are hypostasized and blocked when tied to a coherent structure and system of representability such as the *pueblo*. The theoretical and practical task Negri thus sets for himself is "the construction of a constitutional model capable of keeping the formative capacity of constituent power itself in motion [and] of identifying a subjective strength adequate to this task" (Negri 1992, 25). For Negri, both the subject and structure are the multitude.

In *Commonwealth*, the last installment of their trilogy that began with *Empire*, Hardt and Negri begin to address the issue of the multitude's ability to govern itself. In their account, the multitude must be a force of both "insurrection and institution, structural and superstructural transformation" (Hardt and Negri 2009, 367). However, these gestures toward more sustainable forms of the multitude are more evocative than programmatic, perhaps inevitably so, but in a way that nonetheless restates rather than resolves the fraught relationship of constituent and constituted power. Paraphrasing Sheldon Wolin's pointed implication that democracy only ever *is* when it *is* fugitive, however, we must ask why an ostensibly immanent and democratic force like the multitude would want to govern itself in the first place (Wolin 2004, 602). Are there possible or desirable institutional forms that allow for a constantly expanding becoming of the multitude? Can constituent power exist without constituted power? Or, are both inextricably linked to one another as artifacts of the modern nation-state? Most importantly for the purposes of this chapter, to what extent has the Bolivarian Revolution contributed to the work of finding and supporting alternatives when they emerge? Rather than proposing definitive answers to matters that are contingent, I move now to a more detailed outline of the events and discourses since the Caracazo of 1989. In so doing, I hope to better situate what is at stake in these experiments with political community not only for observers and participants in Venezuelan politics, but for the ongoing reimagining of democracy in the early twenty-first century.

A History of Rewriting Histories:
From the Caracazo to the Reforma Constitucional

At a 2009 event commemorating the twentieth anniversary of the Caracazo, Hugo Chávez argued, "anyone who says the Caracazo was not a political event is simply wrong . . . the Caracazo was not an irrational explosion of the primitive or savage instincts of the masses, nor was it simply the chance for someone to steal a refrigerator." It was rather the moment in which "the pueblo broke its chains" (TeleSur 2009). He went on to resignify the Caracazo in terms of the nation's officially sanctioned iconography. In the symbolic universe outlined by Chávez, the national anthem, the Caracazo, and an explicitly Marxist historical analysis combine to form the subjective force of the Bolivarian Revolution. Drawing from the national anthem, he continued, "the Lord shouted, down with tyranny, and the poor from their shanties demanded freedom in the streets. [This was] a rebellion of the poor, [this was] class war as Karl Marx would say."[2] Chávez has been exhaustively characterized in terms of his charisma and iconoclasm (Hawkins 2003; Marcano and Tyszka 2005; Sunkara 2012). However, what is most striking in this characteristic performance is his adeptness at playing the *bricoleur*—combining, juxtaposing, and rewriting preexisting discourses; speaking both *with* and through the symbols of the nation; navigating systems of signs so as to both reinforce social structures and trigger evental ruptures.[3] However, it is also in this regard that the Chávez years in Venezuela most resemble the experiences of other actually existing democracies.

In his 2009 commemoration, Chávez described the relation of constituent and constituted power in terms of independent but complementary elements that establish the political terrain of the Bolivarian process—much like Dussel's concept of the *pueblo*. By interpreting the revolt through long-standing and officially sanctioned and ritualized symbols, Chávez attempts to rein in a fundamental refusal of the modern social contract, essentially reading the assertion of a foundational ungovernability in terms of the so-called "right to revolt" of modern liberal constitutions. In other words, the discursive celebrations of the Caracazo in Bolivarian Venezuela are attempts to transmogrify a multitude into a *pueblo*.

"Todo 11 tiene su 13": *Coup and Countercoup*

In chapter 2 I argued that the Bolivarian Revolution has attempted to inscribe the Caracazo into a narrative and a timeline in which the governments of Hugo Chávez and Nicolás Maduro stand as realizations of constituent power and the fulfillment of the potentials exposed by an egalitarian rupture. In this way, they posit a relationship of representability between themselves and the people, a move that assumes the transformation of crowd, *turba*, or multitude into *pueblo*. The Bolivarian Revolution also often cites other powerful examples of its affinity to egalitarian events and ungovernability, most frequently, the countercoup that returned Chávez to the presidency on April 13, 2002.

From late 2001 until the day of the coup, the private media, the military high command, the Confederación de Trabajadores Venezolanos (Venezuelan Workers' Federation, CTV),[4] the managerial board of PDVSA, and the Chamber of Commerce (FEDECÁMARAS) colluded to trigger the president's ouster. On April 11, 2002, a march called to protest Chávez's attempt to replace the executive board of PDVSA with his supporters started from the affluent east side of Caracas. During the march, organizers redirected the crowds toward the presidential residence, where a progovernment rally was taking place. When pro- and antigovernment forces met, a clash ensued in which shots were fired and nine people—mostly Chavistas—were killed.[5]

Citing the need to impose order, the military high command took to the airwaves, denounced and deposed the president, and then named the head of FEDECÁMARAS interim head of state. The resulting forty-eight hours of martial law and media blackout were ended by a spontaneous mass uprising of the urban poor and revolt of junior military officials demanding the return of Chávez. The architects of the coup for the most part scattered to Colombia, Peru, and Miami.

Much like the Caracazo, the uprising of April 13 took many by surprise. While organizing by the government in the massive barrios ringing the country's major cities had taken place, it would be a stretch to imply that it had the level of control over the population that many in the Venezuelan opposition, and no small number of political scientists in the United States, often suggested (see, for example, Hawkins and Hansen 2006). Neighborhood self-help networks—nodes of protagonism and *autogestión*— that predate the Chávez government were central to the countercoup. These ties have been strengthened and celebrated in the discourse and iconography of the Bolivarian Revolution in the years since, but in many cases the most radicalized areas continued to demand their autonomy. For example, Martinez observes, "after years of police repression and abuse, 23 de Enero,[6] with the help of the local city government, finally succeeded in kicking the police force out [of] the neighborhood in 2004. The collectives now coordinate security among each other" (Martinez, Fox, and Farrell 2010, 271). In other words, the relation between the Bolivarian Revolution, its supporters, and the state apparatus is far from halcyon. While the Bolivarian Revolution still enjoys a high degree of popularity in places like 23 de Enero, the support of these social networks is contingent on the government's performance.

A brief examination of some mass-produced and distributed popular iconography provides a telling glimpse into the importance of the events of April 2002 for the Bolivarian Revolution. The 13th of April not only reads as a defiant "¡no volverán!" (they'll never come back)—a defensive and reactive posture that is perhaps predictable—it has also been invested with new layers of meaning, particularly to signify support for the forward march toward a socialist future. This is evident not only in the speeches and celebrations that mark the anniversaries of the countercoup, but also on T-shirts, banners, and impromptu murals (see figure 3).

The slogan "Todo 11 tiene su 13" (every 11th has its 13th) displays the historical and political stakes of the coup and countercoup. Blacked-out Venezuelan flags (the seven-starred flag of the Fourth Republic) hover in the background, waving in multiple directions, suggesting chaos, weakness, disorganization, above the "Todo 11" signifying the coup.[7] The 11th is thus depicted as a return to the past, both in the official symbols of the Fourth Republic but also in the perspective of the image. The response "tiene su 13" interrupts with the vivid tricolor the eight stars of the Fifth, Bolivarian, Republic and a unified leftward march on the verge of overtaking the brooding past. The image not only recreates in a snapshot the events of

Figure 2. "Every 11th has its 13th: The Pueblo is still on the street, now on the road to socialism!" (Todo 11 tiene su 13 ¡El pueblo sigue en la calle, ahora rumbo al socialismo!)

April 2002, it warns would-be coup plotters against any future adventures. It also imposes a direction and purpose on the insurrection that, like the Caracazo, was perhaps only latent when the events actually took place. In other words, the uprising of the 13th did not seek a return of Chávez's (at the time, perhaps necessarily) cautious and coalition-oriented policies. Both the Chavista government and the multitude acknowledge this point. Rather, as radical strains within Chavismo emphasize, the countercoup must be seen both as an affirmation of the power of the people *and* a rejection of the state form and all it stood for that emerged during this exception (Gott 2000; Wilpert 2003).

While the Caracazo continues to be commemorated as the original break pitting the majority of Venezuelans against the neoliberal model and state power, the 2002 countercoup is less ambiguous in relation to the Bolivarian Revolution. Unlike the countercoup, the Caracazo is much easier to interpret as a revolt *against* state power than as a revolt *for* a "better" state power. In the multitudinous and excessive moment of the Caracazo social relations were inverted. State power was able to reassert the normalcy it desired and needed only through bloody repression. In the Caracazo, the state itself killed the hope of a new Venezuela.

The April 13 countercoup requires much less retrofitting in order to domesticate it for the Bolivarian Revolution's purposes than does the Caracazo. While I have suggested that a reading of the countercoup in terms of a people's love for their president would be too easy, it is nonetheless more integrated into the statist aspects of the Bolivarian Revolution than its predecessor. It was, after all, Chávez who was returned to power two days after being kidnapped by a nefarious and internationally linked conspiracy. More significantly, the dynamics of constituent power and its institutional realization are much clearer in the countercoup than the Caracazo. The people took to the streets in 1989 and were quashed by the military. They failed to resurface in 1992 when Chávez himself led a failed coup attempt. In 2002 the multitude mobilized and Chávez was returned to the presidency.[8] Thus, whereas Bolivarian discourse must do the work of locating and translating the meaning of the Caracazo before inserting it into its own history, the countercoup of April 2002 is much more ready-made for a reading that ties the current government directly to the constituent power of "its" base.

"El Golpe Petrolero": The Oil Coup and the Democratization of Consumption

Immediately following the April 2002 coup, the Chávez government moderated. The opposition did not. Rather than participating in a process of national reconciliation facilitated by the Carter Center and the Organization of American States, management of PDVSA and transnationals operating in the country immediately intensified their destabilization campaign. The new plan was to bring down Chávez by cutting off the state's access to oil revenues. From December 2002 to February 2003 a lockout paralyzed the national oil industry, which in turn brought the economy as a whole to a standstill (Weisbrot and Sandoval 2009). The lockout, in which this oil-exporting nation found itself in the bizarre position of *importing* petroleum to meet its contractual obligations, only came to an end when retired oil workers, members of the military, and foreign contractors aligned with the government forcibly reopened the oil facilities (Ellner 2008; Kozloff 2007; Sánchez Otero 2012).[9]

As a result of this second opposition-precipitated crisis, moderates within the government and movement were isolated. Radical voices pushing for a more fundamental break with neoliberalism and a more direct form of democracy prevailed. Thus, if the April coup unmasked or exposed the real intentions and alliances of the opposition, the oil coup reinforced the belief among poor Venezuelans and the Chávez government that the opposition was neither loyal, responsible, nor reasonable. The opposition discredited themselves repeatedly, and in so doing, made a more fundamental and less-compromising break with neoliberalism possible (Ellner 2008; Martinez, Fox, and Farrell 2010).

In the aftermath of the oil coup the government began the process of democratizing consumption in earnest. After recovering from the crippling blow to the economy caused by the lockout, the government began distributing the profits of the oil industry through a vastly expanded social welfare system. Illiteracy was functionally eradicated, building on the successful Cuban "¡Yo Sí Puedo!" program. Between 2003 and 2007, the national poverty rate—measured in the purchasing power of a citizen's cash income—was halved (from 54 percent of the population to 27.5 percent) and extreme poverty cut by two-thirds (from 25 to 7.6 percent of the population). School enrollment skyrocketed, up 86 percent in higher education since 1999, 54 percent in secondary, and 10 percent in primary (primary school enrollment was already at 91 percent in 1999). Employment also increased with the expansion of the Venezuelan economy in the first ten years of the Bolivarian Revolution, with two million formal economy jobs being created in the private sector and over six hundred thousand in the public sector (Weisbrot, Ray, and Sandoval 2009).

The key drivers of the democratization of consumption were the Misiones Bolivarianas (Bolivarian Missions) and the Consejos Comunales (Communal Councils)—bodies that not only depended on the spike in oil prices and a benevolent government, but on the self-organization of affected communities. The Misiones and the Consejos are, in other words, examples not merely of populist or clientelist distribution (Hawkins and Hansen 2006; Corrales and Penfold 2011) but are rather experiments in *cogestión*. Once in government, and after another series of popular mobilizations against the 2002 coup and the 2002–2003 Golpe Petrolera allowed him to establish control over PDVSA and the state bureaucracy, this pattern of incorporating protagonism and translating *autogestión* into *cogestión* would be extended into the Consejos Comunales and the Misiones Bolivarianas.

The Misiones, which by 2016 numbered over thirty, are targeted social programs implemented at the neighborhood, municipal, and international levels. They are tasked with providing primary and intensive medical care (Misión Barrio Adentro); education, from literacy to university (Misiones Robinson, Ribas, and Sucre); food security (Misión Mercal); safe, dignified, and affordable housing (Gran Misión Vivienda Venezuela); impetus and support for collective and otherwise noncapitalist modes of production (Misión Che Guevara); and spreading awareness, protecting memory, and encouraging pride for Venezuelans of indigenous descent (Misión Guaicaipuro)—among other goals. The successes of the Misiones have been admirable, especially in their early days. They are so popular that even the opposition has recognized them as important and promised to keep (some of) them in a proposed post-Bolivarian future.

Consejos Comunales aim to be participatory democratic structures that decentralize legislative power spatially—locating administrative power at the level of the neighborhood—and temporally—with them, decision making becomes more equitably shared, mundane, and quotidian. They are formed from existing community organizations and residents and have planning and budgetary control over a defined geographical area. Councils work on everything from building key infrastructure—building staircases and roads to access hillside neighborhoods, installing electricity, improving drainage and plumbing—to building shared spaces such as daycare and community centers, to providing seed loans to collective and communal enterprises. Decision making is open and democratic, and the stated goal of these new administrative bodies has been to root out corruption and bureaucratic inefficiency through direct action and participation. Without question, election campaigns continued to dominate much of the agenda. Furthermore, people form communal councils for a host of reasons; to gain access to state resources and to feel their voices are being heard motivate participation as well as the perhaps loftier aims of protagonism and radical egalitarianism. The point, however, is the councils have redefined democracy in Venezuela. The expectation of politics *as democracy* goes beyond the liberal transfer of power from represented to representative and into a more involved, fluid, and local practice of mutual constitution.[10]

One should not conclude, however, that these developments equal socialism, much less that they represent some sort of unleashing of constituent power or the dismembering of a constituted order. Furthermore, by 2016, many of these gains had been reversed by the collapse in global oil markets and a renewed wave of opposition-led economic, political, and social counteroffensives. Reversals and counterrevolutions aside, even at its height in the years following the events of 2002 and 2003, the Bolivarian Revolution can in many ways be seen as extending the developmental state model it inherited. A glut of oil money in the first decade of the twenty-first century allowed the Chávez government ample political and fiscal room for maneuver. According to Venezuelan government statistics, the Gini coefficient—the statistical measure of income inequality, the closer to zero being the most equal distribution—moved from 0.487 in 1998 to 0.420 in 2007, making it nearly a statistical equal to the United States before the onset of the global recession in 2008 (Weisbrot 2008); opposition figures put the number much higher. In economic and social indicators, then, Venezuela's Bolivarian Revolution made significant inroads but still had much to do to achieve its stated goals of social justice and the elimination of poverty even before the crises that followed the death of Chávez.

At the time of the Golpe Petrolera, Roland Denis was vice minister of planning. He argues that the mobilization against the lockout marked a revolutionary high point in the Venezuelan process. It was, for Denis, worker militancy of December 2002–February 2003 that *forced* the question of socialism back on the table in Venezuela. There nonetheless remained significant institutional strongholds in which the traditional bureaucratic and technocratic elite were entrenched. Most notably, Denis argues that the pro-poor land law was "timidly" enforced, and worse, PDVSA fell back to its technocratic and bureaucratic ways (Denis 2005, 11). In short, the response to the lockout has been celebrated and integrated into the discourse of the Bolivarian Revolution as a coordinated mobilization of state and *pueblo*, but the actual practices that made the popular counteroffensive successful—the *autogestión*, transparency, and workplace democracy of the multitude— remained exceptions to the normal functioning of the statist project, even at high points of revolutionary action. The case of the response to the Golpe Petrolera illustrates not only the potentials of a multitude-becoming-*pueblo* but also its limits vis-à-vis a developmentalist state that approaches the political instrumentally. The consequences of this increasingly top-down and vertical reconfiguration of constituted to constituent power can be seen in the case of the government's failings by 2007.

La Reforma Constitucional: Multitude, Pueblo, Absence

Sometimes the multitude and *pueblo* are best recognized in their absence. Both expressions of egalitarian desire resist routinization and neutraliza- tion—even by ostensible allies. A striking example of the force of a politics of refusal can be seen in the failure of the Reforma Constitucional (Consti- tutional Reform—hereafter, Reforma) of 2007.

In August of 2007 Chávez announced a proposed reform to thirty-three of the 1999 Constitution's 350 articles. The National Assembly later added another thirty-six proposed amendments and the National Electoral Council (CNE) set December 2 of that year as the date for the vote. The reforms, split into two "packages" for the ballots, aimed to implement political, social, economic, and geographic changes according to the "five motors" plan announced in Chávez's inauguration ceremony in January of that year.

While the Venezuelan and international media identified the entire Reforma with the proposal to lift term limits on elected offices, which they described as an attempt by Chávez to make himself president for life, the proposed changes would have among other things extended social security protection to workers in the informal sector, incorporated the Misiones Bolivarianas and Consejos Comunales into the constitution, set the official working day at six hours, and established a legal basis for communal and collective property. Other progressive highlights included attempts to amplify the social inclusion of youth, women, and Venezuelans of African descent in ways similar to the recognitions extended to indigenous peoples in the 1999 Constitution; it called for a "right to the city" to be recognized as a fundamental human right; it prohibited discrimination based on sexual orientation or health condition. However, the Reforma was silent on questions of same-sex marriage, the right to legal abortion, and was, even in the opinion of sympathetic observers, too timid in its protection and support for workplace democracy (Wilpert 2007b).

Not a few regular supporters of Chávez also noted that the Reforma also made too many unnecessary or even concerning moves. The proposal was peppered with the term "socialist," even though the idea was never explicated in any sustained (let alone juridical) form. Barriers against direct democracy via citizen referenda were heightened. The president's ability to promote, demote, and deploy officers in the National Armed Force was increased. Most disturbingly, the executive branch was granted new powers to issue a "state of emergency," and that exceptional period gained expanded meaning (Wilpert 2007b).

The opposition seized on these final amendments. The domestic and international "No" campaigns centered on the proposal to end term limits and the question of socialized property in an attempt to agitate middle-class turnout, painting each measure as steps along the royal road to "Castro Communism" in Venezuela. Left-wing critics of the government, on the other hand, argued that too little was proposed to definitively move the social and productive bases of Venezuela away from the rentier and semi-capitalist economy that has defined the country since the early twentieth century (Denis 2013). Indeed, when Chávez passed twenty-six of the failed referendum's amendments by decree the following summer (July of 2008), the government published a pamphlet that attempted to counter the "No" campaign's red-baiting, underlining the benefits of the laws in terms of opportunities generated for small businesses and entrepreneurs (Ministerio del Poder Popular para la Comunicación y la Información 2008).

In the voting on December 2 the opposition was able to win roughly the same numbers as they had in the 2006 presidential elections—between four and four and a half million Venezuelans. However, while in 2006 over 7.3 million voters turned out to elect Chávez, in the 2007 referendum three million of those potential progovernment voters stayed home. This was the first time Chávez lost at the polls in nine years of government, and it occurred scarcely a year after his most convincing electoral result.

The proposed Reforma captures a complex and contradictory moment in the course of the Bolivarian Revolution, one in which the state attempted to invert its relationship to the *pueblo*, and a multitude responded with silence. Quite distinct from the democratic openings inscribed into the 1999 Constitution, the 2007 process was less an exercise in participatory democracy than a plebiscite. What is more, as Edgardo Lander notes, "to put it in terms that have come to form part of the common vocabulary in Venezuelan politics, [the 2007 Reforma] would have strengthened *constituted power* in its relation to *constituent power*" (Lander 2008, 136; emphasis in original). One can thus see the failure of the 2007 Reforma as either a setback for the Bolivarian government of Hugo Chávez or as a correction, particularly from the perspective of constituent power. This second reading would seem to have been taken on by Chávez himself, who in the aftermath of the failed referendum called for a period of "Revision, Rectification, and Relaunching" of the Bolivarian Revolution.

However, the lessons learned during this moment of rectification did not immediately sink in; if the defeat of the Reforma can be attributed to Chavista abstention, a second example more clearly illustrates the degree to which forces aligned with the government retain a high degree of autonomy. In the December 2008 regional elections, voters rejected unpopular PSUV candidates such as Diosdado Cabello and Jesse Chacón, gubernatorial candidate for the state of Miranda (which includes the massive east Caracas barrio Petare) and mayoral candidate for the Caracas municipality of Sucre (which is situated in Miranda state), respectively.[11] Left-leaning activists I interviewed described both Cabello and Chacón as key elements of the *derecho endógeno* (internal right wing) of Chavismo. Both were from the military, both were too keen on bureaucratic power, both were corrupt, and neither had any radical credentials to speak of outside of their very public fealty to Chávez. They had both also, not unrelatedly, worked to create their own private fiefdoms within the Bolivarian government, opening lucrative state jobs for family members and creating their own cadre of personally invested officials. As a result, they were unable to win their races despite the full-court push of the PSUV that included youth-oriented get-out-the-vote events like a free concert featuring international artists sympathetic to the Bolivarian Revolution such as Spain's Ska-P, Mexico's Molotov, and Jamaica's Ziggy Marley. In the end, however, neither candidate inspired much in the way of votes. Cabello lost by roughly seven percentage points, Chacón by twelve.

The examples of the Cabello and Chacón campaigns illustrate the most important of three reasons why the PSUV lost in the 2007 Reforma and the 2008 regional elections. They also lost, expectedly, in districts dominated by opposition interests—Nueva Esparta, the affluent portions of major cities like Caracas, Maricaibo, and Valencia. These are also patterns that have either maintained or intensified in subsequent elections and mobilizations, including in the PSUV's massive losses in the December 2015 National Assembly elections. The multitude and *pueblo*, the drivers of the Bolivarian Revolution, remain fickle, able to create effects in absence as well as in overt expressions of collective power.

Finally, the PSUV failed to win over the *ni-nis* (neither-nor—a demographic that by 2016 made up nearly half of Venezuelans)—a dynamic that has continued in subsequent elections. There are conflicting lessons to be taken from this pattern: the government could deepen its commitment to socialism for the twenty-first century in deed as well as in word, furthering the decentralization of power to a communal level and prioritizing the diversification of the productive base. Or, the government could (and apparently did) see itself as having to do more to appeal to the middle classes, especially on issues of property rights and insecurity. The election in the state of Carabobo and the loss of Mario Silva, the firebrand host of the popular Chavista television talk show *La Hojilla* (the razorblade), illustrates how dangerous catering to the undecided as opposed to the multitude, *turba*, or *pueblo* can be.

Silva's electoral aspirations and revolutionary credibility were significantly damaged for radical rank-and-file voters I interviewed in the lead-up to the election when he publicly denounced radical Chavistas alleged to have carried out direct action attacks against FEDECÁMERAS and other opposition strongholds in early 2008. Silva's denunciations were seen as part of old-style politics, as a game, and as calculated to make him a more palatable, law-and-order-style candidate for middle class and *ni-ni* voters. In the end, the gesture only served to alienate what was previously considered to be an unshakable base of support. This was also, not coincidentally, the conclusion of the opposition supporters I spoke with: Silva's gestures were cynical, and they wouldn't work. In the end, of course, they didn't: Silva lost to the center-right candidate, Henrique Salas Feo, by 3.5 points.

For many Chávez supporters, the most significant problem with the Bolivarian Revolution was the degree to which it had yet to break with the norms of contemporary liberal democracy. Allowing for the fact that the electoral struggle is one of many—and not the most important one, at that—many rank-and-file Chavistas were tired of the campaigns, compromises, and posturing of elected officials. As one interviewee put it, rallies, elections, and marches are important as a show of force and serve as vital reminders of power, but they don't replace what she called *real* politics. Changing consciousness, changing the physical environment, changing lives—elections could help in these regards, but they could not stand in for self-organization and direct action. A colleague from Misión Ríbas concurred, "the politics we need happens before and after" spectacles, marches, and commemorations.

The sequence spanning the Caracazo to the Reforma and the 2008 elections can be characterized as a series of attempts on the part of constituted power to transform an ungovernable multitude into a more coherent *pueblo*, and to transfer the energies of the *pueblo* into a disciplined and electorally focused bloc. It can also, therefore, be read as a sequence that ends in failure. By the time of the 2008 regional elections, concerns were already being raised publicly by left-wing dissidents about the PSUV's lack of internal democracy, mounting cases of corruption, and mismanagement of the Misiones Bolivarianas. Against this, the slogans among the most radical elements of the rank and file at the time are as telling as they were widespread: "Por un socialismo sin PaBuCo (Patrones, Burocratas, Corruptos)!" (for a socialism without bosses, bureaucrats, or corruption); "Hay que profundizar la revolución bolivariana" (the Bolivarian Revolution must be deepened); "una revolución *en* la revolución" (a revolution *in* the revolution). That these slogans gained special prominence in an election season, ostensibly a time when calls for unity and discipline were most likely to be heeded, when constituted power's demand to hew to the party line was most credible, also suggests the insurmountability of the gap between constituent and constituted power.

These lessons of 2007–2008 were finally acknowledged in 2012's *Golpe de Timón* address. At a minimum, this analysis illustrates that the Bolivarian Revolution is less a consolidated entity than a rich terrain of struggle upon which the meaning and significance of collective life is contested and determined. It also suggests at least three possible readings of the gap between multitude and the *pueblo*.

The first, Negrian reading, points to the multitude's ungovernability. Retaining its autonomy, the multitude continually exposes the limitations of an institutional and elections-focused government. Moments of refusal, even when against its own ostensibly objective interests, suggest the persistence of the multitude as force despite attempts by constituted powers to code, capture, represent, and rationalize its energies. Faced with this stubborn refusal to be domesticated, the state's inherent antagonism to authentic expressions of constituent power will inevitably eventually be exposed.

The second reading, more in line with Dussel's conceptualization of the *pueblo*, sees in the left critique of the PSUV and the Bolivarian Revolution the healthy functioning of *hiperpotentia*. Contention within the ranks is part of the virtuous cycle of the political. It prevents the Bolivarian Revolution from becoming stagnant, autoreferential, or fetishized. Whereas the first reading considers the slogans to be evidence of the perpetual *being-against* of the multitude, this second reading suggests an organic link between constituent and constituted power. For Dussel, the *pueblo creates* the mediations that distinguish the latent power of the community and the expression of that power in the form of institutions. However, these mediations are not and cannot be static or eternal; they must be replaced depending on the demands of the conjuncture. If the *pueblo's hiperpotentia* did not press the limits of constituted power, the political would devolve into tyranny.

Finally, a third, speculative reading: in Dussel's account of the *hiperpotentia* of the *pueblo*, the internal stirrings of revolt come about despite what he describes as the inevitable entropy of constituted power. But what if the state in question *invites* this perpetual pressure to move forward, to change, to adapt? That is to say, the discursive redeployments of ungovernability within the narratives of governance move toward a more open and contingent "weak constitutionalism" (Colón-Ríos 2012) of constituent power. Multitude and *pueblo* demand processes more than they demand *states*. This reading is the government of ungovernability, anchored in Simón Rodríguez's slogan "inventamos o erramos" (either we invent or we fail). Cautioning against the truism that necessity is the mother of all invention, the Bolivarian Revolution has in numerous cases proven extremely willing to experiment with new forms of civic participation and government's role in the lives of the public. This, at a minimum, marks it as a unique experiment in twenty-first-century post-neoliberal governance. The question remains, however, whether this minimum view can keep up with the egalitarian desire and constituent power of multitudes and *pueblos while* navigating challenges from the domestic opposition and a globally resurgent right.

Constituent Power beyond Multitude and *Pueblo*?

After Hugo Chávez's first election in 1998, social movements throughout Latin America have been increasingly willing to work with or as governments. As a result, several critics in the North Atlantic have called for a reconsideration of the left-wing anti-statism (see, for example, Beverly 2011). However, by 2016, the so-called "Pink Tide" of left-of-center governments in Latin America seems to have decisively ebbed, and Venezuela under Nicolás Maduro offers a less compelling location from which to reconsider the potential virtues of constituted power than it did during the Chávez years. Reversals for the electoral left—especially in Argentina, Brazil, and Venezuela—beg the question of constituent power's long- or even medium-term governability. They also importantly reassert the question of whether governability is a desirable goal in the first place.

As Boaventura de Sousa Santos observes, "exercising power to recreate the state is immensely more difficult than taking power" (de Sousa Santos 2010, 109). New configurations of constituent and constituted power have been called for, and perhaps the singular contribution of the Bolivarian Revolution has been its novel restaging of the relations that define the political in Venezuela. That it has done so while openly contemplating the potentials and tensions of the differences between multitudes and *pueblos* mark the sincerity of the manifold experiments that define it, but much remains to be done.

Thus, while mainstream critics of the Bolivarian Revolution are perhaps correct to point worriedly at the overbearing role of the executive branch, they also miss the more fundamental fact that democracy happens elsewhere. Paraphrasing Jon Beasley-Murray against his own conclusions, Chávez was the *beneficiary* of social change, not its source. By the time of his election,

Venezuela had already been transformed; Chávez inherited the Bolivarian Revolution, he didn't create it (see also Ciccariello-Maher 2013). The state is shown to be the residue of insurrection.

Bolivarian discourse, and particularly its celebration of social upheavals like the Caracazo and the 2002 countercoup, emphasizes its dependence on social forces more than other statist phenomena usually consider safe. It articulates a liberatory mythology that codes and recodes the world, looking for moments in which the multitude can be transformed into the *pueblo*. As a result, the Bolivarian Revolution was at least for a time contingent and open in a way that other actually existing democracies, with their reliance on bureaucratic and institutional modes of legitimation, are not.

There is, however, an ambivalent aspect to the state-sanctioned celebration of these ruptures. The official narrative of the Bolivarian Revolution claims these moments in which an established order broke down as its own. The Caracazo is presented as a direct precursor of the Bolivarian Revolution, a demand for the social transformation, necessary but not sufficient for carrying through on its revolutionary potential. The Bolivarian Revolution claims to *follow* the Caracazo as both chronological successor and spiritual heir. While the countercoups of 2002 and 2003 returned Chávez to power and led to the democratization of consumption, they did so from a position outside of government control and relied upon insubordination from the barrios and the barracks for success. Bolivarian discourse legitimates the government not through a historical link to a people or territory, nor to juridical recognition by fellow sovereign states, but rather through its discursive and historical ties to a rupture—to an event. As the failed Reforma illustrates, however, these ties are not guarantees. Governments lose sight of this at their own peril.

The Bolivarian Revolution presents itself as the realization or government of an original ungovernability. In so doing, it also attempts the transformation of a multitude into a *pueblo*. However, this transformation must be seen as open, contingent, and above all else, collective. It is only from the perspective of *processes* rather than the end products of transformation that the political sequence in Venezuela since the Caracazo can be considered a *revolution* rather than a *state*.

CHAPTER 4

The Structures of Constituent Power

The Caracas Metro and the Right to the City

⚬◉⚬

Constituent power gives form to and animates the political. It continually reestablishes the boundaries of the possible, as it escapes the barriers imposed on it. It propels the formation of collective identity and action. Much writing and thinking on constituent power—the present book included—flirts with the mystical. To speak of constituent power is to always touch upon ontology while insisting "it" is less a "thing" than a capacity or relation, encouraging a language freed from existing historical conditions and the messy, quotidian, entanglements of the political. This book has attempted to resist the pull of theory untethered from history. This chapter extends this commitment by examining how the threat and promise of constituent power as ungovernability also shapes the very *concrete* world of the built environment.

Physical infrastructure is typically either considered in functional terms or as a fixed monument to constituted power. One could argue that city planning, at least since Haussmann's Paris, has been preoccupied with preventing any recurrence of the Commune. Cities in North Atlantic modernity are militarized infrastructures, designed to facilitate the flow of goods and peoples, but also to neutralize constituent power (Virilio 1986; Virilio and Lotringer 1997). Latin America's contemporary urban landscape of walls, cameras, and private security are similarly expressions of elites' fear of poor and popular classes (Caldeira 2001; Rothker 2002; Zubillaga 2013). In Caracas, waves of insurrection, ungovernability, and official and unofficial reaction have led to similar spatial expressions of constituted power, but they have also triggered democratizing moves meant to open access to and guarantee a right to the city for all. Multitudes shape metropolises; *pueblos* do more than merely populate.

This chapter explores these dynamics through a study of the Caracas Metro. My primary assertion is that constituent power has physical as well as civic and theoretical consequences: constituent power founds the political, but it also shapes and constructs the physical. Or, as Henri Lefebvre points out, "there is a politics of space because space is political" (Elden 2007). Urban infrastructures are always already marked by constituent power.[1]

This poses a paradox, however, in terms of scale and substance: large infrastructure developments require more lasting coordinating authority and capital to execute than normally considered possible in the virtuosity of the encounter. Moreover, projects like the expansion of subway systems or the construction of housing blocks are by their very nature fixed to a greater extent than found in thinking around constituent power as an effervescent and episodic expression of democratic potential. The metro thus allows us to consider constituent power through its effects on the urban imaginary as well as the built environment of the city itself. Infrastructure is constituted power. Just as in the case of states, parties, and identities, it is reflexively shaped and reliant upon constituent power.

Even before its inaugural journey in January 1983, the Caracas Metro helped to define Venezuela's capital city. In the decades since, it has been constitutive of the desires, frustrations, and identities of *caraqueños*. More than a technical structure of public transport, a response to the traffic and congestion of the city, or an infrastructure designed to facilitate the flow of bodies and commerce, the metro has always been a *social project*. It produces and directs both urban space and the political subjectivity of the city's residents in an open-ended and sometimes antagonistic sequence. It is an object of political contests while at the same time serving as a principle terrain on which the struggles that define the future of Caracas, and of Venezuela, are fought.

By the first decades of the twenty-first century the stakes around these struggles could hardly be higher. The economic collapse of the 1980s and 1990s triggered the implosion of Venezuela's once-praised Puntofijo system of pacted democracy. After a neoliberalizing 1980s and 1990s that largely followed regional trends, the return of record oil prices opened space for the Chávez government to carry out sweeping changes to Venezuela's political, social, and human infrastructures. The expansion of the Caracas Metro (hereafter, MetroCCS) is a key example of these reforms, providing both a concrete way to productively invest windfall oil revenues while at the same time altering the physical terrain of politics in Venezuela for years to come. The twenty-first-century expansion of the MetroCCS system to include modernized busses, extended subterranean routes, light rail networks throughout the Caracas Metropolitan Area (CMA), and a series of cable car routes linking precarious and informal districts along the hillsides of the capital to the city center are not merely public works projects. They are also, and importantly, material projections of an ethical stance vis-à-vis the collective life of the city, democratizing space and amplifying mobility. That is to say, the MetroCCS not only functions as a pedagogical apparatus oriented toward the behaviors of passengers and citizens. It is also, importantly, an egalitarian vector of a right to the city for all who inhabit and traverse it.

For French Marxist Henri Lefebvre, the right to the city extends classical concepts of political, civil, and social rights. Lefebvre, whose theorization was "more provocative than careful," developed the term in response to the global—but especially Parisian—uprisings of 1968 as a way to assert the increasingly social and spatial aspects of capitalist accumulation and antisystemic struggles for equality (Marcuse 2012, 29). The right to the city entails not only access to all that urban life has to offer, but to the processes by which the city is defined. It is a demand for both *appropriation* and *participation* (Harvey 2008; Purcell 2014, 150). Since its original formulation, the demand for a right to the city has been asserted by urban social movements fighting—among other social injustices—gentrification, privatization, police and private surveillance, socioeconomic inequality, and political exclusion. It has, in short, crystallized a multitude of demands and movements against the late capitalist tendency to fragment and commoditize collective life (Harvey 2008; Mayer 2009; McCann 2002; Mitchell 2003; Purcell 2014).

Academic treatments of the right to the city in Venezuela for the most part center on questions of land ownership and infrastructural support in the urban periphery, or on participatory aspects of twenty-first-century democracy (Fernandes 2010; Humphrey and Valverde 2014; Lajoie 2010; Madera 2010). However, significantly less has been written concerning the role of urban transport infrastructure in extending and facilitating these new rights. Even in light of movements' attempts to recreate the city, these have often been isolated by the geographical reality. Despite gains, Caracas still "is not a shared space for social integration and transformation but an increasingly divided one between rich and poor, Chavistas and anti-Chavistas" (Humphrey and Valverde 2014, 158). The MetroCCS cuts across these internal frontiers, physically, carrying with it the potential to open settled spaces and substantiate the right to access, appropriate, and transform the city. This is precisely why it became a preferred target of the more violent sectors of the Venezuelan opposition.

In the following three sections, this chapter examines the MetroCCS as an infrastructural assemblage (McFarlane 2009) that results from contests over space and access. The first provides a brief history of the metro as conceived by elites in the mid-twentieth century. In this moment the pedagogical function of urban infrastructure corresponds with those positivisms that consider citizens and the city to be raw materials for the modernizing designs of technocrats and experts. The second looks at the effects of the Caracazo on the urban imaginary and the emergence of a demand for a "right to the city"—that subjects have the right to access, shape, and themselves be shaped by the urban environment (Harvey 2008; Marcuse 2009). These demands in turn laid the groundwork for a newly conceived role for the MetroCCS in the twenty-first century, discussed in the third historical section. The metro continues to act as a social engineer in Caracas in the Bolivarian moment, and it remains a key instrument of the interventionist state. However, it also reflects the new ways in which this developmentalist state has attempted to position itself vis-à-vis the tensions between constituent and constituted power. I conclude with a brief analysis of 2014's violent protests against the government of Nicolás Maduro. The tactics and targets of these protests—including barricades and direct attacks on public infrastructures such as the metro—illustrate the perceived threat democratized urban space poses to traditional elites in the context of social change. While the metro plays a key, interventionist, role across these moments—the positivist, the neoliberal, and the Bolivarian—each is driven by distinct approaches to collective life and the transformative power of the urban environment.

La Gran Solución para Caracas: Planning, Social Engineering, and the MetroCCS (1926–1983)

The use of infrastructure as social project has a well-established history in Venezuela. The first urban design schemes in the capital city followed French thinking on city planning and aimed to transform Caracas, its confidence bolstered by Venezuela's oil wealth, into a modern metropolis on par with the capitals of Europe (Almandoz 1999; Cartay 2003). The mid-twentieth-century dictatorship of Marcos Pérez Jiménez (1948–1958) pursued what it called the Nuevo Ideal Nacional (New National Ideal) aimed at transforming Venezuela both physically and socially through, in the words of the dictator, the "progressive modification of the natural and historical environment" (D'Imperio 2003, 104). Above all else, it looked to "eradicate mediocrity" through plans that encouraged urbanization, the development of physical infrastructure, and European immigration as means to "enrich the human capital" of the country (Castillo D'Imperio 2003, 107). Venezuela needed to be remade infrastructurally so it could be reborn socially and politically. As Laureano Vallenilla Lanz—a key proponent of the New National Ideal—declared, "the [bulldozer] is the government's most important collaborator . . . it is as respectable a symbol as the horse on the nation's coat of arms" (quoted in D'Imperio 2003, 112).

These precursors to the MetroCCS by military and civilian governments illustrated a positivist social philosophy that aimed to transform the "effective constitution" of Venezuelans—determined by history, geography, climate, race, and the built environment—into subjects responsible enough to enjoy the "written constitution" of a modern liberal democracy (Bautista Urbaneja 2013, 8; Vallenilla Lanz 1980, 369). Urban planning played a key role in these attempts at modernization, and city life was imagined as a means by which elites could "discipline the barbarity" they saw in their conationals (Cartay 2003, 192). Even still, in Venezuela as in much of Latin America, most urbanization has unfolded in a largely unplanned and post facto fashion. The pace of urban growth has far outstripped the ability, or desire, of planners to provide for the basic needs of a majority of the population (López Maya 2011, 44) and by some estimates over half of *caraqueños* resided in informal and often precarious settlements by 2005 (Ocaña and Guardia 2005, 165). As late as 1992, Aristóbulo Istúriz (then newly elected mayor of Libertador, the largest of Caracas's five municipalities) noted with dismay that his office lacked even basic information about the city. The absence of zoning codes, an accurate census of residents, or a reliable map of streets and services all contributed to what he described as the "special anarchy" of Venezuela's capital (Harnecker 2005, 24).

Caracas is situated in a valley, bordered to its north by the El Ávila National Park and coastal mountain range (where construction has been banned since the 1950s) and to the south by the Cordillera de la Costa Central. As the Venezuelan economy became increasingly defined by petroleum, growing numbers of its citizens were pushed and pulled to the capital city. In 1920, 118,000 people called the Caracas Valley home, less than 4.5 percent of a national population that was still characterized by an agrarian economy and the semi-feudal relations of the persistent *latifundio* (Sanoja Obediente 2011). By 1979, over 3.2 million Venezuelans—nearly a fifth of the national population—were *caraqueños* (Marcano Requena 1979). The economic, political, and social turmoil of the 1980s and 1990s did not slow this urbanizing trend. If anything, the lost decades of neoliberal reforms and the collapse of the pacted democratic system only intensified patterns of economic growth without development, and urbanization without industrialization (Fajardo and Lacabana 1989; Lacabana and Cariola 2003).

Precarity and unplanned urbanization also triggered responses recognizable as expressions of *autogestión* and constituent power. By the 1930s lands on the fringes of the capital city—at that time, still involved in coffee and cacao production—were being occupied illegally by rural migrants. By the 1940s, residents of the urban periphery organized into an umbrella group, the Confederación de los Sin Techos (Confederation of the Homeless), to advocate for official recognition of the property claims, for the provision of necessary domestic infrastructure, and to raise concerns over the criminalization of the growing *zonas populares* (working-class districts) (Grohmann 1996, 31).

Due to the spatial constraints of the Caracas Valley, these settlements either occupy the interstices of previously zoned residential areas—as in the case of the detoured modernism of the 23 de Enero superblock apartment complexes in the west of the city[2]—or crawl up landslide-prone sides of hills and mountains. These popular zones are often accessible only by motorcycle, four-wheel-drive jeep, or foot. For residents in farther-flung sectors of the urban periphery—particularly those at higher altitudes—the metro attempted to rationalize a complicated multivehicle journey across the city center.

The effect was often as additive as it was simplifying. For example, in 2008 travel to the center from a residential parish took two to three hours, often more, depending on the time of day or weather. Travel from a parish like La Vega (which, compared to more recent and farther-flung settlements, is located near the heart of the city) to the Central University (UCV)—a journey of less than ten kilometers—involved no less than three modes of formal and informal transport. Residents of La Vega must first walk either up or down hill along winding paths—often next to open sewage drains and in fear of the armed groups of *malandros* that help make Caracas so notoriously dangerous—to stand in line for a 4x4 jeep that will take them to the bottom of the mountain. From there, they then queue again for a bus or car that will carry them through congested roads to one of two subway stations. The subway is a relatively direct route to UCV, though most of the workers who descend from La Vega work another bus ride or two beyond.

The planning and construction of the MetroCCS attempted to bring order to this situation. It originally followed in the path of previous modes of pedagogical developmentalism in insisting order, stability, and a conquered environment were prerequisites for the "moral, intellectual, and material" improvement of the people and the country (Pérez Jiménez, quoted in Ramos 2010, 30). Public infrastructure projects were not only "concrete embodiments of progress . . . transplanted from metropolitan centers to the national soil" but also considered endowed with the power "to bring progress to Venezuela" (Coronil 1997, 173). The MetroCCS followed this penchant for developmentalist monumentality and was rolled out in accordance with constituted power's need to channel, develop, or neutralize the raw potentials of constituent power.

Given the layout of the city, plans for subterranean transit settled on a major East-West conduit shortly after the World Bank published a position paper in 1959 recognizing urban transport as key to economic growth, with explicit reference to Caracas (Padrón Toro 1990, 11–14). It was only with the oil bonanza of the 1970s that construction began, starting with an appropriations bill in 1976 and the foundation of the MetroCCS as a nationally owned utility in 1977. By the following year, ten stations and connecting tracks were under construction, as were massive public works and arts projects, such as the expansion of the Bulevar Sabana Grande and the construction of a monumental water fountain at the Plaza Venezuela (Metro de Caracas 1982). Plans also included two future north-south lines, eventually opened in 1987 at El-Silencio-Zoologico and 1994 at Plaza Venezuela-La Rinconada (Metro de Caracas 1979, 19–35). In 1986 the MetroBús fleet was incorporated into the MetroCCS as a subsystem, though the service map was initially limited to the anticipations of future subterranean routes (Metro de Caracas 2007, 47).

In the two years immediately preceding its opening in 1983, a massive campaign—*La Gran Solución para Caracas* (The Grand Solution for Caracas)—sought to train residents for what planners promised would bring about the most "radical and beneficial changes to daily life that the city had ever seen" (Padrón Toro 1990, 161).

The designers of both the metro and the *Gran Solución* campaign were explicit in their belief that theirs was an endeavor of civic and social as well as civil engineering. These were not merely step-by-step instructions on how to use a new technology. They were rather parts of a coherent vision for Caracas and Venezuela as a whole. Indeed, official MetroCCS publications are explicit in this regard, elaborating a five-point program for its role in this new social project:

1. *Urbanism*—The MetroCCS is a key element of the modern city for reasons both practical (the circulation of people and goods) and symbolic (the overcoming of the city's natural limits, and a means to secure membership among the ranks of world-class cities).
2. *Urban Regeneration*—The MetroCCS would open the city for new waves of economic growth (construction of the metro itself, but also of secondary effects in real estate markets and cross-sector increases in efficiency), and a means by which to transform "the cultural life of Caracas."
3. *Stable Source of Work*—the MetroCCS promises a steady source of income for future operators, support staff, and construction workers. It would also create new economic hubs around stations that would also stimulate employment.
4. *Testimony of Progress*—The MetroCCS illustrates Venezuela's national development and progress.
5. *Acts of Government*—The MetroCCS shows the "institutional commitment on the part of the state to benefit the collectivity, but especially for the popular sectors. (Adapted from Padrón 1990, 163)

Figure 3. "It's very easy to travel on the metro . . . if you follow these simple instructions." (Viajar en El Metro es muy fácil . . . siguiendo estas sencillas instrucciones.) (Metro de Caracas, SA n/d)

Figure 4. "We're safe on the metro! The metro's conductor is an authority that cares for your well-being and wisely guides you. Respect him, and follow his orders." (¡En El Metro estamos seguros! El Conductor del Metro es la autoridad que cuida por su bienestar y le informa acertadamente. Respételo y siga sus instrucciones.) (Metro de Caracas, SA n/d)

Figure 5. "Feel pride in the metro . . . ! And help keep it clean: by following the rules as a user you'll be contributing to the upkeep of the metro. Remember not to throw garbage on the ground, or to enter the system with food or beverages." (Sienta orgullo de El Metro . . . ! Y ayude a conservarlo limpio: Respete las normas del usario y así estará colaborando a mantener El Metro en buen estado. Recuerde no botar basura en el suelo ni entrar al Sistema con alimentos o bebidas.) (Metro de Caracas, SA n/d)

Before the first passengers entered a subway car, the MetroCCS was a political and civilization-defining achievement; a tool of the economically interventionist state; and, perhaps most important, a means to transform the city and its inhabitants. As a disciplinary apparatus it altered the behaviors and consciousness—the very subjectivity—of bodies "accustomed" to what planners described as the reigning "casual lawlessness of urban transit" into manageable, orderly, and rule-abiding citizens (Padrón 1990, 164–165). It was constituted power attempting to sculpt ungovernable bodies into manageable subjects and citizens. The MetroCCS was thus at one and the same time conceived as a practical solution to traffic, a symbol of national progress, *the means of achieving said progress*, and a motor for the production of modern subjects.

This modernity was a wholly imported entity. As one observer reporting for the *Washington Post* put it in 1983, "nothing in Caracas compares with this. It is the mark of a big league city. It is Venezuela's piece of space-age technocracy . . . the Metro, you see, is not just a beautiful new national toy. It is also the one thing in this great urban tangle that really seems to work." As if to drive the developmentalist narrative home, and to underline the position of Caracas, of Venezuela, and of Venezuelans in the global circle of civilized nations, he concludes, "it is as if such a Metro, in Caracas, could only ever be borrowed from another place" (Diehl 1983, A10). Or, as President Carlos Andrés Pérez said to a North American researcher a few years earlier, "someday soon . . . we will look like you" (quoted in Karl 1999, 32). In other words, the MetroCCS was not only a civilizing and disciplinary project, it was an attempt to help Venezuela gain recognition as an equal from the North Atlantic.

What is most striking, then, about the *Gran Solución* campaign is not so much its content—safety advisories, instructions for use, anti-graffiti and anti-litter messages, cues on how to navigate the mechanical and physical environments of the subway—but rather the way in which it updated existing grammars of power for a new configuration of infrastructure and subjectivity. New modes of authority and affect were grafted onto the city, with smiling and uniformed conductors ensuring an orderly and almost familial extension of the pedagogical state-citizen dynamics of the past. The *Gran Solución* incorporates riders into the mechanics of the MetroCCS as responsible and autonomous individuals and as part of a collective endeavor, but it does so treating them as passive bodies in need of instruction, called upon to obey as beneficiaries of a massive technological feat. Thus, while its egalitarian aim of promoting access for all *caraqueños* can be said to have potentially democratizing effects, at this stage the MetroCCS cannot be said to be democratic or participatory. It operates *on* citizens, and perhaps, it looks to operate *through* them. At this stage, the MetroCCS does not act *with* *caraqueños*.

In the end, the *Gran Solución* would be among the last attempts of the pedagogical state in Venezuela to pursue development through massive infrastructural investment. By 1981 the project neared financial insolvency, requiring another round of emergency funding and another opportunity for the siphoning of public funds by unscrupulous officials (Padrón 1990, 133). When it opened in 1983, the total cost reached over $1 billion USD (in 1983 dollars) (Diehl 1983, A16). Beyond the perhaps predictable fiscal issues surrounding such a massive endeavor, the MetroCCS opened as Venezuela's Puntofijo social, political, and economic order disintegrated. With neoliberalization in the 1980s and 1990s, long-simmering racial and economic tensions boiled over and dominated urban and national imaginaries. The poor were increasingly cast as threats and as the vectors of the barbarity and ungovernability—of a darker side of constituent power—that elites had been struggling to discipline, redirect, and stifle for decades (Cartay 2003; González 2005; Rothker 1993). The MetroCCS was an attempt to rationalize traffic and transit in the capital and to impose a more modern and metropolitan mode of life among *caraqueños*. These aims and the political order they reflected would not survive the coming crises that began in earnest a few short months after the pomp and ceremony of the inaugural journeys of the *Gran Solución para Caracas*.

From Pedagogical Infrastructure to a "Right to the City": The Caracazo and After (1989–2000)

After nearly fifty years of plans, proposals, and half-starts, the MetroCCS opened amid a slow-burning economic collapse, in 1983. The oil bonanza of the 1970s dissipated with alarming speed due to a toxic cocktail of mismanagement, predatory lending practices from abroad, and notorious corruption across every level of government (Días, Cipriano, Villegas 1996, 96–101). In short order, Venezuela went from Latin America's richest nation to one of the region's most indebted (López Maya 2005).

This deteriorating political, economic, and social situation was more than the Puntofijo system could navigate. As elites were dislodged from their traditional roles as "messengers of the future" and "brokers between Latin America and the 'civilized' or 'modern' world," so too was the positivist-pedagogical program for top-down modernization (Coronil 2011, 245). Austerity accompanied a global fall in oil prices, nullifying the "right to have rights" of the growing ranks of Venezuela's poor and rendering democracy a "pantomime" of itself (González 2005, 113). Cracks in Puntofijo—apparent from its very beginning, as seen for example in the abortive guerrilla campaigns of the 1960s—became increasingly unmanageable. By the early 1980s elite consensus had emerged on the need to open the Puntofijo system. However, the proposed reforms—for example, allowing for the direct election of mayors—never matched the scale of the mounting crisis. The inadequacy of these proposals was laid bare by the Caracazo. In its aftermath, popular pressures accelerated the rate and scope of change—moving from reforms to the Puntofijo system of pacted democracy to calls for the convocation of a constituent assembly and an overhaul of Venezuela's socioeconomic order (Denis 2001; López Maya 2011, 22).

The Caracazo highlights the degree to which urban space itself has become both the terrain and the objective of struggles over the future of Venezuela. Opposing tendencies took shape: an isolating and increasingly militarized fear of violent crime and the "other" (Rothker 2002 met with countervailing and democratizing forces that attempted to break down barriers, to move, and to interact with the city and its inhabitants. Pitched battles were fought over access, over transport, over visibility, and over participation—in short, over the very meaning and practice of shared urban life.

Models of urban life and governance based on liberal principles of private property, accumulation, and developmentalist designs reinforce the familiar exclusions of constituted power. Multitudes and pueblos are, at best, expected to enjoy the fruits of enlightened policy making, but are expected to remain outside of the active decision making process beyond the regularly scheduled election of representatives. These dynamics are intensified with neoliberalization. Against this the right to the city envisions the urban as a work in progress "in which all citizens participate" (Mitchell 2003, 17). The "all" in this formulation is of central importance. To assert a right to the city is also to continually ask *Whose Right? What Right? What City?* As Peter Marcuse insists, "it is not everyone's right to the city with which we are concerned . . . there is in fact a conflict among rights that needs to be faced and resolved, rather than wished away. Some already have the right to the city, are running it now, have it well in hand . . . it is the right of the city of those who do not have it now" that animates right to the city movements (Marcuse 2009, 191). The demand for the right to the city is transformative and antagonistic, but it is also protagonistic and partisan. The Right to the City takes sides in social conflicts. As opposed to liberal conceptualizations that treat rights as the private property of sovereign individuals, the right to the city is a contested and collectively articulated demand. It is a demand to be part of a future city that will necessarily supplant the unequal present (Marcuse 2009, 193).

David Harvey adds that to demand this right is to pose a fundamentally dialectical relation between the city and its inhabitants. He writes, "the right to the city is an active right to make the city different, to shape it in accord with our collective needs and desires and so remake our daily lives . . . to define an alternative way of simply being human" (Harvey and Potter 2009, 49). The right to the city is thus "far more than the individual liberty to access urban resources: it is the right to change ourselves by changing the city. It is . . . a common rather than an individual right since this transformation inevitably depends on the exercise of a collective power to reshape the process of urbanization" (Harvey 2008, 23). The right to the city, then, is more than a demand for access to an actually existing polity, but a collective process aimed at the transformation of social relations and urban space. Ontologically, it asserts the division between the city and its inhabitants, between the objective and subjective world, between the environment and the human—is contrived. We are entangled not only with others, but with the worlds we create, and by which we are created. The right to the city is in other words similar to the generative, creative, and constantly moving attributes of constituent power. Like constituent power, it is an assertion of equality and a refusal to accept separation and exclusion. It relates to the actually existing constituted order as an exterior, revolutionary, and revolutionizing force.

The most obvious expressions of a right to the city emerged as local projects in *autogestión* and *cogestión* (self- and comanagement) as well as the growing incidences of protest over deteriorating public services, police repression, and access to the city (López Maya 2005). In effect, expressions of *autogestión* and *cogestión*, in which "people manag[e] collective decisions themselves rather than surrendering those decisions to a cadre of state officials" (Purcell 2014, 147), decentralized key functions of the modern nation-state "from below" as the official neoliberalization in the 1990s forced administrative decentralization as best practices throughout the 1990s. They are expressions of constituent power. Innovative responses to economic decline and political implosion—such as the Mesas Técnicas de Agua (Water Working Groups), the Comités de Tierra Urbana (Urban Land Committees), the Círculos Femininos (Women's Circles), and the Asamblea de Barrios (Neighborhood Assemblies)—elaborate different aspects of a *collective* right to appropriation and participation that is vital to any articulation of a right to the city, even when that specific framework is not invoked (see for example Azzelini 2010; Ciccariello-Maher 2013; Fernandes 2007; García-Guadilla 2011; Grohmann 1996; Martinez and Fox 2010; Motta 2013). In this respect, the 1999 Constitution both recognized and concretized but did not found demands for greater autonomy and *cogestión*, notably in Articles 26, 82, and 182 that promote popular participation in municipal and regional affairs and a fundamental human right to housing.

Calls to transform the unequal city of the 1990s would not have grown in strength and volume were they not consistently faced with countervailing economic, political, and social tendencies. As the crises of neoliberalization deepened, security increasingly became a preoccupation, and the wealthy especially developed a festering siege mentality in the face of what they saw as threatening and racialized "hordes" menacing their civilized parts of the city (Duno-Gottberg 2013). Violence—and the fear of violence—increasingly shaped an urban and national imaginary haunted by highly publicized murders, kidnappings, and robberies, all shadowed by a proliferation of walls, security checkpoints, and armed guards (Ciccariello-Maher 2007b; Rothker 2002; Sanjuán 2002; Zubillanga 2013).

In the decade between the Caracazo and the election of Hugo Chávez, the social role of the MetroCCS, of urban transit and planning, and of the pedagogical state moved in contradictory and ultimately untenable directions. Above all else, in the context of fiscal austerity and the consolidating neoliberal common sense, the MetroCCS lost much of its previous imagined and practical role in shaping the infrastructure and subjectivity of the city and its residents. While Venezuela certainly followed the regional trend toward the decentralization of administrative functions (García-Guadilla 1997; López Maya 2005), this was also the moment—in 1989 and 1991—that the central government implemented integrated national transportation plans for the first time. Rosa Virginia Ocaña and Inés Guardia note that while these plans ran against trends toward decentralization, they were nonetheless neoliberal in orientation and were directed by the architects of key privatizations, such as that of Cantv—the national telecommunications company—in late 1991 (Ocaña Ortiz and Guardia Rolando 2005, 166). Urban transit plans, furthermore, were increasingly marked by buzzwords of marketization and a general freeze in construction due to fiscal constraints. Plans prioritized "efficiency" and piecemeal improvements to existing infrastructure while allocating funds for private-sector operators in the hybrid public-informal sector transit systems of Venezuelan cities (Ocaña Ortiz and Guardia Rolando 2005, 168). In one such plan, the state offered loans and grants to entrepreneurs and public-private enterprises in the hillside communities inaccessible by conventional means of mass transit like busses and subterranean rail (Ocaña Ortiz and Guardia Rolando 2005, 172; Ocaña Ortiz and Urdaneta 2005, 198). However, in so doing, these initiatives tended to replicate rather than replace entrenched patterns of bureaucratic bloat, inefficiency, and clientelism—particularly in the capital (Ocaña 2005, 174).

As the MetroCCS transformed itself in step with the rest of the Venezuelan state, it also exhibited traits of what María Pilar García-Guadilla has characterized as a process of decentralization without democratization. In some cases, these reforms had the perverse effect of demobilizing the democratizing movements of the 1980s and early 1990s (García-Guadilla 1997, 47). Adding to this potentially destabilizing moment of fiscal austerity and administrative overhaul, internal and international immigration patterns to the capital city took on a more impoverished and precarious character as privatization, deregulation, and trade liberalization evaporated middle-class jobs (Portes and Roberts 2005, 76). In Venezuela, the artificially large public sector shrank as oil prices dropped throughout the 1990s, contributing to an explosion of the informal sector to over half of the working population and a by now generalized, cross-class, obsession with insecurity (Humphrey 2014, 256).

The demand for a right to the city in Caracas responds to the social and political crises of neoliberalization. Just as economic adjustment rolled back the project of the city as a shared (if hierarchical and managed) space, new social movements created counterpublics and alternative visions of collective life. With the electoral successes of the Bolivarian Revolution and Hugo Chávez in 1998, this uneven and contested process of negotiating life in the city entered a new stage, as the state attempted to reassert its historically strong position in Venezuelan polity and society by capturing and institutionalizing expressions of autonomous constituent power (Azzellini 2010; Beasley-Murray 2010; Kingsbury 2013). These processes can be observed in the reconstruction of the built environment of the city of Caracas and the reimagined role of the MetroCCS in processes of social transformation that pick up the pace by 2006. However, and just as important, we can assess the implications of attempts to spatially reorganize the city in the forceful counterattacks of those who, recalling Marcuse's diagnosis, have historically already enjoyed a privileged access to the city, and who are doing everything in their power to maintain that exclusive prerogative.

Bolivarian Infrastructure? *Un Metro en Revolución* (2006–2014)

The demand for a right to the city has been implicit but constant across the actions of a number of urban social movements since the 1990s. Expressions of *autogestión* and *cogestión* resulted in renovated expressions of civic identity and participation beyond the circumscribed representative Puntofijo system. Many of these political transformations were institutionalized in the 1999 constituent assembly and the constitution of the now *Bolivarian* Republic of Venezuela. Even more fundamentally, the new constitution acknowledged its basis in a constituent power where "democracy . . . trump[s] constitutionalism" (Colón-Ríos 2011, 378). The same forces reflected in alterations to the juridical scaffolding of the Venezuelan republic have also been at work in reshaping the physical transformation of the city of Caracas.

Of course, *concretizing* political visions through massive public works and construction projects is nothing new to Venezuela. Indeed, one could plausibly argue that converting oil profits into spectacular feats of social engineering has been a preferred mode of public policy since at least the mid-twentieth century (Coronil 1997; Velasco 2015). However, if construction was in many ways predictable given the early twenty-first-century flush of oil money, its direction and social role were not. Priority was given to housing and transit policies and projects that facilitated access to the city for its poorest and most vulnerable residents. Public transit fare schedules of the MetroCCS and MetroBús—as well as public mass transit projects in other cities—remained far below market price for transport, even by the low standards established by Venezuela's almost free consumer gasoline. Perhaps *the* most emblematic of these policies and projects—the MetroCable in Caracas—operates at a loss. Indeed, it never sought to justify itself in economic terms, citing instead the need to provide access to the city for those with the least resources (Urdaneta 2012, 458).

The MetroCCS entered a new moment in its role as social project. In response to violent opposition attacks on transit infrastructure as part of extraparliamentary attempts to overthrow the government from 2002 to 2004, the MetroCCS initiated a series of internal reforms aimed at carrying out a more protagonistic role for itself within the wider Bolivarian process. In accord with national reforms to the military, its employees formed a workers' militia (Metro de Caracas 2007, 151). In the typical fashion of Bolivarian iconography, the MetroCCS revised Simón Bolívar's maxim and proclaimed that "all of the metro is a classroom" (170). Workers convened reading groups on socialism and Latin American history, among other topics (175). In addition to monies invested in social and cultural infrastructure around subway and MetroCable stations, the public company also developed mobile libraries to serve less accessible corners of the capital (133). These projects took place at the prerogative of the MetroCCS's Gerencia de Coresponsibilidad Social (Office of Social Co-responsibility), which was created in 2006 with the aim of integrating riders, workers, and residents in the shared management of urban and transit spaces "according to principles of cooperation, solidarity, knowledge, and shared social responsibility" (128).

While the MetroCCS has always seen itself as a "cultural and social system" embedded in the greater urban environment, what this means has changed over its lifetime (Metro de Caracas 2007, 57). Changes in both its internal corporate structure and the scope of its services suggest a shift from neoliberalization to a retooled developmentalism proclaiming its fidelity to the *pueblo* and a general politicization of what planners might prefer to think of as neutral or at least benign public transit infrastructure. The Bolivarian MetroCCS imagined itself an active and visible participant in the social transformations that characterized Venezuela at the time. That is to say, the MetroCCS was not only a way for the state to sculpt the population into its preferred image, it also took sides in the internal social struggles between the Bolivarian Revolution and the opposition in Venezuela.

By 2006, as the system expanded to include cable cars, light rail, and regional transit, the metro outlined four orienting goals for itself in relation to the larger processes of the Bolivarian Revolution:

1. To produce functional public spaces and order to their constitutive elements.
2. To produce cultural public spaces that provide urban landmarks and shared protected sites.
3. To conceive of public space as an instrument of social redistribution, of community cohesion, and collective self-esteem.
4. To promote public space for the formation and expression of the collective will of the citizenry. (Adapted from Metro de Caracas 2007, 92)

In contrast to the previous mission statement of the metro and its role in the life of Caracas that emphasized modernization, economic growth, and a symbol of government prowess, the Bolivarian MetroCCS emphasizes social justice, the formation of shared public space, and participation. As opposed to the monumental approach of public works of previous models, new stations along the expanded network were to serve as cultural and educational hubs for community participation and empowerment. Along the San Augustín MetroCable line, for example, the metro built sports fields, communal kitchens, meeting spaces, and schools directly adjacent to its five stations. Before, during, and after the construction process, the metro sought out the direct participation of local communal councils and other grassroots assemblies for planning and grievances and to fully integrate the community not only as passive beneficiary of public works but as an active participant in an ongoing process of urban *cogestión* (Metro de Caracas 2007, 98–100).

Starting in 2006, the MetroCCS expanded both within the city of Caracas—through a relief line in the east, light rail lines around Petare, more stations, and a series of MetroCable gondola lines linking hillside settlements to the center of the city. The first MetroCable installation linking the area of San Augustín to the Parque Central district was inaugurated in 2010. A second line was opened at El Mariche in the east of the city in 2012, and several other cable car projects are currently in development. The MetroCCS

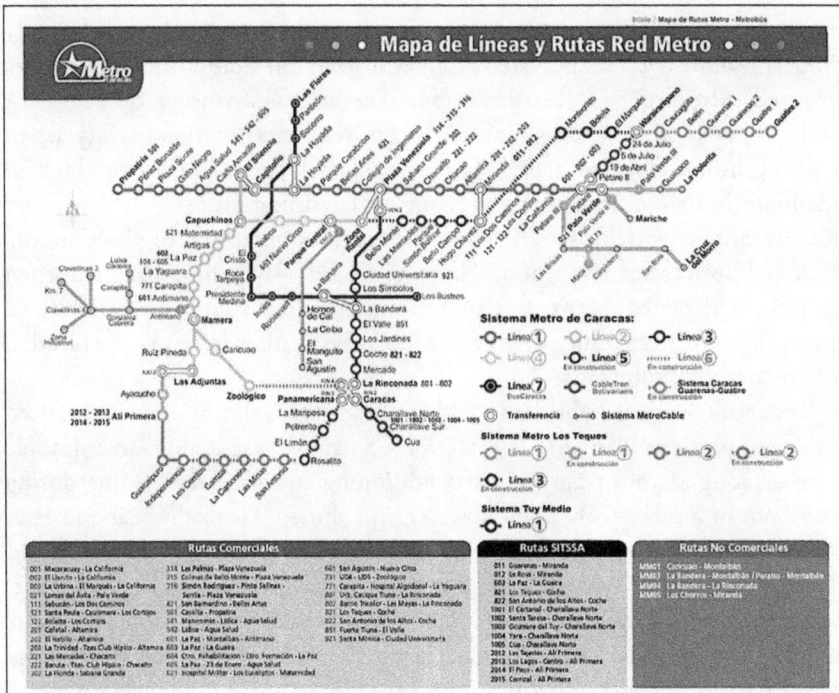

Figure 6. Caracas Metro and Metrobús System Map, 2015

has also worked toward integrating the Caracas region, with commuter rail service to satellite cities such as Los Teques, Guarenas, and Guatire. The company has, finally, expanded its Metrobús fleet with vehicles that meet heightened safety, emissions, and disability accessible standards in an attempt to ease the perennial congestion of the capital and rationalize its anarchic and aging network of private buses (Metro de Caracas 2007, 48). By 2007 there were no fewer than ten new public mass transit projects—subterranean metro lines, light rail, cable car routes, and busses—in the works (Urdaneta 2012, 458).

There have, of course, been bumps in the road. The stated goal of *cogestión* has often held more in principle than practice. The centralizing tendencies of the Bolivarian Revolution as constituted power has certainly been observable in the massive public works and operational necessities of the MetroCCS. Justin McGuirk (2014) contends that corruption, petty politics, and government paranoia have contributed to projects going over budget, opening late, or not happening at all (162–173). The construction of the cable cars and the expansion of subway routes have all but universally been carried out by foreign firms—Swiss, Austrian, and especially Brazilian—thus missing a potential opportunity to meet the need to develop and diversify domestic industry. Finally, MetroCable projects inevitably find themselves inserted into larger issues that impact the city as a whole. By 2014, for example, residents in San Augustín expressed fears for their safety when walking home from MetroCable stations after dark—either for lack of adequate lighting, *malandros* preying on tired commuters, or absent or equally untrustworthy security forces. Special operations of the Guardia Nacional Bolivariana (Bolivarian National Guard, GNB) have been launched to address these concerns, but in a climate of persistent and generalized insecurity in Caracas, such steps can only hope to offer temporary, episodic, and incomplete solutions.

The result is more hybrid and additive than the uniform and modernized visions of previous planners. The MetroCCS can be wonderful—an enjoyable ride—as long as your train has air conditioning and you aren't riding during rush hour or a protest. By 2016, however, this shifted. Generally rising fears of insecurity have become particularly concentrated in the subway. Chavistas and the opposition alike will warn you against using a smartphone in plain sight. Stories of sexual assault are common, and the growing population of beggars and hawkers are registered by many as vectors of a criminality that was once—before Chávez, insisted opposition riders—not tolerated on the metro.

These are in many ways, however, inherited and unavoidable problems of the capital city itself. Attempts to physically transform Caracas and to ensure a lasting right to the city occur despite entrenched corruption and worsening insecurity, and these blights were by no means caused by attempts to democratize space in Venezuela. More importantly, and enduringly, the very concrete nature of expanded public transit infrastructures extends the democratizing potentials of constituent power into an uncertain future. The demand for a right to the city—implicit but forceful *and prior to* the Bolivarian government—becomes an emplaced fact on the ground with the expansion of the MetroCCS. In this way constituent power extends beyond its immediate expression, outliving any given political regime and affecting the mobilities, expectations, and behaviors of subjects far into the future. It is an emplaced act of sabotage against any future attempt to roll back the sociospatial gains won by poor *caraqueños*.

If infrastructures force future reactions and form subjects in ways that cannot be predicted, the way in which the MetroCCS figured in antigovernment protests of 2014 is far less open and ambiguous. On January 23, 2014—the anniversary of the fall of the Pérez Jiménez dictatorship in 1958—two prominent figures of the Venezuela opposition, Leopoldo López and Maria Córina Machado, denounced the "dictatorship" of the government of Nicolás Maduro and called for Venezuelans to take to the streets until they could provoke the fall of the regime. At a press conference ready-made for the Twitter age, they launched their brand, La Salida (the exit, or, alternatively, the solution), and distanced themselves from the electoral strategy of the mainstream opposition Mesa de Unidad Democrática (MUD, Democratic Unity Coalition). Over the following months, Venezuela's major cities were rocked by violent street protests called *guarimbas*. Antigovernment protestors erected barricades of burning cars, tires, and trash. Pitched battles were fought with police and national guard forces. Many government supporters reported formal and informal pressures from the *guarimberos* and their supporters—a friend in Caracas recounted worriedly that *guarimberos* told her family to either support them or, ominously, to be put on a list for when the neighborhood would be "cleaned." Driving through Merida, another pointed out the precision with which second- and third-floor apartments where Chavistas lived had their exterior windows smashed by projectiles from the street. Adjacent residences, belonging to pro-opposition families, escaped the disturbances unscathed.

The *guarimbas* of 2014 were a reboot of a 2004 campaign called for by Cuban émigré Robert Alonso, which were themselves a reboot of a tactic utilized by Communist Party youth during the Puntofijo years). *Guarimbas*, as Alonso outlined, aimed to "totally paralyze the country" and precipitate a terminal crisis for the Chávez government (Alonso nd). The 2004 wave of *guarimbas* left nine people dead, and over two hundred injured (López Maya 2006, 41). In the aftermath, Alonso fled to Miami (TeleSur 2014).

The MetroCCS was a constant target of these protests. In the first weeks of the protests, at least forty busses were singled out for attack by protesters (Padrino 2014). From February to May, stations were often closed as a result of antigovernment protests. Kiosks, stations, and bus stops in the opposition strongholds of eastern Caracas—the municipalities of Chacao, Baruta, and El Hatillo—were regularly vandalized and set ablaze (Noticias24 2014). By April, *guarimberos* had attacked a number of Metrobús vehicles with Molotov cocktails—often with passengers aboard, hospitalizing two drivers in May alone. On May 6, Minister of Transport Haiman El Troudi reported that over one hundred busses had been firebombed (YVKE Mundial 2014) and at least fifty-seven employees of the MetroCCS system suffered various injuries (Correo del Orinoco 2014). Protesters also attacked the Parque del Este (Miranda) subway station during operating hours with flaming tires and Molotovs (Noticiero Digital 2014).

Opposition mayors in eastern Caracas condemned specific incidents—for example, the May 26 attacks on the Ministry of Housing and Habitat in Chacao (Bautista 2014)—and publicly exhorted their residents to engage in peaceful protest (Smolansky 2014). Indeed, by late 2015 the *guarimbas* and the La Salida campaign exposed emergent divisions within the MUD when former presidential candidate and governor of Miranda Henrique Capriles Radonski described the radical and violent protests "a massive national *fracaso* (failure)" (Amaya 2015). Government officials and supporters, however, maintained that opposition mayors like David Smolansky in El Hatillo, Carlos Ocariz in Sucre, and Ramón Muchacho in Chacao contributed to disturbances *at the very least* by validating protester claims that they were fighting a dictatorship and foot dragging when it came to enforcing the law (Agencia EFE 2014; Correo del Orinoco 2014). By the time the wave of *guarimbas* ebbed in late May, forty-three people from both sides of the political divide were left dead, hundreds more were injured, López was jailed for inciting violence, millions of dollars in damage was recorded, and the sharp polarization of Venezuelan politics was once again forcefully underlined.

Of course, *guarimberos* burned and attacked anything associated with the government and its social programs. Antigovernment protestors burned food delivery vehicles, medical facilities, schools, cultural centers, and the headquarters of the Gran Misión Vivienda Venezuela (Great Venezuelan Housing Mission), betraying their opposition to *any* attempt to expand access and democratize consumption. However, the destruction of metro stations, kiosks, and busses not only attacked visible representations of the government, but also asserted a specific configuration of intraurban territorial sovereignty, refusing right of passage to citizens of other zones.

On April 16, 2014, MetroCCS workers initiated a campaign against the *guarimbas*, calling for protestors to respect their right to a safe work environment as well as the right of all *caraqueños* to safely traverse the city. They distributed flyers that included photographs of masked protesters burning installations as a reminder of the competing projects of the opposition and the MetroCCS. In a statement marking the start of the campaign, Edison Alvarado, president of the union of MetroCCS workers, said, "While the opposition is destroying busses and attacking our workers and other public institutions, we are making a call for peace and love. We say to them that the only road is that called for by President Nicolás Maduro, that of dialogue and peace" (quoted in Venezolana de Televisión 2014).

The tenor and trajectory of actions carried out in response to the *guarimbas* by the MetroCCS reflect a politicized institutional culture. Most obviously, statements in support of the president against the La Salida campaign are partisan and explicitly take sides in the ongoing struggles between the opposition and the government. It should be little surprise that a public company integrated into the national government would follow the orders of the chief executive.[3] More interesting, however, is the way in

Figure 7. "We want Peace! Workers and riders of the metro say NO to violence." (¡Queremos Paz! En el Metro los trabajadores y usarios decimos NO a la violencia.) http://www.vtv.gob.ve/articulos/2014/04/02/con-actividades-culturales-y-entrega-de-volantes-trabajadores-metro-iniciaron-jornada-por-la-paz-4079.html.

which the MetroCCS responded directly to attacks by attempting to mobilize ridership in defense of the transit infrastructure and publicly shaming those opposition officials it deemed responsible for the violence. By directly entering the fray, the MetroCCS acted more like a participant in a complex social struggle than inert infrastructure. It was defending not only itself, but the vision it had adopted for its role in a present and future Caracas.

In a country that is over 90 percent urban, it borders on banality to suggest protests shape and are shaped by cities. What is striking about the opposition protests of 2014, however, is the degree to which they both physically exemplify the content of their demands and the way in which they appropriate and redeploy tactics often associated with more progressive ends. First, the 2014 protests exclusively occurred in opposition and affluent sectors of the city, leaving traditionally restive barrios silent as middle- and upper-class youths spoke to foreign news crews, in English (Neuman 2014). The barricade, a tactic perhaps most romantically associated with the New Left of Paris 1968, was in the Caracas of 2014 a means of protecting established zones of privilege from government supporters. They are symptomatic of a deeper siege mentality, a blocking off of a protected zone from a dangerous invasion or contagion. Perhaps the most grisly and medieval manifestation of this mentality occurred on February 20, 2014. Retired general Ángel Vivas, a vocal critic of the Bolivarian Revolution, which he likened to a "Cuban Invasion," tweeted instructions on how to "neutralize criminal hordes of *motorizados*" by stringing razor wire across streets at head level. *Motorizados* had by then become—and remain—a specter that haunts the Venezuelan opposition. Seen as motorcycle vectors of criminal Chavismo, *motorizados* are often blamed for all manner of injustice, from roughing-up and intimidating innocent antigovernment protestors, to dealing drugs, to occupying or stealing homes (Ciccariello-Maher 2014a). At least two people were decapitated at the barricades by these razor-wire traps. After a televised standoff with police, Vivas remained sequestered in his heavily fortified home until 2017, when he was finally arrested.

The *guarimbas* thus can be seen as extending a decades-long practice of erecting borders at the internal—racial and class—borders of the city. Pro-testers sought to destabilize the government, and their actions in that regard carried a clear, instrumental, and organized meaning. However, in actions such as burning dark-skinned and red-shirted effigies at their barricades, they also betrayed a more crassly racist motivation to their desires to interrupt ongoing social reforms (Ciccariello-Maher 2014b, 2014c; Tinker Salas 2014).

Events since 2014 highlight the degree to which the city of Caracas has become both the object and terrain of political struggle in Venezuela. The city is a physical instantiation of constituent power's encounter with constituted orders. They also illustrate the importance of transit infrastructure in this conflict. The MetroCCS has served to physically shape and transform the city and to provide access to its processes and services in accordance with the desires of inhabitants previously excluded from the life of the metropolis. It has also become a prominent and representative site of contestation and antagonism, in the military-strategic sense of opposition actions as well as in the imaginary of a city that has been struggling to redefine itself for generations.

Conclusion: Infrastructure and the Right to the City as Constituent Power

Like most Latin American cities, Caracas is a traffic nightmare. Bound by geography and demographic pressures, the city is congested, polluted, and difficult to traverse via surface transportation. The MetroCCS is a necessary response to the practical difficulties of urban life.

However, in each of its the three dominant modalities since planning and construction began in the 1970s, the MetroCCS has also been part of a larger social project, shaped by or responding to expressions of constituent power. In the early moments of planning and the *Gran Solución* campaigns, the MetroCCS extended a positivist-pedagogical relationship of the state to the citizenry established in the early twentieth century. As such, the cultural politics occasioned by the construction of a subway, like other public works, recreated familiar developmentalist hierarchies in which the inhabitants of Venezuela's capital were so much raw material, wanting in the cultivation and training necessary for modern citizenship. In this positivist phase, constituent power is a threat to which the MetroCCS responds and attempts to transform into modern urban citizenship.

The second moment of the MetroCCS stepped away from this emphasis on training. During the economic downturns of the lost decades, the tradition-ally interventionist Venezuelan state followed regional trends in privatization and decentralization, and while the MetroCCS remained a public company providing a vital service during this era, it did so in a larger discursive environment dominated by the language of efficiency, entrepreneurship, and austerity. It was also during this moment that Venezuelan politics saw a long-standing national project—that of the Puntofijo state—collapse. The resulting vacuum was replaced by local projects in *autogestión* and *cogestión* and the demand for access and inclusion characterized thematically by the right to the city.

With the electoral success of the Bolivarian Revolution, the MetroCCS again played a key role in a statist project contoured by a worldview that ultimately remains developmentalist, but in importantly different ways. First and foremost, the positivistic consideration of passengers as passive pupils has been realigned according to principles of *cogestión*. The MetroCCS has accordingly become more overtly politicized, reflecting changes that have shaped Venezuela since the 1990s. The MetroCCS increasingly acts as a guarantor of a right to the city, and as such, should be recognized as a terrain, object, and indeed, a protagonist in processes of social transformation.

During the unrest of 2016, as the opposition again mobilized for the ouster of Nicolás Maduro in the context of political, economic, social, and ecological crises, the MetroCCS closed subway stations and cancelled bus routes through opposition strongholds. The MetroCCS cited concerns that the infrastructures would again be targeted by violent protests and vandalism. In an ironic twist, it was the opposition's turn to claim their rights were being violated (Meza and Castro 2016). Without validating or refuting their claim, this episode illustrates the changing dynamics of constituent and constituted power in Venezuela, as well as the changing meaning of what a right to the city entails in Bolivarian Caracas. As the MetroCCS has become a protagonist in the Bolivarian Revolution, it has ceased to entertain the notion that it is simply a neutral infrastructure. It thus has its own set of answers to Marcuse's question—*Who's right? What rights? Whose city? What city?*—with an insistence that it will not contribute to the opposition's project to end the Bolivarian Revolution. The MetroCCS is in this way an expression of constituted power that declares itself in the service of what it recognizes as constituent power.

Transit lines, public services, and the built environment shape the time and space of daily life. Strategies of users and the demands they make on planners and operators shape these vital aspects of the built urban environment. The movements of the 1990s levied political and ethical demands for a future—more inclusive, accessible, and open—city. The resulting boom in infrastructural development in Caracas can be seen as an extension of this political sequence, creating facts on the ground that preemptively sabotage future attempts to restore the old order of the segregated city. The backlash to the Bolivarian Revolution in the twenty-first century has sought to defend and reinforce a Caracas in which a besieged privilege is protected, fortified, and exclusive. With each new sequence in the political life of the city, the MetroCCS has been recast as a component in this struggle. However, unlike the constituent power of social relations and political positions—which, to be sure, engender inheritances, identities, and worldviews that structure politics in real and often seemingly immutable ways—there is something about the quite literally *concrete* nature of these infrastructures that projects a present ethical commitment into the uncertain waters of the future. This is precisely why opposition attacks on the MetroCCS have been so violent.

Returning, finally, to one of the questions with which this chapter opened—*Can multitudes build metros?*—the answer is of course both yes and no. While urban infrastructural development may indeed be beyond the scope of crowdsourcing, voluntary association, collective being-against, and virtuosic collaboration, the discussion of the Bolivarian MetroCCS and the response to opposition attacks suggests a third possible conclusion. The multitude, as a creative, innovative, expansive force of constituent power is always impure, always contaminated by aspects of the situations from which they emerge, including those defined by constituted and state power (Arditi 2008,79). In forms of infrastructural politics such as those illustrated by the MetroCCS, in other words, we can glimpse moments in which constituted and constituent politics correlate and project an egalitarian desire—the right to the city—into the uncertain future *as the built environment*. These are the structures of constituent power.

Escuálidos

The Opposition, Constituent Power, and the Problem with (and of) Democracy

In a 2010 event marking the anniversary of Misión Barrio Adentro, Hugo Chávez joked to an auditorium of white-coated doctors, "to be an *escuálido* is to be ill." He continued, riffing on the location and the event, that "only in a few cases" could the "grave sickness" of *escuálidismo* be cured. "What is bad for the country is good for them," he observed, noting how the opposition had capitalized on recent energy shortages for their narrowly conceived political gain (Noticias24 2010). Later, and with his typical flourish, the president defiantly announced in 2012 that the cancer that would soon take his life had returned *escuálido*—and that he would "fight without truce" to vanquish it (Noticiero Digital 2012).

These were not the first times Chávez pathologized the opposition. Nor would they be the last. Indeed, one of the chief characteristics of the social and political conflict that has deepened and become ever more insurmountable since his election is the belief that the enemy is sick, mad, or otherwise afflicted. Both sides level this accusation. For its part, Chavismo's medicalization contends the *escuálidos'* illness makes them incapable of national pride. They are parasites, benefiting from the Bolivarian Revolution's project of national development while actively undermining and sabotaging it. *Escuálidismo* is a cancer.

Escuálido doesn't translate elegantly into English. It means "squalid"—thin, weak, and incapable. In the tangled and evolving political lexicon of the Bolivarian Revolution, *escuálidos* are seen as motivated by the basest self-interest. They are holdovers from the old order. Rich, white, more loyal to the United States than to Venezuela. Short-termism and individualism isolates them from the power of the collective. They are shadowy figures that must rely on sabotage since they lack the strength or appeal for the rigors of an above-board, democratic, contest. Escuálidos are the enemies of the Bolivarian Revolution.

While it has become common practice to refer to *the* opposition in Venezuela in the singular, it is also common to point out this is a convention that obscures as much as it illuminates. The shorthand simplifies a diverse field of antigovernment forces and personalities, but it also implies an internal unity to the opposition. *The* opposition projects a coherence, shared vision, and common agenda on what has throughout the history of the Bolivarian Revolution more resembled a fractious pool of would-be-presidents-in-waiting than a viable political bloc. What is more, *the* opposition implies a mirror opposite: *the* government. These are reflections of constituted power; they may hold true in contingent moments, but in both cases they inevitably fail to capture the constituent energies they claim as their own.

The various parties that make up the Mesa de Unidad Democrática (Democratic Unity Coalition—MUD) span the ideological spectrum. Among the most prominent members, Henrique Capriles Radonski and Julio Borges's Primero Justicia declares itself progressive-liberal while promising economic reforms closer to the neoliberalization of the 1990s than the Pink Tide of the 2000s. Un Nuevo Tiempo (A New Era, UNT) was formed after its founder, Manuel Rosales, left AD in 1999. The party has a similar social democratic mission statement to the former cornerstone of Puntofijo (the remnants of which also joined the MUD), and their stronghold remains in his home state of Zulia. Voluntad Popular (Popular Will, VP) is largely organized around the electoral ambitions of Leopoldo López—the conservative former mayor of Chacao who was imprisoned in March of 2014 for incitement. Vente Venezuela (Let's Go Venezuela, VV), another conservative party, is the electoral vehicle for María Corina Machado, the former National Assembly representative from Baruta who, after joining López in the 2014 call for La Salida, traveled throughout Latin America, North America, and Europe calling for international intervention to bring down the Maduro "dictatorship." She was removed from office in 2014 (El Mundo 2014). Many Chavistas consider them all fascists, another less than helpful simplification. While there is little in the way of programmatic cohesion among the member parties of the MUD, and while none of the parties' leaders have hidden their personal ambitions to the presidency, for a short time they managed to operate in a tactically unified manner.

Emboldened by the death of Chávez in 2013, they stepped up coordinated efforts to depose Nicolás Maduro. They renewed violent street blockades and protests costing lives and resources while damaging the already flimsy sense of social cohesion. According to government accounts, they waged a ruthless economic war of financial sabotage, exacerbating the consequences of already existing mismanagement and corruption, triggering shortages in hospitals and on grocery store shelves. Opposition figureheads claimed they were forced into confrontations by an obstinate government that wantonly manipulated institutions to retain its hold on state power. As such, they carried out an international campaign calling for diplomatic isolation and even armed intervention while threatening a civil war at home and calling for the military to choose a side. They also, finally, used the constitution in a failed attempt to recall the president in 2016.

By 2016 the forces of the opposition faced an increasingly isolated Maduro government. Electoral reversals for the regional left throughout 2015, a constitutional coup in Brazil in 2016, and the complete collapse in oil markets have left the Bolivarian Revolution both with fewer allies and fewer resources to attract new friends. In the National Assembly elections of December 2015, MUD candidates swept to power in dramatic fashion, winning 109 of 167 seats. The government subsequently moved to neutralize the legislative branch, with the president openly referring to the assembly as "bourgeois-Adeco"[1] and the formation of a Congreso de la Patria (Congress of the Fatherland)—though this second move was aimed more at shoring up support for the Maduro administration than actually replacing the representative state (Venezolana de Televisión 2016a). Indeed, as economic and political crises deepened in 2016, protests and disturbances—usually focused on shortages in food, medicine, and consumer goods—grew with such rapidity that some antigovernment intellectuals in Venezuela like Margarita López Maya drew parallels between the Maduro years and the 1990s (León 2016). In 2014–2016, however, these spontaneous responses to shortages by and large remained separate from the more explicitly political marches led by official opposition parties. While the MUD capitalized on, publicized, and in some cases orchestrated these disturbances, they have not organized the sort of social movements that emerged in the collapse of Puntofijo. In the years immediately following the death of Hugo Chávez, *both* government and opposition have acted as if they would best like to forget the centrality and unavoidability of constituent power.

This book has traced the many faceted trajectories of constituent power in Venezuela since 1989, from egalitarian rupture, to collective subjectivity, to the physical constitution of urban space. In these manifestations, constituent power has been an inclusive and creative force. But it has also, and perhaps primarily, been *disruptive*. Constituent power is most easily recognizable in expressions of resistance and refusal, in moments of rebellion against a constituted order that has become autoreferential, entropic, and fetishized. What then of the forces of the Venezuelan opposition? How do they relate to state power and, more pressingly, to spontaneous expressions of dissatisfaction with the status quo of Maduro's Venezuela? Not quite constituted power, it would seem that if any common ground among the opposition exists, it is their shared being-against in relation to the Bolivarian Revolution. Might then the opposition, or at least some part of it in body or spirit, also be considered a contemporary vector of constituent power?

Can the dogged resistance to attempts from above and below to impose a new social order be interpreted as moments of ungovernability? Can one differentiate among moments of the opposition—if it is more or less clear that the opposition was a force of reaction in the early years of the Bolivarian government, does that certitude diminish given the state's later distances from the constituent powers that made it possible? If the opposition does not yet *represent* the *pueblo*, does it nonetheless pose the problems of the *multitude* for the constituted powers of the Bolivarian Revolution?

This chapter approaches these questions of the opposition in Venezuela and its relationship to the idea of constituent power with three interrelated aims in mind. First, examining the opposition in terms of constituent power allows for a more differentiated understanding of antigovernment forces in Venezuela. All too often, analyses of the Bolivarian Revolution fall into polarized camps that reify the diverse fields of contestation in Venezuela based on one's position vis-à-vis the regime. Focusing on constituent power allows for reading the political field in terms of the potentials posed by the competing tendencies that comprise it—a more dynamic reading that focuses on capacities for collective action rather than identity or position. An examination of the opposition that privileges their relation to constituent power also, secondly, offers a possible contrapuntal periodization of the Bolivarian Revolution. Editorial positions of major North Atlantic media outlets aside, it would be quite a stretch to conclude that the Venezuelan opposition is a champion of democracy and inclusiveness. Far from it. However, understanding their relation to the government as forming a triangle between the state, the opposition, and constituent power commands a critical reading of the Bolivarian Revolution. If the government must be increasingly less identified with or allied to constituent power, what are the alternatives? The opposition's rhetorical and tactical turn to democracy, especially after 2012, highlights not only their own deficiencies but, I will argue, the limits of democratic theories based in liberal procedure, deliberation, and agonism. Thirdly, a deeper consideration of the opposition forces a reconsideration of the political theory of constituent power. Analyses of constituent power all too often settle into the very binaries they originally meant to disrupt. Debates around constituent power frequently settle into polemics for or against a given regime, discussions of identity, and an overemphasis on tactics. This critical appraisal of opposition, state, and constituent power in Venezuela is aimed at disrupting these tendencies, while also, finally, turning the question back onto the inquiry itself: What if the problem of actually existing constituent power is less a given political sequence and more a matter internal to the concept of constituent power itself?

Finally, what if the constituent doesn't always or automatically align with a progressive, universally liberatory, or left political project?

The chapter is comprised of three sections. The first addresses the social and political composition of the opposition in Venezuela, attending to the distinct tendencies and tactics of anti-Bolivarian movements since the election of Chávez in 1998. From an initial position calling for the complete rejection of all Bolivarian era reforms, by the second decade of the twenty-first century the opposition has softened aspects of its program. I contend that this has more to do with changing macroeconomic paradigms and the tactical recognition that the discursive universe in Venezuela has been definitively altered by the Bolivarian Revolution than with any sort of conversion to progressivism by the opposition. By 2016 hardliners in the opposition returned the anti-Bolivarians back to a purely tactical-political focus on ousting the president, seeking to capitalize on deepening economic and social crises.

In the next section I use the opposition's increasing deployment of democracy as a goal and antagonistic position vis-à-vis the government to interrogate key components of contemporary democratic theory. Given the social makeup, economic proposals, and liberal approach to democracy of the opposition, I contend that democracy as a self-sufficient value offers much to be desired. Too many questions—poverty, inequality, exploitation, for example—are left unaddressed or actively obscured by both democratic theory and the opposition. This is of course part of the discursive political universe of the early twenty-first century. However, this is also part of the problem to be challenged, setting aside for a moment the degree to which the Bolivarian Revolution's approach to democracy has shifted between 2013 and 2016.

With these concerns in mind, the chapter then concludes with a critical consideration of the relationship between democracy, constituent power, and the political in the twenty-first century. Despite the ubiquity and all but universal valorization of democracy—or perhaps *because* this celebration has now passed on to common sense—I argue that the concept has been emptied of meaning. More pressingly, I argue that the analysis of the opposition and democracy illustrates the extent to which the latter is no longer a threat to injustice, inequality, and exclusion. When such a conjuncture presents itself, a return to the political theory of constituent power becomes increasingly necessary.

Los Escuálidos: Who (and What) Is the Opposition?

By 2014, when opposition *guarimbas* challenged the government, a shift in anti-Bolivarian discourse in Venezuela and throughout the world began to shape headlines. Summed up in one *New York Times* headline as "Slum Dwellers in Caracas Ask, What Protests?" (Neuman 2014), even editorial boards in the North Atlantic recognized that Venezuela's opposition was not made up of poor, struggling, masses. Familiar narratives about Latin America in which a humble *pueblo* fights against an out-of-touch oligarchy, or against a murderous military junta, had to be revised: in Venezuela it was the rich and middle class rebelling against a socialist government that proposed to distribute the country's oil wealth and to provide free health care, education, and housing for all. A string of economic crises and scandals and, perhaps most importantly, the death of Chávez, allowed the opposition and their allies in the North to argue that this redistributive bent was as impossible as it was, for them, ideologically unpalatable. The Bolivarian Revolution could no longer rest on its results and had become corrupted, stagnant, ossified. It had, recoding editorial lines of the *New York Times* and *The Economist* for our purposes, become *the worst kind of constituted power*. As such, the opposition could attack the government without having to hide its class and racial composition as rich, white, and cosmopolitan. The real issues at the heart of good governance were once again electoral democracy and economic efficiency. Social justice, national development, and equality had again been relegated to extrapolitical or technical matters.

Electorally, the ranks of opposition voting Venezuelans has grown since the 1998 race for the presidency first ushered the Bolivarian Revolution into power. This is of course a generalized phenomenon, as perhaps "the most important political story from Venezuela [since 1998] is one of unprecedented electoral mobilization" on both sides of the political divide (Kutiyski and Krouwel 2014, 93). After its nadir in the 2006 presidential elections, in which Manuel Rosales lost to Chávez by over three million votes, the secular trend has favored opposition candidates and causes. Though Chávez continued to enjoy a bedrock of support among the most impoverished and marginalized, concerns about the national economy and perception of one's position therein, deteriorating security, and understandings of democracy and democratic practice all contribute to the PSUV's patchy record at the polls. Venezuela was suffering, or seen as suffering, in all these categories even before Chávez's death, with the result that the opposition was able to capitalize on growing discontent with the Bolivarian project, especially after tempering the more overtly neoliberal aspects of its platforms (Kutiyski and Krouwel 2014). Even as votes for the opposition grew—from 4.2 million in 2006 to 7.2 million in 2013—Chávez was able use his tremendous personal appeal to shield himself and shore up the Bolivarian Revolution in the poles (94). Maduro has not been able to do the same.

In demographic terms, the opposition has always had strongholds in traditionally affluent parts of the country. From places such as the eastern Caracas municipalities of Chacao, Baruta, El Hatillo, and Sucre as well as much of the city of Maracaibo (the historical heart of the oil industry) in the west and the state of Táchira in the Andes, the opposition has maintained footholds in the Venezuelan government even in moments of near-total Chavista hegemony. These are also places most traditionally associated with whiteness in Venezuela's racial imaginary, a position that has increasingly seen itself as under siege in the context of the Bolivarian Revolution's very proud, vocal, and visible *mestizaje* (mixed-race identity) (Duno-Gottberg 2011; Tinker Salas 2014).

As support flagged for the government, the opposition could be distinguished at the very least among two groups. First, there are the traditional elites—white, affluent, and cosmopolitan. This bloc has *always* fought against the Bolivarian Revolution, attempting to dislodge it by any means at their disposal. It should be emphasized, if only in passing, that by 2016 all political leadership of the unified opposition—from hardliners like Leopoldo López and María Corina Machado to ostensible moderates like Henrique Capriles—come from these sectors. Secondly, more recently converted voters, who are at least *potentially* disaffected Chavistas frustrated with the slumping economic, political, and security situations in Venezuela, gave the opposition its first tastes of popular support and legitimacy. It remains to be seen if the affective ties between these two groups run deeper than a protest vote against Maduro, but from an electoral-political standpoint, the death of Chávez and the moderation of their message, coupled with the steady decline of economic and security situations, allowed the opposition in Venezuela to swell its ranks and better its position in the 2010s.

In the early days of the Bolivarian government the opposition was weakened both by its identification with the Puntofijo order and by its own failed attempts to recompose itself after the political and economic implosions of the 1990s. In the absence of viable political parties—both AD and COPEI survived Puntofijo, but neither generate the sort of loyalty or confidence they once did, nor do they enjoy their previous institutional dominance—NGOs, the private media, the national chamber of commerce, the Catholic Church, and issue-oriented local campaigns cobbled together a coalition against the government of Hugo Chávez. Heterogeneous in composition and in tactical vision, this coalition—typified by the Coordinadora Democrática (Democratic Coordinator, CD) of 2002–2004—never mounted a convincing *legal* challenge to the Bolivarian Revolution. It never recognized the legitimacy of the Chávez government, effectively calling for street resistance in a state of exception (Cannon 2014, 54).

Even when more coherent political challenges to Chávez eventually emerged, the distinction between the electoral and the violent has often been more contrived than real, as seen for example in the reaction to the 2013 election to replace Chávez. When the votes were tallied, and Henrique

Capriles of the MUD lost by a mere 235,000 votes, the candidate who had presented himself as a centrist initially refused to recognize the result. Instead, he called for a recount of paper ballots and encouraged his supporters to take to the streets and "unleash their rage" (*descarga toda esa arrechera*). In the ensuing violence, eight government supporters were killed, dozens more were injured, numerous PSUV offices were burned, and government buildings—including Barrio Adentro clinics, which radicals in the opposition maintain are the advance waves of a Cuban invasion—were attacked (Cannon 2014, 62).

Police forces offer another example of the blurring of tactics between the institutional and the illegal. In 2002 the Metropolitan Police—at the time under opposition control—were implicated in the killings that provided immediate justification for the coup of April 11 (Márquez 2009). In late May of 2016, federal police forces and the Guardia Nacional Bolivariana (Bolivarian National Guard, GNB) raided the police headquarters for the municipality of opposition controlled Chacao in Caracas after it emerged that the PoliChacao were behind a string of politically motived assassinations (Venezolana de Televisión 2016b). Each of Caracas's five municipalities has its own police force and elected mayor. Those areas under opposition control have regularly been accused of aiding and abetting violent protesters, including among other events, the siege of the Cuban embassy led by Leopoldo López (then-mayor of Chacao) during the 2002 coup. In sum, through complicity or outright support, the division between an opposition of election campaigns and one of violent street confrontations in Venezuela is not hard and fast.

In Zulia, where Chávez's sacking of over eighteen thousand mid-sector, white-collar, and other PDVSA employees who supported the 2002–2003 Golpe Petrolera guaranteed the oil-rich state would remain a stronghold of antigovernment sentiment well into the future. While some of this anti-Bolivarianism resulted in emigration to the United States, Canada, and Europe, others formed the Rumbo Propio (Our Own Path) movement to secede from the country. Highlighting their belief in limited government and philosophical liberalism, the organization called for "limited government, free markets, and social institutions separated from the state" (Rumbo Propio 2006). They supported Manuel Rosales, governor of Zulia, during his 2006 bid for the presidency, and they also officially supported the short-lived government of Pedro Carmona during the 2002 coup against Chávez. Rumbo Propio was in other words equivocal in its separatism: they were more than happy to remain in a post-Bolivarian Venezuela. Principles of democratic self-determination were instrumental rather than absolute, more partisan ploys to protect established privilege than fidelity to principles of participation, equality, or autonomy. The high tide of the Rumbo Propio movement was arguably reached in 2006 and 2007, when overtures by Rosales to then–US ambassador William Brownfield transformed Rumbo Propio's partisan regionalism from a matter of regional identity to one of national security and a threat to Venezuela's sovereignty (Steinsleger 2007).[2]

Politics further complicates the already volatile relationship between the Bolivarian government, the opposition, constituent power, and democracy in Zulia. Neither the state nor the capital city can be considered captive territory for either the PSUV or the opposition—voters have instead often alternated elected officials among relatively familiar faces. Manuel Rosales was mayor of Maracaibo from 1996 to 2000, and again from 2008 to 2009, when he fled the country while under investigation for corruption and for alleged ties to the Colombian paramilitaries that have long operated on both sides of the porous border. His wife was elected mayor in 2010. In the interim of Rosales's mayoral terms, Gian Carlo Di Martino, a lukewarm Chavista of PODEMOS and then the PSUV, served from 2000 to 2008, when he lost a bid for the governor's mansion in a race against Pablo Pérez, of Rosales's Un Nuevo Tiempo (A New Era, UNT).

I pause on these details of elected office not to comment on electoral democracy in Venezuela but rather to indicate the degree to which voters in Zulia—as a stand-in for the variegated field of opposition to the Bolivarian Revolution—also often make non-ideologically driven calculations in a given sequence to address their most pressing needs. For example, when visiting Maracaibo in 2008 and discussing regional separatism with an opposition activist, I asked how a Chavista like DiMartino could maintain his position as mayor. With a shrug and a wink, the activist lamented that since the city was such a prized possession for either side of the political divide, it was rational for people to play each party off one another for a greater share of both local and national resources. With a Chavista in office, the opposition would have to promise more to voters to sway them from an increasingly hegemonic project. Likewise, the government needed to make sure voters were happy in Zulia and Maracaibo to further consolidate their control over the country and the oil industry. We were, in other words, far from the excessive if inconsistent rhetorical liberalism and regional nationalism of Rumbo Propio (or conversely, the solidarity of twenty-first-century socialism) and rather squarely on the terrain of pork barrel politics.

In addition to rejection and pragmatism, another influential tendency of the Venezuelan opposition looks to replicate key aspects of the Bolivarian platform and retool it for their own purposes. After the 2006 elections, opposition parties and activists entered an extended period of reconfiguration and message management. Elements of a new strategy emerged in Primero

Justica's attempts in 2007 to replicate the government's Misiones Bolivarianas with what they called the Casas de Justicia para Todos (Houses of Justice for All) in barrios around the capital. The aim of the Casas de Justicia was explicitly to identify the political brand of Primero Justicia with social welfare among Venezuela's poorest citizens, as well as to highlight shortcomings in the operation of the Misiones. In this way they were not only trying to appropriate government discourse for their own, but also attempting to replicate the government's activities, to "out Chávez" the Chavistas.

Barry Cannon notes the way in which this deceptively "continuist" discourse became the organizing platform of the opposition coalition in 2008 with the foundation of the MUD, even while economically and politically this opposition can be characterized as "a neoliberal project with a pro-poor emphasis, similar to post–Washington Consensus policy formulations as opposed to a 'shock therapy' style of neoliberal adjustment" (Cannon 2014, 64). As typified by the presidential campaigns in 2012 and 2013 of Henrique Capriles Radonski, this opposition recognizes the popularity of the Bolivarian Missions, of the participatory democratic reforms of the 1999 Constitution and the Communal Councils, and the need to construct a more inclusive polity. However, the MUD claims, they are more capable of achieving the goals of social justice and national development than the Bolivarian state.

By 2016, the official platform of the MUD included many of the explicit aims of the PSUV and the Bolivarian Revolution. Indeed, both formations share many of the goals of nearly *every* government in Venezuela since the boom in the petroleum industry in the early twenty-first century. Chief among these ambitions is the diversification of the local economy and lessening Venezuela's dependency on oil while pursuing an international agenda to guarantee stable prices in petroleum markets. The MUD has also recognized the popularity—and at least for many, the need—to maintain state control of PDVSA and to sustain the Misiones Bolivarianas and Consejos Comunales as local organs of the national government. However, in so doing the platform also promises to decentralize and depoliticize these institutions, to streamline the public sector, to return expropriated businesses and properties to previous owners, to reengage with multilateral financial institutions like the IMF, and to carry out a massive public education campaign explaining the "connection between property, economic progress, political liberty, and social development" (Cannon 2014, 57–58). In other words, the MUD proposes to keep the Bolivarian Revolution's most popular policies *after* a thoroughgoing process of purge and reprogramming.

What this suggests is that ideologically speaking the opposition in the MUD era is more liberal than *neoliberal* in the sense the latter term accrued in Latin America with the shocks and austerity regimes of the 1980s and

1990s. However, the nature of the opposition's liberalism also illustrates the limits of liberalism as a potentially progressive, egalitarian, or transformative ideology. While there can be no room for doubt that theirs is a project aimed at shoring up the class power and position of elites in Venezuela—as all capitalist economics are—the agenda of the mainstream opposition is more in line with the Santiago Consensus on neostructural development than with its predecessor from Washington.[3] Despite neostructuralism's promise to prioritize pro-poor economic growth, Fernando Ignacio Leiva insists it shares neoliberalism's aim to depoliticize the economy—also a key position of the MUD.

Both neoliberals and neostructuralists see the need to correct what they contend are the errors of state interventionism—either in the ISI strategies throughout Latin America in the mid-twentieth century or the democratized consumption of the Bolivarian Revolution in Venezuela. Neostructuralism as a development strategy emphasizes social cohesion, consensus, and other *bons mots* of the present face of economic globalization. However, as Leiva insists, "instead of offering tools for better understanding and redirecting powerful economic forces, Latin American neostructuralism plays the historical role of contributing to emplace new and more effective forms of stabilizing, legitimizing, and regulating the status quo" (Leiva 2008, 237). This ultimately conservative move, Leiva insists, is all the more insidious in that it has in many cases *deepened* the de-democratizing effects of the first wave of neoliberalization in the region.

In particular, neostructuralism relies on a consensual model of political and social democracy in which managed participation within a consolidated liberal order precludes attempts to effect substantive changes to class structures or relations of production (Leiva 2008, 118). It is, in other words, democratic, but only in a limited sense. It is a model of consensus-making in which the most important conclusions have already been reached: all questions of organization, value, and form must be subordinated to the uncontestable equation of economic growth as the basis for all social goods. For example, neostructuralism recommends building "a new type of labor movement" oriented toward its goal of attaining "systemic competitiveness," which takes the place of the neoliberal principle of comparative advantage. Within this paradigm, the particular task of the labor movement becomes one of fostering and enforcing "participatory wage regimes" (read: performance-based pay) and an expansion of labor flexibility in the service of the export-oriented economies (5–11).

Similar criticisms could be made of neostructuralism's attempts to "civiliz[e] the poor as consumers of services and self-regulating citizens" (Leiva 2008, 118; see also Schild 2013). In both positions we can see how the consensus of neostructuralism is a *fait accompli*. Rather than a process by which the direction of communities is to be determined, consensus has here already been achieved. The matter at hand for neostructuralism is to then create the conditions on the ground whereby this consensus-in-principle can become a reality. To the extent that neostructuralism is articulated to democratic politics, then, it must be understood as a wholly defanged democratic politics. Democracy is the practice of legitimating constituted power rather than the generative potential of the constituent.

This new relationship to development, democracy, and globalization can be seen in a widely circulated opposition tactical analysis, *Como Ganar o Perder las Elecciones Presidenciales de 2012 en Venezuela* (How to win or lose the 2012 presidential elections in Venezuela). In it, José Antonio Gil Yepes illustrates the lengths—and limits—of the opposition's attempts to reform and reconstitute itself since the coups, absenteeism, and general rejection that once defined the anti-Bolivarian camp in Venezuela. Gil's analysis stands out from a number of opposition tracts in its honesty and self-criticism. He calls for a moderation of the opposition's tendency to reject everything having to do with the Chavista regime, contending that certain institutions—such as the Consejos Comunales—could be reorganized as local instruments of representative rule (Gil 2011, 105). The previous tendency to claim any Chavista victory resulted from fraud, he admits, is both wrong and self-defeating (136). Most damningly, he attacks the opposition for lacking democratic credentials and political vision. "An old adage," he writes, "says that 'you can't give what you don't have' . . . the MUD is going to have difficulties in opening itself democratically to other sectors and parties if the parties that direct it are not themselves internally democratic" (131). He accuses the opposition of operating as a *partidocracia*, approaching the political arena only as a means to capture and retain power, not as a means to organize public life and secure collective needs (116). Opposition leaders have no program, no vision, their message amounting to "Vote for me, when I get to power, I'll give you solutions" (94) while discounting or willfully ignoring that even if Chavismo is democratically bankrupt, it nonetheless consistently secures the support of voters for "utilitarian"—that is, material—reasons (59). For Gil, writing against the grain of much prevailing opposition wisdom, the masses were not duped by Chávez's charisma, nor is the country locked in a zero-sum battle between irreconcilable enemies. With vision and moderation, pluralism and deliberation, he insists, the opposition can secure the presidency and set about dismantling the Chavista state from above.

Como Ganar o Perder should be read as a sincerely liberal manifesto and roadmap to what it hopes will be a post-Bolivarian Venezuela, no small feat for an opposition characterized for its all but complete lack of theoretical production. It is so full of advice for building a "pluralistic" and "democratic" country that it even offers suggestions for the Bolivarian Revolution to reform itself into a "modern, European style socialism," despite the author's obvious doubts such a reform was possible under Chávez or any likely successor (Gil 2011, 22). Gil is a sociologist at the Universidad Central de Venezuela (Central University of Venezuela, UCV). He is also, among other things, director of the polling firm Datanálisis—one of the most cited sources for public opinion and market research information on Venezuela. This focus group and market research pedigree organizes much of the book: Chavismo and the opposition both offer "products" to "consumers" (voters), and the dire necessity of crafting a coherent brand capable of converting the *ni-nis* into consistent voters—or buyers (32).[4] Quite simply, the opposition needs to be "pro-something" (23), and that something, for him, must be what is arguably the biggest brand in the world's political "marketplace": democracy (111).

It appeared that several prominent figures in the opposition took this advice in the lead up to the 2012 presidential elections, which eventually coalesced around the candidacy of Henrique Capriles. Capriles compared himself to Brazil's Luiz Inácio Lula da Silva and even proposed conditional cash transfer programs modeled after Fome Zero (Zero Hunger) in Miranda—gestures that were vehemently rejected by Lula and the Workers' Party (O Globo 2012). While Capriles presented himself as a "progressive and moderate" (Goldstein 2012) foil to Chávez and the Bolivarian project, even more conservative and hardline opposition candidates found themselves forced to update their message.

In 2002 María Corina Machado founded Súmate (Join Up!), a US-funded NGO that organized the campaign to recall President Chávez in 2004. For her efforts, she was received by then–US president George W. Bush in the Oval Office for an ill-conceived photo opportunity. That she did so at a point when no Venezuelan official of any rank had met with any senior representative of the US government, and the fact that even many anti-Chavistas considered Bush a danger to regional stability, did little to help the campaign or to counter the Bolivarian claim that the opposition is made up of foreign agents.

Throughout 2011 Machado, by then a deputy in the National Assembly representing the state of Miranda—which includes both the richest districts in the nation as well as Petare, one of the largest slums in Latin America—also campaigned for the opposition nomination. Her campaign was in many ways shockingly honest—centering on the defense of capitalism and private property—but found itself having to translate these principles for mass consumption, as seen in her promise of a capitalism for the people in bold, Bolivarian-red letters.

Figure 8. "Here comes the People's Capitalism. Here comes María. Opportunity for the people." (Viene el Capitalismo Popular. Viene Maria.) (http://venezuelanalysis.com/analysis/6709)

The point of interest here is not that Machado is attempting to sell the virtues of the free market but the fact that she does so in a language defined by Chavismo. It is no longer possible to pursue office in Venezuela without an appeal to the national-popular, and preferably in the bold, red script of revolution. In the past, politicians ran on platforms of national development and, as was more often the case, their personalities. Between 1998 and 2006, opposition candidates tended to establish their credentials in purely reactive terms, painting themselves as anti-Chávez and consistently winning the same number of votes from the same demographic.

The 2012 opposition primaries and the shift in discourse suggests the opposition has at least partially taken on some of the lessons of *Como Ganar o Perder* and learned from its past failures. Attempts to moderate and present themselves as uniquely capable of realizing the Bolivarian Revolution's own goals intensified with the crises of 2014–2016, even while the *guarimbas* of 2014 exposed the depth of the divide between hardliners like López and Machado and moderates like Capriles. By mid-2016, however, attempts to replicate government programs and to pose a liberal challenge to an illiberal Chavismo had fallen by the wayside in favor of the procedural-electoral campaign for the recall of Maduro. Tactics shifted accordingly, and the traditionally fractious opposition pressed with a remarkably unified voice for the referendum to be held in 2016,[5] while engaging in an intense local and international media campaign to publicize and sensationalize worsening economic and social crises in Venezuela. The continuism and moderation of the new, *democratic*, opposition should thus be viewed with a degree of skepticism. More opportunistic than principled, they proved themselves perfectly willing to switch "brands" when they perceived the political winds to have shifted direction.

Even still, as a brand or framing, Chavismo versus democracy still implies a rather particular notion of democracy, one reflecting the hegemony of North Atlantic liberalism in the aftermath of the Cold War. While Gil's economic proposals and Capriles's campaigns of 2012 and 2013 reflect neostructural attempts to embed capitalism within a larger social matrix, they also share the latter's tendency to privilege markets over people in the first and final instances. Capitalism is common sense. There is no alternative, no way imaginable to develop a country without free markets and foreign investment (Gil 2011, 148). Among their most pressing tasks, then, is to "sign a social contract" among opposition parties and with the sectors of civil society not aligned with the government: "Accept responsible capitalism as the economic model. . . . Accept unions as the model for workplace organization . . . accept political parties as the model for political organization" (Gil 2011, 147). The social and political visions of *Como Ganar o Perder*, while more detailed and sincere than that of a vast majority of the opposition in Venezuela, is thus rather limited in scope and originality. Chavismo is for Gil an antiquated project that replicates the state socialisms of the twentieth century. His antidote is to import to Venezuela the sort of representative, liberal, and market-oriented capitalist democracy from the North Atlantic that has been experiencing its own escalating crises of confidence since the 2008 global recession.

Como Ganar o Perder marks an important rebranding of the opposition in terms of liberal pluralism and democracy. The Bolivarian Revolution is now considered bad because it is realizing its autocratic potential—tendencies Gil admits are also found in the opposition and that need to be purged if they are to present Venezuela with a viable alternative. This proposal, however, opens into new theoretical and critical terrain and the need to discuss the *limits and potentials of democracy itself*—both democracy as an alternative to the Bolivarian Revolution and democracy's relationship to itself, as seen in contemporary democratic theory. Both approaches tend to replace, obscure, and displace questions of human social equality with formal political equality and representative government. Gil's account is no different in the way it demands capitalist modes and relations of production be accepted as common sense, effectively closing off the political in favor of liberal democracy. While pluralism may indeed be important for healthy societies, pluralism as a supreme political and social value offers little help in situations where some paint injustice and inequality as virtues—as in the case of a politics of the market, as in the case of liberal capitalism.

This is not meant to be an argument in favor of the sort of postliberalism that leads to the consolidation of single party, or single person, rule. It is rather a suggestion, explored in greater detail in the following section, that liberalism and democracy have great difficulty responding to the challenges of equality and creativity posed by constituent power. Liberalism limits. It is a politics of the enforced present in a global historical moment that demands inventiveness and collaboration with an urgency that grows with each passing day. If, according to Gil, liberal democracy escapes the trap of power's autoreferentiality, where it becomes the ends of politics regardless of the cost or consequence (Gil 2011, 116), it does so from a self-satisfied belief that there is no alternative. Liberal democracy escapes one expression of constituted power's inward gaze only to find a circumscribed universe that is both more generalized and absolute. Rather than viewing the political as instrumental, liberalism defines itself as politics *tout court*, jealously denying the viability of any alternative modes of organizing public life and social power. Any counterproposal for liberalism is either antiquated—Castro in Cuba before the 2016 thaw in relations with the United States, for example—or evil—as with the various "fundamentalisms" that emerged with globalization. If the political is a space of human collaboration and creation, and politics the negotiation of difference, then liberalism is their negation. Liberalism doesn't view politics instrumentally because it refuses to see, to allow for, to engage with, politics *at all*.

This foray into the social and ideological composition of the second wave of anti-Bolivarianism illustrates a need to reconsider the status of democracy—its discursive weight, its theoretical composition, its popular salience—in contemporary Venezuela. We can appreciate the diversity of the opposition field, both demographically and temporally in Venezuela—from rejection to continuism, from neoliberal to neostructural, from a narrow band of elites to disaffected Chavistas—but what does the composition of an opposition that champions democracy suggest about the status of democracy? What does it mean when *both* the government and the opposition claim to be operating according to democratic principles, and when both accuse the other of being democracy's antithesis? How does this shared claim reflect on the relationship of democracy to constituent power? What do these relationships mean, *practically*, for the realization of egalitarian desires in Venezuela and beyond in a global twenty-first century that by 2016 is already shaping up to be more brutal, unequal, and polluted than its predecessor?

Democracy, Democratic Theory, and *Escuálidismo*

"Woah, the neighborhood has changed!"

Miguel* only grunted in response.

"You don't like it?"

"Some yes, some no," he replied. We were walking his dog through the Plaza Andres Bello, along the street of the same name, in the summer of 2014. Miguel was an old friend; a middle-class, middle-aged man who loved to share a laugh, though we disagreed on most questions concerning politics. We hadn't seen each other in a few years, and in my absence, the street had been transformed. This plaza, for example, had been completely revitalized and was now vibrant and full of people where it was once for all intents and purposes a vacant lot. Across the street, a few Gran Misión Vivienda Venezuela towers (Great Venezuelan Housing Missions—the flagship of the mega-missions that aimed to accelerate the physical, social, and political infrastructure of the country) towered above the tree-lined center boulevard. *Motorizados* buzzed through the plaza, on the street, in and out of the circle of plastic chairs and Venezuelan flag set up to coordinate neighborhood patrols, part of a campaign against insecurity or—depending on who you asked—to show force and intimidate opposition residents.

"You don't like your new neighbors?" I teased.

Just then, one of the *motorizados* yelled at Miguel. I tensed, fearing the worst. Miguel wasn't a hardline opposition supporter. He mostly wanted to be left alone, he always said. But reading opposition accounts circulated in the North Atlantic media of a government crackdown before the visit, even with a grain of salt, I was nervous for my friend.

As it turned out, I needn't have been concerned. Miguel and the *motorizado* laughed, hugged, casually swore in that Venezuelan way when they caught up on work, family, weather—the usual end-of-the-day chatter. I was introduced, jokes and small talk were exchanged, and Miguel, the dog, and I eventually continued on our way.

"Wasn't he a Chavista?" I asked, when we were a few paces away.

"Yeah, but he's a good one. An old friend."

"I thought all these *motorizados* were thugs and drug dealers?"

"Not him."

Despite the widely circulating common sense that Venezuela is irremediably polarized, I often encountered examples of this sort of dissonance. Opposition supporters who insisted that *all* Chavistas were illegal immigrants, Cuban fifth columnists, lazy, corrupt, narcos (this list could be extended)—*except* so-and-so, who was just confused. Similarly, Chavistas insisted all the *escuálidos* were rich, white, *pitiyanquis* (more or less, wannabe Yankees)—*except* cousin so-and-so, who might be an asshole, but wasn't a *golpista* (coup-monger).

To be sure, there are many on either side of the divide who do not make such exceptions. I am not suggesting that political and social divisions in Venezuela are not real, entrenched, or violently contested. Far from it. My walk with Miguel rather illustrates the sort of everyday incoherence French Marxist Louis Althusser once suggested (in a rather different context) was a telltale sign of a functioning ideology: the reconciling of contradictory elements into a nonsensical common sense (Althusser 2001a, 100). Ideologies interpellate subjects as subjects in their particularity, not as generic categories.

Even if the lived experience of *escuálidismo* is not an ideological state apparatus in the exact sense formulated by Althusser, it should be seen as a proto-statist formation and an aspiring state authority. It organizes lifeworlds around the promised goal of (re)capturing state power and positions subjects in various relations of authority and contestation. It is, furthermore, a thoroughly bourgeois ideology that assumes and reproduces the liberal subject as the basis of the social order. In this way, *escuálidismo* both resonates with and provides a unique light on the limits of much contemporary democratic theory. Democracy functions within and as ideology; it marks subjects and ethical systems while it obscures others. *Escuálidismo*'s deployment of democracy avoids more thoroughgoing and structural analyses of Venezuela's woes. Miguel and the *motorizado* are able to remain friends not *in spite of* ideology, but rather *because of it*. Democracy as ideology sees subjects as individuals, divorced from context and stable as property. Indeed, in liberalism, the individual is the first and fundamental piece of property a subject can own. Democracy as ideology functions within and as part of liberalism when it naturalizes the individual as the basis of all sociopolitical organization and all ethical judgment.

This section builds on the opposition's evolution and rebranding as purveyors of democracy's wares to consider the implications of political change in Venezuela for democratic thought more generally. Through an inquiry of democracy as an instrument of regime change backed by North Atlantic powers and, more substantively, of democracy's liberal, deliberative, and agonistic variants, the section asks in theoretical terms what democracy is being asked *to do* in twenty-first-century Venezuela. Imperial democracy is easily recognizable as cynical and limited. However, liberal and deliberative democracy's promise of political equality and agonism's valorization of difference offer a more challenging position from which to reconsider the relationship between democracy, social justice, and constituent power. Radical democracy, finally, provides a more critical dialectical turn: democracy turned against itself to regenerate its liberatory potential. As we shall see, however, all these subtypes in their own way risk replacing principles with procedures, and, against stated intents, subordinating constituent to constituted power.

In the bitter and ultimately thwarted campaign to recall Nicolás Maduro in 2016, Henrique Capriles remarked, "How things have changed! Today, the same people who used to talk about participatory and protagonistic democracy don't want elections. The people have a solution to the crisis, it is the recall referendum of Article 72 of the constitution. Government spokespeople are horrified to consult the people, horrified of Venezuelans making a decision" (El Nacional 2016). Capriles was responding to government efforts to stall and invalidate the opposition's push to recall Maduro. His remarks are significant indictments of the creeping proceduralism of Bolivarian government. They also, however, presume a notion of democracy contained within voting booths, which is a rather limited understanding given the snapshot they also offer of democracy's shifting meaning in Venezuela since 1989.

For example, the Puntofijo system advertised itself as a functioning representative liberal democracy, though in actual practice it was much more of an "inter-elite consensus" in which decisions were made "behind closed doors without popular participation" (Curato 2014, 114). The 1999 Constitution promised a democracy that would be "participatory and protagonistic, multiethnic and pluricultural in a federal and decentralized state of justice that strengthen values of liberty, independence, peace, solidarity, the common good, territorial integrity, coexistence and the empire of the law for this and future generations." Subsequent articles (e.g., 62 and 70) assign to the state the responsibility to generate conditions under which such a multifaceted democracy can be realized. Expropriations and workplace occupations saw the economy democratized along a participatory framework (Azzellini 2010). The renationalization and reconfiguration of the oil industry in 2003 allowed for consumption of the nation's oil revenues to be democratized, just as one could suggest the valorization of historically marginalized peoples democratized the imagined community of the nation along more representative and inclusive lines. Even if we accept, finally, Capriles's reduction of democracy to voting, we can also conclude that the scale of Venezuelan democracy has expanded vastly, with more contests and greater turnout since 1999 than in any other moment in the country's history.

The opposition was rather late in considering democratic tools to turn back the Bolivarian Revolution. Even still, their deployment of democracy has been decidedly liberal and procedural in nature. While opposition rhetoric admitted the need for some redistributive programs to benefit the majority of Venezuelans after 2012, and while calls to respect democratic rules of the game sometimes take the place of ideological denunciations of socialism, the policy prerogatives and assumptions of anti-Chavismo remain opposed to experiments in protagonism and constituent power that animated the most progressive elements of the Bolivarian Revolution. Democracy, in other words, is important only as a means for the capture of institutional power. As an egalitarian desire for the transformation of social relations, *substantive* democracy is a threat that must be managed and confined to electoral cycles.

In this way, the opposition's relation to democracy in Venezuela illustrates key debates within the country on democratic practice in the Bolivarian era. It also provides an important counterpoint to debates within Latin American and North Atlantic political thought on the nature, normative value, and limits of liberal democratic pluralism, consensus, and deliberation. The opposition aligns itself with liberal and neostructural emphases on procedural democracy and a market free from public interference, rebranding and extending elements of neoliberalism's "postpolitical" world. While the Maduro government retains the rhetoric of communal and workers' democracy, iterated social and economic crises from 2013 to 2016 saw it increasingly center its energies on retaining con- stituted power. In either case, constituent power's place is obscured by two fac- tions claiming to be "democratic" as a means for maintaining or aspiring to rather familiar—top-down, representative, extractivist, developmentalist—state power in Venezuela.

Democracy is the main principle of political legitimacy in the twenty-first century. It has been "considered the panacea to all the world's political ills . . . employed by the West as both stick and carrot" (Gagnon and Chou 2014, 1). Even as powerful, ostensibly extrapolitical forces reshape, subordinate, and erode institutions like the modern nation-state, usually accepted as necessary to make democratic practice possible, democracy and its variations occupy a commanding place in global political theory (Bray and Slaughter 2015, 2). The liberal triumphalism in the North Atlantic that followed the Cold War has been followed in the twenty-first century by many so-called mature or consolidated democracies stumbling over problems "often of their own making" (Gagnon and Chou 2014, 1). There have also been, throughout the North Atlantic and beyond, new variations of an old theme: liberal democracy is an increasingly hybrid phenomenon, incorporating plebiscitary, imperial, and participatory aspects (among others) in a complicated global context in which the powers of the sovereign nation-state—the modern "home" of democratic community and practice—have been significantly weakened by transnationalizing economic, ecological, demographic, and political realities.

In response, a growing cottage industry has emerged in the social sciences to catalog and in some cases contain democracy's popular, participatory, hybrid, authoritarian, or otherwise illiberal variants. For a number of these accounts—methodologically and disciplinarily distinct from but sharing many of the normative assumptions of democratic theory—democracy remains in much of the world a fleeting horizon, and is usually under threat. While North Atlantic liberal variants of democracy are by no means considered perfect in this tendency, their institutions, procedures, and subject positions are nonetheless deployed as normative measuring sticks for politics outside of Europe. Even some self-professed radical democrats like Chantal Mouffe (1992) see their task as one of pressing actually existing democracy into a deeper realization of its principles and ideals (1). Liberal democracy is, finally, often an interventionist position. Publications like the *Journal of Democracy*, for example, are tied to the National Endowment for Democracy, a US State Department International NGO that has sponsored right-wing causes in Venezuela and Bolivia, for example, under the aegis of "democracy promotion" (see, for example, Corrales and Penfold 2011; Diamond 2002; Levitsky and Way 2002). It is a theory and a politics that celebrates diversity and pluralism, but only on its terms.

Yet, even in the forms most celebrated in the North Atlantic and among the opposition in Venezuela, it remains misleading to discuss actually existing democracies as democracy. "At best," writes John Burnheim, "we have what the ancients would have called elective oligarchies with strong monarchical elements" (1985, 1). When twenty-first-century democrats justify or even celebrate these regimes, they are effectively penning apologies for what William Robinson describes as a "low-intensity" or polyarchic arrangement in which elites maintain power but periodically legitimate their rule though regularly scheduled elections. "In contrast to more popular conceptions of democracy, which see political power as a means for transforming unjust socioeconomic structures and democratizing social and cultural life," he writes, "the polyarchic definition explicitly isolates the political from the socioeconomic sphere and restricts democracy to the political sphere. And even then, it limits democratic participation to voting in elections" (Robinson 2007, 100). Under conditions of polyarchy—promoted by Northern NGOs and multilateral forums in Latin America since regional neoliberalization began in the 1970s—key aspects of people's lives are removed from the table of democratic contestation and debate. Elites have their privileged status protected from scrutiny or antagonism, and the exercise of political power in this Imperial democracy becomes routinized in increasingly opaque institutions and bureaucracies. Its ostensible legitimacy rests on geopolitical concern rather than the interplay of constituent and constituted power.

Deliberative approaches are harder to dismiss. They contend democracy provides a framework for incorporating difference into a given society and that democracy is uniquely suited for peaceful encounters with "the other" (Curato 2014, 113; Tucker 2008). Deliberation emphasizes interaction in or beyond formalized institutions, and in or beyond liberal notions of civil or political rights (Dryzek 2009, 1380). It is a politics based in the communication, debate, and negotiation of competing worldviews among subjects in a public sphere that more or less corresponds to the idealized case of modern Europe (Benhabib 2006; Habermas 1991).

In Venezuela, proponents of deliberative democracy contend that the participatory excesses of the Bolivarian Revolution—communal councils, recall referenda, factory occupations, and so forth—need to be tempered by deliberative institutions for both normative and practical reasons. In addition to making democracy "more inclusive," institutions that guarantee opportunities for moderation and incorporation of opposing views provide the losers of a given deliberative process recourse other than "uncivil actions" such as coups, blockades, or other forms of extraparliamentary violence (Curato 2014, 120; O'Flynn and Curato 2015). Democracy, in this light, is the key to peace and stability, but it also provides escape valves to mitigate social tensions.

Within this moral universe the Bolivarian Revolution's democratizing reforms are guilty of "including the people but excluding elites," which some democratic theorists have likened to an obverse of the Puntofijo era (Curato 2014, 119). This sort of conclusion is common among liberals, where any position threatening to break from the consensus of the consolidated center is a dangerous extreme, and all such extremisms are rendered equivalent. Among the many problems with such an approach that equates left and right, communists with Nazis, or even inclusive egalitarianism with racist xenophobia, is that while accepting the deliberative democrat's presumption that democracy can only exist among equals, it also defines equality in terms of the narrowly *political* equality of citizens (Brown 2008). Matters of social, economic, epistemological, or geographical inequalities are shunted to the side. Politics is a regulative procedure that balances—if only contingently and without an enforceable consensus—the demands of rich and poor rather than upturning a system that requires, reproduces, and naturalizes these inequalities. Such an attempt at ethical equivalence is galling on democracy's own grounds, let alone from the perspective of any project oriented toward social justice, equality, development, and solidarity. This sort of deliberative approach either assumes actually existing social organizations as inevitable and ahistorical, or at least fails to adequately account for structural inequalities (Young 2001).

Transformative action oriented by the desire for a world without elites and subalterns, or politics and the political as creative exercises of constituent power, are precluded by many democratic theorists, deliberative or otherwise, as too radical and divisive. Similarly, many agonistic democrats propose to contain any antagonisms that might unsettle order. While they reject the artificial conclusions of the end of history, or that there is no alternative to the constituted liberal order, they nonetheless insist on a domestication of antagonism. Chantal Mouffe, for example, contends:

> Modern democracy's specificity lies in the recognition and legitimation of conflict and the refusal to suppress it by imposing an authoritarian order. Breaking with the symbolic representation of society as an organic body—characteristic of the holist mode of organization—a pluralist liberal democratic society does not deny the existence of conflicts but provides the institutions allowing them to be expressed in an adversarial form. It is for this reason that we should be very wary of the current tendency to celebrate a politics of consensus, claiming that it has replaced the supposedly old-fashioned politic of right and left. A well-functioning democracy calls for a clash of *legitimate democratic political positions*. . . . The danger arises that the democratic confrontation will . . . be replaced by a confrontation between *essentialist forms of identification or non-negotiable moral values*. . . . Antagonisms can take many forms and it is illusory to believe that they could ever be eradicated. This is why it is important to allow them an agonistic form of expression through the pluralist democratic system. (Mouffe 2005, 30; emphasis added)

In this passage, Mouffe sets out a position for agonism's alternative to the neutralization and consensus of liberal democracy. In it, she replaces one series of neutralizations with another. She contends that democracy needs to be the location of disagreement and contention rather than their resolution or pacification (see also Mouffe 1999). All well and good; however, the constraints she places on the ideal, pluralist, democratic order are telling in their absences and qualifications. Here, the purpose of democracy is tied into the organization of the state. The state as constituted power is tasked with providing institutions capable of hosting *legitimate democratic political positions*—though the ultimate determining authority on the question of legitimacy goes unsaid, the reader is at least assured that everything is negotiable. Constituted power is in other words equated with the political. *Essentialist* positions, as in, for example, the demand for absolute equality, must be given up in the spirit of negotiation and compromise. In short, democracy is for the agonists a way of mitigating extremes, which in the twenty-first-century context of extreme inequalities in wealth and quality of life can only be a conservative gesture.

Much democratic theory—and these considerations of liberal, deliberative, and agonistic iterations only barely scratch its surface here—is in other words above all else concerned with domesticating democracy, with stripping away any transformative potential it might yet have left. Against these neutralizations and domestications, any number of radical democrats have implicitly or explicitly echoed Sheldon Wolin's assertion that democracy only ever *is* when it is "fugitive"—fleeting, moving, escaping rationalization, routinization, and containment. Democratic moments are in other words wholly exceptional (Wolin 2004, 602). Temporally and spatially, Alexander Hirsch concludes democracy only occurs in "sporadic and eruptive flash[es] of memory that cal[l] into being the constituent power of the demos" (Hirsch 2011, 184). For one strand of radical democracy, in other words, democratic possibility is a rare thing, an expression of constituent power that punctuates the normal functioning of constituted order.

For another school of radical democratic thought, democracy is made of much more mundane and much less messianic stuff. Douglas Lummis (1996), for example, insists democracy "is not a kind of government, but an end of government; not a historically existing institution, but a historical project" (22). For Lummis, democracy is a position from which to criticize the present from "the side of the people" that informs the constant labor or constructing of a better world (25). Radical democracy, then, is labor tied antagonistically to and even within an actually existing constituted order.

Dario Azzellini and Marina Sitrin (2014) emphasize radical democracy as perpetual critical motion and activity based in the horizontal (that is, immediate and equal) encounter in which "democracy is at the heart of both the new social creation and the refusal" of the existing liberal representative order (9). In their far-ranging study of anticapitalist movements and experiments—including in Venezuela—they locate democracy as a key practice in a constellation that also includes autonomy, *autogestión*, and horizontalism. This is, however, a decidedly contrarian democracy. It is a democracy that speaks its own name to illustrate the deficiencies of prevailing liberal democracy. For them, this critical gesture, which will by its nature vary from case to case and moment to moment, is more a relationship than an established order. As democratic horizontalism, this resistance and creation is what Sitrin (2006) elsewhere described in terms of "preconfigurative movements" that "create the future in their present social relationships" rather than wait for a solution to be handed down from on high.

Radical democrats thus explicitly pit themselves against liberalism's attempts to neutralize democracy's potential for reshaping the world. As French intellectual Jacques Rancière notes:

> Democracy initially stirred up political philosophy because it is not a set of institutions or one kind of regime among others but a way for politics to be. Democracy is not the parliamentary system or the legitimate State. It is not a state of the social either, the reign of individualism or of the masses. Democracy is, in general, politics' mode of subjectification if, by politics, we mean something other than the organization of bodies as a community and the management of places, powers, and functions. Democracy is more precisely the name of a singular disruption of this order . . . it is the name of what comes and interrupts the smooth working of this order though a singular mechanism of subjectification . . . it is the introduction of a visible into the field of experience, which modifies the regime of the visible. It is not opposed to reality. It splits reality and reconfigures it as double. (Rancière 1999, 99)

Democracy as politics is the eruption of the "part with no part" and the expression of the "unsayable" that reconfigures what we accept and assume as possible. It is a dispute, a disagreement with the consensus of prevailing liberal democracy and its "regime of the perceptible" (Rancière 1999, 102). For Rancière democracy cannot be reduced to a particular mode of social organization or a catalog of rights and responsibilities. It is, rather, a location from which politics as the emergence of novelty and unforeseen possibility can occur. Democracy is the interruption of the crowd, multitude, or *turba* in the Caracazo. It is constituent power's egalitarian desire. As opposed to the Venezuelan opposition's "brand" of democracy as an alternative to the Bolivarian Revolution in the marketplace of political choice, for Rancière, democracy is the possibility of politics.

Of course, this possibility of politics occurs *in spite of* democracy just as if not more often than it has been occasioned *by* it. Furthermore, possibility of course is a far cry from the inevitable. In Uruguayan philosopher Yamandú Acosta's estimation, democratization in Latin America, what Robinson described in terms of polyarchy, brought with it a naturalized and global condition of "capitalism without citizenship," where democracy was reduced to the representative functions of parties wholly integrated into a constituted state apparatus, usually inherited from the anticommunist dictatorships of the 1960s–1990s (Acosta 2008, 183). In Venezuela, this citizen-less capitalism resonates with proposals to depoliticize PDVSA and the state bureaucracy. Against this, social movements moving through, against, and beyond the state have transformed politics in Latin America. The protagonism—direct action, *autogestión*, absolute resistance to the neoliberalization of state and society—confronted two possible outcomes: subordinating capitalism to the needs of the people or constructing alternative models for the organization of collective life beyond markets and abstract individual citizenship (Acosta 2008, 185). That is to say, the radical democratic assertion of *democracy against democracy* in the twenty-first century moves against the imposed consensus of democracy as liberal, representative, and market-oriented as promised by the opposition in Venezuela. It insists that there are indeed alternatives to neoliberalism in the post–Cold War world.

Finding these alternatives has of course been an uneven and contradictory process, and, by 2015–2016, a wave of restoration and crisis ended hybrid projects of the mainstream left in Argentina and Brazil while economic crisis and internal contradictions stalled governments of the left in Venezuela and Bolivia. In all cases—revolutionary or reactionary—democracy has been upheld as the defining principle of often mutually exclusive worldviews. Writing shortly before his death, Fernando Coronil diagnosed the situation as one in which democracy has become a "value in itself" irrespective of its social content or potential for disruption (Coronil 2011, 240). The result has been "a rather peculiar articulation between practices and ideals in the short and long terms" in which "leftist governments proclaim socialist ideals for the long term, [and] promote capitalism in the short term. And while they promote capitalism in the short term, they regard capitalism as unviable for the long term. Thus we have capitalism for a present without a future, and socialism for a future without a present" (Coronil 2011, 250). Inward-looking democracy as a value in and for itself contributes to this short termism by allowing procedure—necessary, horizontal, participatory, and inclusive as they may they be in some cases—to take the place of guiding principles and ethical ideals such as equality, or sustainability. This autoreferentiality is further entrenched, weakening democracy's potential guiding or disruptive potential, when both the government and the opposition deal in slogans without concrete measures—the celebration of socialism in word but not deed in the case of the government, or the promise of an alternative to the present while disavowing the class content of the project in the case of the opposition. Democracy thus presents itself as a powerfully effective empty signifier, perfect for the Twitter age, but politics needs something more than a hashtag to press beyond the political, social, economic, and ecological impasses of the twenty-first century.

Azzellini and Sitrin (2014) contend the Bolivarian project has always addressed this question of democracy "from two sides," thus offering a more nuanced but no less problematic response to liberalism's evacuation of meaning from democracy. This two-sided approach can be seen, for example, in the civic-military alliance that has always defined the process that emphasizes coordination and discipline for a shared goal (Chávez 2013), as well as in the intensification of direct and autonomous actions *from below*. In Azzelini and Sitrin's words, "the state and institutions are reinforced, and pursue a policy of active economic regulation, in a mixed (capitalist) economy. However, according to the normative orientation of the Bolivarian process, the popular movements must assume a central role in the development of change, and at the same time remain autonomous with respect to the state" (214). As we have seen in the case of the PSUV, however, the process might be more accurately considered "lopsided" than "two-sided," as the horizontalist ethos of autonomous action has often been overshadowed by the verticalist call for order and institutionalization—all in the name of Bolivarian democracy.

It should be added, if only in passing, the triangulated strategy of the opposition from 2013 to 2016—seeking to isolate Venezuela internationally both from multilateral institutions like the Organization of American States or making direct bilateral appeals via sympathetic presidents and legislatures in Latin and North America and Europe; obstructionism in the National Assembly after the elections of 2015, including declarations unseating President Maduro; and above all else, violent street confrontations that have left many dead and millions of dollars in damages—have also contributed to Bolivarian democracy's increasing verticalization as calls for discipline prioritize defending past gains over deepening or accelerating the stalled revolutionary transformation of Venezuela. By 2016, the Bolivarian government effectively painted itself into a corner. The emphasis on democracy and its identification with electoral campaigns has paradoxically closed space for politics as the expression of constituent power against *both* political *and* economic subordination—that is, against capitalism. Worse still, during this period the government had a rather inconsistent, often manipulative, relationship with the procedural, electoral, and representative democracy it prioritized (Buxton 2016). The resulting situation allowed opposition strategies based on liberal, low-intensity, and North Atlantic modes of democratic politics to stand as democracy *tout court*. The government, as it has increasingly dedicated itself to channeling constituent into constituted power, has ceded this territory without struggle and was ill-suited by 2016 to win it back. This does not mean the opposition has become the *pueblo* or the multitude; it rather means that the threat democracy as politics poses to the class power of Venezuela's traditional elites, the *escuálidos*, or to the holders of state power, Bolivarian or otherwise, has been effectively neutralized.

Politics versus Democracy: Constituent Power and the Opposition

The relationship of the opposition to democracy, or of a government to democracy, should not be reduced to debates over procedures, institutions, or settled definitions. It is, rather, borrowing from radical democracy theorist C. Douglas Lummis,

> a critique of centralized power of every sort—charismatic, bureaucratic, class, military, corporatist, party, union, technocratic. By definition it is the antithesis to all such power. Though we may find other reasons—order, efficiency, the necessities of struggle—to justify the centralization of power, these give radical democracy no reason to yield in *its* critique: "justifiably" undemocratic remains undemocratic. (25)

Democracy is in other words for Lummis a critique of constituted power. Constituent power exists as a tarrying negativity, an action exerted upon established order—within and pushing toward better, more inclusive and just, horizons. Put slightly differently, constituent power makes actually existing democracy *better*. It is Dussel's *hiperpotentia*, regenerating a constituted power that has forgotten its roots.

And yet, as Burnheim reminded us earlier, it is misleading and even falsely reassuring to characterize any of the various regimes in the contemporary world as "democratic." Sheldon Wolin takes this observation a step further and concludes that democracy can never be a regime. "Democracy," he writes, "is an ephemeral phenomenon rather than a settled system" (2004, 602). It is, at best, "about forms rather than *a* form or constitution; and, instead of an institutionalized process, it should be conceived as a moment of experience, a crystallized response to deeply felt grievances or needs on the part of those whose main preoccupation—demanding of time and energy—is to scratch out a decent existence" (603; emphasis in original). For Wolin, democracy is a political rupture, fleeting and *fugitive* in nature and experienced primarily in a small localized demos in the face of neoliberal powers that are ever more technocratic, arcane, and opaque to the society they are charged with representing (605).

The preceding conversations surrounding democracy, constituent power, and the opposition in Venezuela demand we push these insights of Wolin, Rancière, and Burnheim farther. Democracy is a moment. It only *is* when it is fugitive—resisting the call to institutionalize, regularize and regulate, and subdue its disruptive potential (Wolin 2004, 602). Alternatively, democracy is a constant work in the common—its meaning shifts with each encounter, necessitating an autonomous horizontally situated and protagonistic sociality of creative resistance. As such, we should be ever skeptical of attempts to pin it to a settled meaning or electoral cause, be they Bolivarian or from the MUD. So too must we, in pursuit of new, more egalitarian politics question if a theory of elusive and effervescent ruptures is sufficient. Events leading to the impasses of 2016 suggest the need for a better vocabulary, and a better imaginary than those on offer from a democracy of stalled Bolivarianism or the discredited liberalism of the opposition. Indeed, democracy itself is overdue for a critical overhaul and examination—one that does not end by affixing yet another adjective (radical, deliberative, and so forth) to the hallowed term, nor with the pious affirmation of our democratic credentials.

In an essay that asks in its title "When Is Democracy Political?" R. Radhakrishnan concludes, "if democracy functions at all, and that indeed is an eminently contestable issue, it does so only on the basis of its inherence in dominance. It is precisely because democracy is instrumentalizable as a sure way of controlling the relationships between national peoples in the name of dominant national interests that it is able to survive, that is, it survives as a guarantor of an uneven world" (2006, 103). Democracy's primary function in the twenty-first century is to retroactively legitimate elite rule, to replicate our profoundly unequal world. Alain Badiou echoes the sentiment: "the only way to make truth out of the world we're living in is to dispel the aura of the word *democracy* and assume the burden of not being a democrat and so being heartily disapproved of by 'everyone'" (2010, 7). However, Badiou's call to have the courage to stand against democracy is tempered by his subsequent attempt to redefine it. He warns the reader:

> what I have aimed to do here is to set brackets around the authority [of] the word *democracy* . . . but, as a coda, we can go right back to the literal meaning of democracy if we like: the power of peoples over their own existence. Politics immanent in the people and the withering away, in open process, of the State. From that perspective, we will only ever be true democrats, integral to the historical life of peoples, when we become communists again. (2010, 15)

Badiou contends the name and practice of democracy can be rescued from its contemporary status as the guarantor of inequality only when what one means by democracy is replaced by communism and militancy in a world now overrun by "the triumph of miniscule ideas" (2007, 3).

More concretely, Jodi Dean argues that democracy can only ever be radical or political when it stands "against an order constituted through the exclusion of democracy." She continues, "in contemporary parliamentary democracies . . . for leftists to refer to their goals as a struggle for democracy is strange. It is a defense of the same. Democracy is our ambient milieu, the hegemonic form of contemporary politics. . . . Left use of the language of democracy *now* avoids the fundamental antagonism between the 1 percent and the rest of us by acting as if the only thinking really missing was participation" (2012, 57). The drive to self-identify with democracy has a credentialing function. It makes politics legible and legitimate, defanged and domesticated—it is, paradoxically, an antipolitics in that the celebration of one's democratic identity reinforces a constituted power that declares itself democratic and all other politics evil, totalitarian, antiquated, or unthinkable.

For Slavoj Žižek, politics as democracy fails in the contemporary moment because "the name of the ultimate enemy is not capitalism, empire, exploitation, or anything similar, but democracy itself. It is the 'democratic illusion,' the acceptance of democratic mechanisms as providing the only framework for all possible change, which prevents any radical transformation of capitalist relations" (2011, 450). Žižek calls in other words to de-fetishize democracy, but also and perhaps more importantly, to de-fetishize the modern democratic state's declared "other"—violence. By decentering democracy and by having the audacity to think about alternatives, including but not limited to Žižek's preferred egalitarian terror, we open new ground for collective life beyond the static and pious pluralism of the sort of North Atlantic liberalism on offer from the Venezuelan opposition. This critical act of exposing and rethinking the fetishes of the present, in other words, approaches collective life in all of its fullness, contingency, and openness, terrifying though they may be. It clears space for constituent power, for egalitarian desires, currently occupied by democracy.

The Venezuelan opposition, before or after its democratic rebranding exercises, presents precisely the opposite of egalitarian rupture. It presents, rather, the prospect of a reaction whose only legitimacy comes from the Bolivarian Revolution's failure to resist its own transformation into constituted power. Being-against constituted power is not the only characteristic of constituent power; when it doesn't open, when it isn't based in the common, when it isn't oriented by egalitarian desires, resistance is nothing more than constituted power in waiting—a proto-state conducting the violent work of separation and exclusion in a nonsovereign setting.

Returning to a question that framed the outset of this chapter: Can the opposition be considered bearers of constituent power in the Venezuela of 2016? I have argued that the answer is a definitive no. Nonetheless, reading the opposition's social and ideological composition, and their increasing deployment of legitimating notions of democracy, illuminates important limits of both the opposition as well as prominent strains of twenty-first-century democratic theory in the North Atlantic. By 2016, both the opposition and much democratic theory promise separation, regulation, and a more or less conservative attachment to the present global and local divisions of power and wealth. Constituent power, on the other hand, is the expression of creative, expansive, and inclusive egalitarian desires that arise from collective life. It refuses constraint and preconfiguration. Constituent power violently refuses any legitimation of separation and inequality. It is for this reason that constituent power must be seen as opposed both to the political and social aims of the Venezuelan opposition *as well as* the democracy on offer from contemporary democratic theory.

And yet, after all of this, we have no choice but to conclude that constituent power in Venezuela faces two counterrevolutions at once: that of a Bolivarian Revolution increasingly reduced to an autoreferential Chavismo and that of an opposition promising the restoration of elite class power. The space for politics as creation, as generation, as equality, is closing. This space will not be reopened democratically. Only constituent power, with the violence of its relentless egalitarian drive, can do that.

CHAPTER 5

Conclusion

Rethinking Constituent Power

⤜∂∾

Plowing the Sea

Shortly before dying in 1830, destitute and exiled from the republics he helped found, Bolívar wrote to the president of Ecuador, General Juan José Flores:

> You know that I have ruled for twenty years, and from these I have derived only a few certainties: (1) America is ungovernable, for us; (2) Those who serve a revolution plow the sea; (3) The only thing one can do in America is to emigrate; (4) This country will fall inevitably into the hands of the unbridled masses and then pass almost imperceptibly into the hands of petty tyrants, of all colors and races; (5) Once we have been devoured by every crime and extinguished by utter ferocity, the Europeans will not even regard us as worth conquering; (6) If it were possible for any part of the world to revert to primitive chaos, it would be America in her final hour. (Quoted in Lynch 2006, 276)

Bolívar's failure was total in almost every aspect, and his words reflect a profound disillusionment with nearly everything he had said, believed, and fought for in his life. After twenty years of conquest, founding, and innovation, an age of civil wars (which would last in his native Venezuela for at least the next seventy years) had arrived. Worse still, in this moment of his defeat, he concluded, América was so abject, for reasons of its own making, that even the Europeans would pass on the opportunity to subjugate it once again. Rather than fostering popular sovereignty, political independence, continental solidarity, and a republican government ruled by virtuous and prosperous citizens, the wars of independence brought about the political, civic, and economic implosion of the continent.

Here too the limits of his Enlightenment vision, always present but often obscured, come to the fore. Bolívar was a republican, not a democrat (Drake 2009, 65; Urueña 2007). Either governmental form offers opportunities and

159

challenges to the realization and cultivation of constituent power. Pressed by a situation in which foundation clashed with reconstruction and incipient disintegration and civil war were perpetually on the horizon, the racialized worldview of El Libertador consistently pressed for stronger centralized authority to navigate the stormy waters. Democracy, distinct here from constituent power, existed for Bolívar in that gap between anarchy and tyranny. On his deathbed, Bolívar feared América would be unable to pull itself from this gap, doomed to shuttle between these two miserable poles beyond the foreseeable future.

But what if we read Bolívar's terminal pessimism against itself? From the perspective of constituent power, the ungovernability unleashed in the Americas is less a virtue or a demerit than an *inevitability*. As was the case for most thinkers of the Enlightenment, Bolívar saw the pursuit of republican government as an *ars politica* that meant a constant navigation of the turbulent waters between despotism and anarchy. The task this final Bolívar put to himself, then, was not defined by an abstract fidelity to the ideal of popular sovereignty, but rather the acknowledgment that political power is, in the first and final instance, human, constituent, power. It is neither divinely ordained nor engineered and thus wields the potential for infinitely productive as well as infinitely destructive actions. In this light, we can see nineteenth-century Bolivarianism as yet another failed attempt to harness and direct constituent power.

And yet, Bolívar, even in his defeat, did not give up. Bitterly attuned to the forces at play in the postcolonial Americas, he persisted in his insistence on the need to build a better republic, impossible though such a task may ultimately be. There is then, in the gloomy conclusion he had attempted to "plow the sea" a lesson: Press forward and fail, but keep pressing onward. Adapt, experiment, and create in the spaces opened by constituent power, but lose any attachment to what you have created—institutions were never meant to be permanent.

There is, after all, little alternative.

Only the People Can Save the People

This book started with the assertion that constituent power is not a thing, but rather a social relation, a capacity for action that arises from and demands more being in common with others. Constituent power, especially values like inclusion, egalitarianism, cooperation, and autonomy that are associated with it, is perhaps the most powerful legitimating principle in circulation today and has been since the spread of mass democracy. However, despite the platitudes states evoke when discussing the power of the people, in practice actually existing democracies have done more to check constituent power than to enhance it or follow its lead. While the comparative history of constituent power has seen it deployed with a number of competing meanings—from principle to capacity to vitalistic drive and cultivated practice—in all cases it retains a tortured but seemingly inextricable relationship to the constituted power of states and institutions.

Chapter 1 highlighted how the liberal tradition dominant in the North Atlantic since the twentieth century relegates constituent power either to the routinized cycles of representative democracy or, more maximally, to extreme moments of political experience at the birth and death of regimes. The historical course in Venezuela, on the other hand, considers constituent power as a capacity to be cultivated, trained, and then followed. This second tradition is by no means linear or constant—not a simple "good" alternative to the North Atlantic's "bad." Elites, even ostensibly progressive ones, have been as distrustful of constituent power in Venezuela as anywhere else. It is persistent, but often effervescent and subterranean. Even in sequences like the Bolivarian Revolution, which claim to foster a constituted power at the service of the collective energies and egalitarian desires that brought it into being, constituent power is most clearly marked by its stubborn refusal to accept limits, containment, or mediation.

Its subterranean, spontaneous, and insurrectionary capacities make constituent power an event. In the second chapter we saw how constituent power forces a departure from a given reality, an accepted common sense that naturalizes hierarchy, exclusion, enclosure. Constituent power is an eruption of the unthinkable and unseeable onto a constituted order that requires a complete overhaul of existing boundaries, practices, and desires; it is an absolute rupture with inequality. It is a persistent if subterranean social relation that is periodically and inevitably reshaped by the conditions of its self-expression. In the case of the Caracazo, the refusal to abide by a law and order that enforced inequality and imposed structural adjustment could only be quieted by brutal state repression.

The power of the constituent moment that was the Caracazo did not die on the streets in late February 1989. It instead became a subjectivizing force, reshaping social relations and rewriting the normative and practical rules of public life in Venezuela. It issued a challenge to any would-be ally to construct constituted forms capable of realizing and enhancing its potential. However, by the mid-2000s familiar contradictions troubled the move from protagonism to the party. The PSUV has never fulfilled its potential to become an organ capable of making the multitude transparent to itself, to prolong and sustain the constituent energies of the Caracazo. Instead, it became an electoral vehicle, wholly colonized and willfully reproducing the logic of the state.

Constituent power's expression is often fleeting, retroactively recognized, and disruptive, but its effects outlast its immediate expression. Chapter 4 looked at the transformation of the built environment of the city of Caracas as an example of constituent power's ability to physically reshape the world. More than just an abstract principle or the fear of mass democracy, constituent power contours the city, as seen in the early 2000s expansion of the Caracas Metro. However, this also highlights a potential limit of constituent power. The degree of coordination, funding, and planning needed for large-scale infrastructure developments suggests constituent power faces a problem of scale that would seem to favor the state—multitudes, it would seem, can't build metros. And yet, without at least the tacit cooperation of a city's inhabitants, the sorts of transformations seen in Caracas in the early 2000s would not have been possible. We can glimpse evidence of this reality in the opposition's violent attempts to fragment urban space, to curtail the right to the city of all *caraqueños*, to demolish the concrete effects of constituent power that will act as facts on the ground far into the future.

Attacks on the metro and the securitization and privatization of space illustrate the extent to which the opposition, even when rebelling against a government that illustrates some of constituted power's worst attributes, cannot be considered a vector of constituent power in Venezuela. In chapter 5 this analysis of the opposition opened into a more thoroughgoing consideration of constituent power and democratic theory. Democracy has established itself in North Atlantic political thought as an unassailable principle against which all forms of collective life must be judged. To the extent, however, that democracy has become a regulative ideal and enforceable consensus, it also jealously limits the space for critical thought, limiting innovative action and collective roads toward a more just and inclusive society. If constituent power manifests in the relentless drive to destroy all separation and inequality, its primary target by 2016 must be the democratic forms that legitimate and even celebrate the liberal-capitalist world system. Constituent power against democracy, even if only to revive democracy's potential for egalitarian rupture, means *los escuálidos* must not be mistaken for the harbingers of a better Venezuela.

This book has argued that above all else, and certainly before the museum piece principle ostensibly underlying representative democratic constitutions, constituent power is a possibility of collective life. It makes collective life possible, but it also pushes us beyond our present selves. It is potential, which begs the question: As practical as it is philosophical, can that ever be enough? In other words, is constituent power better understood as a supplement to constituted order? Can constituent power rule itself? And, paraphrasing Sheldon Wolin, why would it even want to? Is constituent power only ever a legitimating adjunct to constituted power?

The early twenty-first century has yet to offer a form of political organization not yet solidified into the alienating and exclusionary organs of state power, a form of individual and collective life not conceived as a mere appendage of the market. This book has argued that the travails of constituent power across revolutionary and counterrevolutionary Venezuela offers insights into what such a republic might resemble. They are, inevitably, contradictory lessons, emphatic and yet slippery, and above all else persistent. Constituent power persists in being—its manifestation as ungovernability, as disruption, is less the signal of a fault in the system, less a technical matter of improving practices of governance, and more a constant attribute of collective life.

Taken as a whole, *Only the People Can Save the People* argues that Venezuela's Bolivarian Revolution offers a compelling, if uneven and contradictory, geohistorical location from which to consider the implications of taking constituent power seriously in the twenty-first century. Globally, the twenty-first century is marked by a dichotomy. Among elites and opinion makers in government, the media, industry, and education reigns a seemingly unquestionable assumption that liberal democracy and globalized, if post-neoliberal, capitalism are not only the best but *the only* way to organize collective life. For the vast majority of the planet's population, on the other hand, democracy and capital have only ever reproduced exclusion and inequality. Constituent power—as seen before, throughout, and after the Bolivarian Revolution—offers a necessary alternative to democratic consensus and the liberal marketplace of ideas.

This conclusion isn't meant to be a comfort. It is, rather, a challenge. In some ways, it does not matter whether states choose to embrace and follow constituent power. As it is both evental and constant, a social relation and force of egalitarian desire more than a "thing," constituent power will always find ways to realize its potentials, if only fleetingly and explosively. The challenge implied in the maxim *solo el pueblo salva el pueblo* is that of finding ways to extend these explosive experiences into a sustained practice. Prevailing currents in North Atlantic political thought tend to identify constituent power as a threat to constituted orders—considered either as benign or better than uncertain alternatives. Venezuelan politics in the aftermath of the Caracazo begin from a realization that dominant order and common sense are threats to life itself. Constituent power is the conceptual way of identifying the praxes that emerge in the construction of a better—more equal, inclusive, and sustainable—world.

Constituent power is both ellipsis and exclamation point. It is an opening. In that spirit, *Only the People Can Save the People* closes with three theses, three openings, three contingent conclusions, on constituent power and the Bolivarian Revolution.

Toward a Constituent (Bolivarian) Republic?

Antonio Negri and Enrique Dussel have been our constant theoretical companions throughout this book. While they come to different conclusions on the necessity of state power, transcendental ideals, and the possibility of a virtuous dialectic between constituent and constituted power, both break with the liberal emphasis on the latter over the former, and both have been influential in Bolivarian Venezuela. Negri's position has been consistently more forceful in its rejection of the state form, despite his insistence that constituent power does not equate, create, or trigger simple chaos. Dussel concludes there is no other choice but to persist in the dialectic of constituent and constituted power. The power of the people holds infinite potential, but it needs settled and rationalized forms to pass into cohesive, positive, and effective existence. Rather than try to synthesize these mutually exclusive positions, my approach has been to locate them as two poles or modes of thinking and acting in the Bolivarian context. The actual praxes of protagonism shuttle between these two relations to state power: rejection of the state as fetishized and autoreferential, and cautious engagement with the state as a contingent tool for securing social change.

Of course, neither Negri nor Dussel is ultimately interested in outlining the ideal state form. Both are concerned with developing a theory of collective freedom and liberation from the prevailing order of exclusion, inequality, and alienation. For both, to be free means to have access to possibilities. Freedom is a practical power that sidesteps all other ethical concerns other than how to maximize its potential: to be fully and inextricably immersed in the world of others, to be and become in common. This is what the phrase "egalitarian desire" that has appeared so often throughout this book means: the drive to dismantle separation and inequality is a drive to collaborate, to construct, and to interact with others free from artificial and imposed constraint.

In a chapter on the notion of the "constituent republic" Negri begins with an analysis of eighteenth-century republican thought, and specifically with Condorcet. For Condorcet, from whom Negri borrows the maxim "to each generation, a constitution," the republican moment recognizes that "any restraint of liberty that goes beyond the requirements of the present necessarily leads to despotism. To put it another way . . . once the constituent moment is past, constitutional fixity becomes a reactionary fact in a society that is founded on the development of freedoms and the development of the economy" (Negri 1996, 213). The enduring lesson of Condorcet's insight, for Negri, is the need to base constitutional forms on "life in a constant process of renewal" rather than static legal *doxa* (214). The point, or rather, the possibility of the constituent republic is thus a form of collective governance based in shared and collaborative action rather than on constituted state order. It is a

> position that avoids absorption within the opaque and terrible essence of the State . . . [that] is able to maintain the thread of genealogy, the force of constituent praxis, in its extensiveness and its intensity. This point of view exists. It is the viewpoint of daily insurrection, continual resistance, constituent power. It is a breaking-with, it is refusal, it is imagination . . . we are beginning to arrive at a situation where we are no longer condemned to think of politics in terms of domination. The very form of the dialectic—that is, mediation as the content of domination in its various different forms, is thus brought into question. (220)

In slightly more concrete terms, he continues that this viewpoint lends itself to the constituent republic,

> a republic that comes before the State, that comes outside the State. The constitutional paradox of the constituent republic consists in the fact that the constituent process never closes, that the revolution does not come to an end, that constitutional law and ordinary law refer back to one single source and are developed unilaterally with a single democratic procedure. (222)

For Negri the task with which everything begins and ends for this constituent republic is that of "destroying separation, inequality, and the power that reproduces separation and inequality," concluding by admitting that his outline for a constituent republic of ceaseless rebellion against the injustices of modern liberalism is too "general and abstract" but assuring the reader that "the event, the untimely, the *Angelus Novus*—when they arrive—will appear suddenly. Thus our generation *can* construct a new constitution. Except that it will not be a constitution. And perhaps this event has already occurred" (222). Constituent power never ceases, meaning a constitution capable of coexisting with and amplifying it must also be an open-ended process. His proposal is nothing short of jettisoning the "voluntary servitude" of the social contract, to end the naturalization of politics as domination and subordination. For Negri, this constituent republic based in free collaboration is already the basis for actually existing capitalism, and especially in the immaterial labor that drives capital accumulation in post-Fordism. All it will take, he concludes on a rather hopeful note, is an event powerful enough to punctuate and reconfigure the present, a catalyzing moment that will accelerate a future republic beyond the state. Like all events, this coming of the new can only be recognized retrospectively, such that we may already be living in the aftermath of capitalism.

Here Negri is evocative as ever, but his assertions carry more questions than answers. Politics and philosophy penetrate one another; an end to domination requires and comes about as a result of the end of the dialectic. A liberatory politics for Negri must get beyond simple anti-statism, which even in its Leninist and early Soviet variations resulted in "a negative dialectic of state [in which] the nucleus remains, in the absolute and reactionary way in which the power of the State is affirmed. 'All the same old shit,' as Marx had it" (Negri 1996, 220). It remains elusive how exactly a "viewpoint" rooted in constituent power escapes this dialectic other than to unsettle the necessity of the state. But then again, does not a permanent refusal, a sequence of perpetual insurrection, need something against which to rebel? The "viewpoint" of constituent praxis, of a constituent republic, still requires the state, at least for the time being. What, though, can this permanent being-against mean other than permanent crisis and permanent exception—both of which situations *also* presume some sort of norm against which to be judged.

Paolo Virno offers a more fully elaborated rendering of constituent power's potential futures as a diffuse, mobile, and contingent mode of the political. The monopoly of decision-making power can only be taken away by a democracy of the multitude (his term) from the State when decision-making is no longer considered a monopoly (Virno 1996, 202). Instead, he envisions associations of "the Soviets of the Multitude" that "eat away" at the existing power of the state, "translat[ing] into republican praxis—knowledge, communication, a "relation-ship with the presence of others"—that are the order of the day in post-Fordist production. They emancipate *virtuosic cooperation* from its present connection with waged labor, showing with positive action how the one goes beyond the other (Virno 1996, 203). One is left wondering if post-Fordism is a prerequisite for these constituent republics and their twenty-first-century Soviets. That is to ask, are these sorts of anti- and non-statist politics possible outside the post-Fordist North Atlantic? What about places like Venezuela, where Fordism never prevailed in the first place?

For reasons such as this, Enrique Dussel's call to decolonize thought is particularly useful for thinking the dynamics of constituent and constituted power (Dussel 2007, 552). Here and elsewhere he draws important lessons from the Zapatistas of Chiapas, Mexico. For Dussel, the 1994 revolt against the Mexican government and the imposition of the North American Free Trade Agreement (NAFTA) builds on the lessons of a Latin American left that has at least since the Cuban Revolution moved away from the Eurocentrism of an Orthodox Marxism of vanguards, working classes, and laws of historical change. Instead, from Fidel Castro and Che Guevara onward, the *pueblo*, "concrete, historical, oppressed, and excluded constitutes the principle reference of the political" (Dussel 2007, 482). This is not to rehash the limits of the debate between multitude and *pueblo*, as examined in chapter 2 of this book. It is, rather, to echo Dussel's insistence that capitalism has not traveled along the same trajectory in Latin America as it did in Europe. Any politics seeking a liberatory exit from the contemporary condition must begin from an honest and direct engagement with the histories, relations, and subjects that produced it.

This is why the Zapatistas are so important for Dussel and for the larger community of Latin American political thought. The former's insistence that their struggle dates to 1492 is just as central to their praxis as is the development of a *poder obedencial* (obediential power) that Dussel contends can also be practiced by certain state formations—his example here is the early years of the Cuban Revolution—once cleansed of their colonial trappings (Dussel 2007, 492). This decolonized obediential power is Dussel's response to the question of how best to sustain constituent power beyond the rupture and event. It is an "essentially moral, ethical" relationship between the *pueblo* and its representative institutions, one that goes beyond the "distribution of wealth or the expropriation of the means of production [but rather] begins with the possibility that human beings can have a space for *dignity*" (Dussel 2007, 502; emphasis in original). The realization of constituent power is in other words tied to the self-valorization of human community, a process Dussel likens to the political maturation of *pueblos* (2007, 504).

It is precisely this sort of "maturation"—of a growing sense of dignity that transforms into self-determination and the expression of delegated, obediential power—that Dussel sees as having taken place throughout Latin America in the early twenty-first century. The so-called "Pink Tide" of left-of-center governments that started with the election of Chávez in 1998 is for Dussel not only an electoral phenomenon. It is also, and perhaps even primarily, the production of a new way of politics based in the deconstruction and reconsideration of "the entire system of categories of bourgeois political philosophy" that has enforced and legitimated Latin America's subordination to Europe (Dussel 2007, 504). And while he admits that these movements that have spawned what he sees as obediential governments can fail, as previous attempts to liberate the *pueblo* have, they will nonetheless "remain as ineluctable references in the future" (Dussel 2007, 505). Concrete expressions of constituent power in a given political sequence—like the Bolivarian Revolution—can be derailed, neutralized, captured, even extinguished. Their example, however, lives on and remains as a resource for the time ahead.

What Negri and Virno see as a republic without a state with perpetual insurrection to guaranteeing and underwriting constituent power, Dussel describes as the cyclical ethic of political practice. Constituent power is expressed as a *pueblo* emerges from exteriority and matures into the directing force of collective life. Whereas Negri and Virno are at pains to distance themselves from any and all mediation—seeing mediation as the royal road to separation, inequality, and exclusion—Dussel insists on its necessity. Without mediation we are left with pure potential, and no way to transfer egalitarian desire into modes of sociality and new forms of individual and collective subjectivity.

In treatments by both Dussel and Negri and Virno constituent power has a dual character. It forms a political practice within a given sequence *and* it serves to reconstitute political orders: the generational constitution of Negri (by way of Condorcet) or the "ineluctable example" that a politics outside the normative universe in Eurocentric liberal modernity is not only possible, but actual and actually attainable. In either case, however, constituent power forms its own limit. The constituent republic—or obediential delegated power—is a constant process of remaking. It is a perpetual engagement with egalitarian desire and a will for the new, but as we have seen in the case of Bolivarian Venezuela, there are no guarantees of its success or iron laws leading us progressively toward its realization.

A final interpretation of the constituent republic and the Bolivarian Revolution: The slogan "Comuna o Nada!" (Commune or Nothing) is in many ways typical of the sorts of exhortations that have marked politics in Venezuela since the Caracazo. Chavistas are regularly encouraged to push forward in a final offensive, to give their all, and to be relentless in the perpetual battle that pits them against the revolution's internal and external enemies. The worldview from which these slogans emerge is decidedly martial—reflecting the movement and government's composition as a "civic-military alliance" as well as the longer Bolivarian tradition dating back to the wars for independence from Spain.

"Comuna o Nada" echoes Bolívar's Decree of War to the Death of 1813. In the decree, Bolívar effectively declares year zero for the Venezuelan republic and its citizens. A general amnesty is offered to Spaniards, "even to the traitors who have most recently committed acts of felony, and it will be so religiously fulfilled that no reason, cause, or pretext will be sufficient to cause us to break our promise, no matter how grievous and extraordinary the motives you give us to arouse our loathing" (Bolívar 2003, 116). The effect of this amnesty is to establish the new lines of friendship and enmity, and to proclaim from that point on "even if you profess neutrality, know that you will die unless you work actively to bring about the freedom of America"

(Bolívar 2003, 116). In short, from the moment of the decree, there can be no turning back. "Comuna o Nada" works in a similar fashion: it states the Bolivarian Revolution has always pressed toward the realization of the *Estado Comunal* (Communal State) and that Venezuelans find themselves in the moment of a final heroic battle where everything is on the line.

From a perspective rooted in constituent power there is still another reading of "Comuna o Nada." It is an expression of the constituent republic. It states, emphatically: *without the commune, we don't want your state.* It is a powerful expression of a protagonism in Venezuela that has worked with but beyond the state and a reminder that thinking of the relationship of constituent to constituted power exclusively in harmonious or antimonious terms is itself an artifact of the modern and especially North Atlantic liberalism. In those moments where the Bolivarian Revolution has been most revolutionary, it has constantly challenged both our thinking of constituent power while allowing constituent power to force itself into more sustainable *and* dynamic manifestations. These are precisely the moments to which it must return if there is to be any hope of a Bolivarian future in Venezuela.

The Bolivarian Revolution in the Postliberal Moment

Liberal and North Atlantic observers have long sounded alarms over the Bolivarian Revolution's ostensible anti- or illiberal tendencies. These accounts are concerned with ways in which Chávez either triggered or accelerated the collapse of representative institutions, centralized power in the executive, diminished the role and stature of political parties, and meddled with the economy (see, for example, Cameron 2002; Mainwaring 2006). These criticisms share much in substance and normative orientation with the booming literature that treats Chavismo as a populist sequence in its focus on the executive branch as cause and catalyst of representative democracy's unraveling in twenty-first-century Venezuela (Castañeda 2006; Corrales and Penfold 2011; Hawkins 2003). The aftermath of Chavismo, from these perspectives, is a postliberal landscape in which would-be reformers and their allies in the North Atlantic must practice patience as they rebuild a pluralist liberal order (Hawkins 2016). As we saw in chapter 5, by the end of the Chávez years the opposition in Venezuela attempted to rebrand itself along these lines as the torchbearer of liberal civil society, promising to reverse what it described as the deepening authoritarianism of the Bolivarian Revolution (Gil Yepes 2011).

Takes on postliberalism divide along normative-critical and theoretical lines. The former, typified by liberal and opposition critiques of the Bolivarian project, bases itself in the defense of modern liberalism, and especially of the rule of law, separation of powers and the public and private spheres, free market capitalism, methodological and moral individualism, and representative government. From this standpoint, while liberal orders are rarely perfect, they at least provide stability and transparency, which are necessary preconditions for prosperous societies (Diamond 2002).

A less normative and more descriptive social science line of inquiry into postliberalism focuses on recent events in Latin America, and especially the mobilization of indigenous groups in the late twentieth century. Particularly prominent in the Andes and Central America, these movements have mounted a challenge to modern liberalism's functioning presuppositions of homogeneous subjects, structures, rights, and responsibilities. They demand "a different kind of political mapping—one that would secure individual rights but also accommodate more diverse identities, units of representation, and state structures" (Yashar 1999, 88). While these studies highlight the ways in which liberalism is being challenged in Latin America, particularly in the aftermath of neoliberal restructuring (see, for an overview, Goodale and Postero 2013; Smith 2007), they are often focused most squarely on changes and challenges to citizenship as an institution. As such, they are additive in nature, attaching concepts of ethnic or cultural citizenship to familiar positions and structures of the modern liberal and democratic state (Canessa 2012).

Yet looking at Bolivarian Venezuela admiringly or admonishingly through the lens of postliberalism can mistakenly lead one to think Venezuela was liberal in the first place. It was not. Even before the petrostate normalized rent-seeking and a heavily centralized patron-client dynamic among the represented and their representatives, before the Puntofijo order centralized power within a highly constrained electoral framework, the liberal project in Venezuela was more a fashionable idea among elites than the organic result of transitions from feudal rule (Cameron 2002, 139). Indeed, liberalism has always been something of a paradoxical hybrid in Venezuela. In the late nineteenth and early twentieth centuries, it was an authoritarian project imposed from above, coupled with a governing style of exclusionary and technocratic positivism. Far from a doctrine of the separation of powers and secular government, the sanctity of the individual citizen and the right to private property, or the civil rights of free expression and association, liberalism in Venezuela has more often than not been experienced as an *illiberal* ideological veneer apologizing for dispossession and justifying elite rule (Cameron 2002).

More useful for the concerns of this book have been the more theoretically oriented accounts of Benjamin Arditi and Arturo Escobar. For Benjamin Arditi, the early twenty-first century can only be characterized as postliberal. Arditi suggests that the hybridity one can observe in the politics of the so-called left turn in Latin America tend to *combine* elements of conventional liberal democracy with other practices rather than *replace* them outright. Regimes like the Bolivarian Revolution are, conceptually speaking, additive in character. It "still draws its inspiration from the socialist imaginary, whether in its cultural orientations, the enactment of distributive demands, or the general vindication of those who are excluded because they are poor, indigenous, or women. Yet, unlike their Leninist predecessors, the left tends to demand equality without necessarily seeking to abolish capitalism, international trade, or liberal citizenship" (Arditi 2008, 73). Postliberalism for Arditi has an unsettled relationship with the liberal consensus, its status "cannot be decided outside a disagreement or polemic," insisting, for example that democracy does not only occur in the context of elections, but is rather embedded in our relations to ourselves, to each other, and to the world (Arditi 2008). Along with multiparty, electoral, and representative democracy, private property rights, and the same formal acceptance of individual rights and freedoms and the rule of law as can be found elsewhere, hybrid regimes of the so-called left turn in Latin America add to democratic experience modes of collective and group citizenship, collective property rights, popular mobilizations and plebiscites, and in Ecuador, the granting of legal citizenship status and protection to the earth itself (Ari 2014; de Sousa Santos 2007).

These hybrid formations all occur within a political-structural context of a state Arditi characterizes as "generally bigger than it needs to be and far weaker than the left would like it to be given the (often) modest range of resources it can command and its limited capacity to implement agreed-on policies" (Arditi 2008, 78). It is perhaps the status of the state that has shifted most radically in the postliberal twenty-first century. After attacks on its capacities and sovereignty during the neoliberalizing 1980s and 1990s, and despite the traditional skepticism of state power exhibited by many on the traditional left—especially after decades of military dictatorship, endemic corruption, and police violence, for many on the regional left the representative state seems to have definitively returned as a terrain on which to pursue social change. Arditi observes: "the point is that a post-liberal politics of the left refuses to perceive contamination between the multitude and representation as something particularly problematic" (Arditi 2008, 79). Such a seeming reconciliation has little to do with a capitulation by rebellious forces. It is, rather, because today social subjects always-already bear traces of the state, are formed by its disciplinary institutions, and have internalized part of its common sense—even (especially?) in the context of insurrectionary mobilizations the search for a somehow "pure" revolutionary subject is farcical.

Arturo Escobar builds on Arditi's analysis, adding what he describes as a deconstructive element. Starting from his own work on postdevelopment, Escobar characterizes the early twenty-first century in Latin America as dwelling between the twin crises of neoliberalism's unraveling and the larger failure and increasing rejection of Eurocentric discourses of modernity, modernization, and development (Escobar 2010, 3). A wide array of cultural and political movements has stepped up since the 1980s and 1990s to challenge the boundaries, exclusions, and inequalities of conventional governance. The resulting postliberal milieu is one in which "'post' signals the notions that *the economy is not essentially or naturally capitalist, societies are not naturally liberal, and the state is not the only way of instituting social power as we have imagined it to be*" (Escobar 2010, 12; emphasis in original). As with Arditi's characterization, Escobar sees the postliberal moment as one of hybridity and experimentation. The forms that postliberalism produces in society and the economy, furthermore, are not settled places at which a movement can arrive. "It is not a state to be arrived at in the future but something that is always under construction" (Escobar 2012, 12). Postliberalism, rather, implies perpetual motion and constant creation.

This has, however, been a profoundly uneven and contradictory process. Speaking directly about Venezuela, Escobar concludes,

A main question remains pending: Is the State an effective vehicle for the transformation of society towards post-capitalism and post-development? There are serious doubts that this is the case. However, it might well be the case that all the pillars of the process—endogenous development, popular economy, and the new geometry of power anchored in the community councils and other forms of popular power—should be understood as *horizons* guiding a different path rather than as fully worked-out alternative models. . . . whereas post-liberalism is not on the radar of the State, there are two important developments that erode cherished liberal principles (at least in its "really existing" forms); the first is the introduction of more direct forms of democracy. The second is the transformation of what could be called the spatiality of liberalism, that is, the commonly held political division of the territory into regions, departments, municipalities, and the like, and which the "new geometry of power" seeks to unsettle in principle. It should be added that post-liberalism seems far from the scope of most popular organizations, partly a consequence of the strength of the developmentalist oil imaginary with its individualistic and consumerist undertones; in other words, the society defined by the Bolivarian revolution and twenty-first century socialism still functions largely within the framework of the liberal order; for post-liberalism to emerge the autonomy of the popular sector would have to be released to a greater degree than the current government is willing to do. (Escobar 2010, 19)

In a tone that resonates with the criticisms found in this book, Escobar concludes that the Bolivarian Revolution has been limited by its statist standard operating procedure, a trait he ties to the cultural imaginary of the oil industry in Venezuela (see also Kingsbury 2016a). Here liberalism moves beyond its classical narrow political conceptualization and into territories of subjectivity, desire, and expectation. While Escobar sees the Bolivarian Revolution as offering potentially useful institutional innovations for the path of postliberal politics in Latin America, he nonetheless concludes that neither the state nor the popular movements have the vision, will, or desire to move more decisively in that direction.

More encouraging postliberal practices have emerged, for Escobar, among urban and indigenous movements in El Alto, Bolivia. Drawing heavily on the work of Uruguayan theorist Raúl Zibechi, Escobar writes, "the struggles are characterized in terms of self-organization aimed at the construction of non-state forms of power; these are defined as 'forms of power that are not separate nor divided from society, i.e., that do not create a separate group in order to make decisions, to struggle, or to deal with internal conflict'" (Escobar 2010, 32). Against the understanding of constituent power as incapable of sustaining or amplifying itself without the constituted power of states and institutions, this perspective

> takes the social relations created from below with the goal of survival as a point of departure and then follows the movement, flows, and displacements of this type of society. Theoretically speaking, this entails prioritizing "displacement over structure, mobility over fixity, society in flow rather than the state's codification of such flows" (Zibechi). There is always a tension between movement-displacement and movement-institution. At play in the wave of insurrections are veritable *sociedades en movimiento* [societies in movement] rather than *movimientos sociales* [social movements]. This is an important distinction that is at the crux of the argument about post-liberalism. (Escobar 2010, 33)

At its most promising, postliberalism is in other words a perpetual process of resistance and construction. A new form of politics is required to address the crises and paradoxes of the present, "emancipation becomes a praxis of both overturning and flight (*trastocamiento y fuga*): material *overturning* of the existing order and *flight* from the semantic and symbolic contents that confer meaning upon that which is instituted (*éxodo semántico*, or exodus from dominant discourses)" (Escobar 2010, 34). In other words, postliberalism allows for movements to push against and beyond the modern nation-state but highlights the fact that this line of flight cannot cease, that it must continue to strike out toward new—also unreachable—horizons created by the very bodies toiling to survive in the present.

There are a few important historical and theoretical caveats that must be considered. It was precisely the sort of "society in movement" that Escobar locates among indigenous movements in Bolivia that made Chávez possible in the first place. That is to say, Escobar starts his analysis of the Bolivarian Revolution a decade too late, thus inadvertently reinforcing the very modern-statist myopia he seeks to redress. While Escobar is correct to point out the deeply embedded nature of developmentalism in both the state and popular identities, his analysis's conflation of political liberalism and the "individualistic and consumerist undertones" of the collective imaginary misses a key aspect of Venezuelan politics before, during, and after Chávez. The Puntofijo era was never itself liberal. Politically, it was a highly centralized and closed system of patron-client networks. Economically, the same oil industry Escobar blames for later deficiencies in civil society meant that the dominant economic activity has for decades been the capture of rents, and a labor theory of value has never defined Venezuelan capitalism.

In other words, it is not just a lingering liberalism that limits Venezuela's ability to move beyond the crises of the early twenty-first century. It is rather paradoxically the fact that Venezuela has in key aspects always been postliberal that both allowed for the Bolivarian Revolution's expansive social vision and that—as Escobar is correct to insist—has tied it to the state form. Puntofijo promised a "Grand Venezuela" for all, one in which something approaching an equitable distribution of the nation's oil wealth—what I have described in this book during the Bolivarian moment as the democratization of consumption—is possible without regard to social status or the degree to which one can successfully alienate her labor. The popular if often ironic conclusion that *Dios es Venezolano* (God is Venezuelan) in many ways survived the collapse of Puntofijo, informing a popular political and social vision that dismisses the constraints of necessity and the commonsensical limits placed on the political by modern liberalism.

In other words, it is not that the Bolivarian Revolution is a post- or illiberal "turn" in Venezuelan political history. Venezuela has always been postliberal. The Bolivarian Revolution is a sequence within this larger genealogy, one that was occasioned by explosions of constituent power and protagonism. In those moments, postliberal Venezuela reached toward the egalitarian horizons of the constituent republic, of an obediential power opposed and constructively other than the politics of the modern, liberal, nation-state. Just as postliberalism is a hybrid of forms and practices, so too is the Bolivarian Revolution a heterodox and often contradictory process. The question demanded of the Bolivarian Revolution by the multitude, *pueblo*, and *turba* that produced it is not if it can sustain itself despite these contradictions. After 2016 it is, rather, if the Bolivarian Revolution can have the courage to once again open itself to constituent power.

Constituent Power and Counterrevolution

Henrique Capriles's call, after losing to Nicolás Maduro by a slim margin in 2013, for his followers to "unleash their rage" resulted in eight deaths and a series of attacks on government infrastructure. In 2014, when Leopoldo López and María Corina Machado called for La Salida, forty-three people were killed and millions of dollars in damages were the result of the ensuing clashes. The opportunity presented by a weakened president quickly doused any chance of a more moderate opposition, one that confined itself to electoral politics.

One of the more striking things about the opposition protests is that the Maduro administration weathered the unrest without the sort of mobilizations that defined the Chávez years, especially in its early phases. More to the point, the Chavista or Bolivarian publics failed to mobilize autonomously and spontaneously in support of the president. By the summer of 2016, that sort of protagonism—of the government working with social forces it recognizes as beyond its control to transform Venezuela—seemed unlikely to return to its engagement with constituted power.

Of course, there are plausible potential reasons why Maduro did not call for mobilizations to counter the *guarimbas* when none materialized independently. He could have sincerely feared the risk of the situation devolving into civil war, with the government forced into an unstable third position and locked into the impossible task of mediating the conflict. He could have made the calculation that allowing the *guarimbas* to continue would strengthen his standing by illustrating the violence of the opposition. He also might have calculated the *guarimbas* would reopen divisions within the opposition, as seen in the uproar caused by Capriles's comments that the *guarimbas* had been a tremendous failure and a political error, in December of 2015.

Just as likely, Maduro may have been less than certain people would answer a call to mobilize on his behalf. After all, he only won the election by less than 1 percent the previous year, and his administration emerged hamstrung by growing inflation, debt, falling oil prices, and ecological crises that exacerbated all these dynamics. A failure at such a moment would have likely been fatal to his career, and potentially to the Bolivarian Revolution *tout court*.

There is a still more damning possibility. Maduro did not want to rely on constituent power to find its own exit from Venezuela's deepening crises. Since 2014 his government increasingly centralized state power, relying increasingly on the military and all but criminalizing social movements outside the immediate control of the PSUV. By July 2016, the Misiones and Consejos Comunales have also fallen prey to these centralizing moves with the announcement of the Gran Misión Abastamiento Soberano y Seguro (Great Sovereign and Safe Supply Mission, GMASS) in response to scarcity and black markets in food, medicine, and basic consumer goods. With the announcement of GMASS Maduro placed all government ministries and institutions, including the Misiones, communes, and Consejos under the direct command of the minister of defense, Vladimir Padrino López. The crises faced by Maduro were dire and worsening. The IMF estimated an inflation rate for 2016 of over 700 percent, while the market price for petroleum leveled off at historic lows fully $100 per barrel less than its high-water mark during the Chávez years. After opposition gains in the National Assembly elections of 2015, the state apparatus was literally internally divided and at war with itself. A historically unprecedented drought crippled Venezuela's hydroelectric power system, which provides over 70 percent of the country's electricity, forcing prolonged blackouts and shortening the official workweek to two days. Venezuela continued to register some of the world's highest violent crime rates, and gains made in lessening inequality since 2003 were eroded by mismanagement and the collapse of the economy.

In the face of all these challenges, the Maduro government increasingly looked to constituted power to rescue itself.

Conditions and prospects are bleak for the expression of constituent power in Venezuela. The Maduro administration is now all but completely militarized. Both the government and the opposition remain focused on retaining or securing state power by whatever means necessary. While some elements of the opposition softened its discourse and incorporated elements of the Bolivarian Revolution's ethical worldview into its own platform for the 2012 elections—Henrique Capriles going so far as to compare himself with Brazil's Lula—even ostensible moderates have consistently promised a return to the neoliberalizing 1990s. The 2016 campaign to recall Maduro quieted any gestures toward moderation, dialogue, or collaboration with the government. Only when the government successfully manipulated institutional means to prevent the recall from taking place did mediated dialogues between the government and the opposition begin. Each side immediately declared the other to be acting in bad faith. More disconcerting, however, is the degree to which moves toward international mediation of the political stalemate in Venezuela suggest a return to the pacts of the past. In the best-case scenario, the government and opposition meet in secret to decide the fate of the nation; the people are relegated to the role of passive observers—extras in a serialized political drama.

Protagonism illuminates and presses beyond the limits of liberal or populist democracy as irredeemably implicated with the violences of the modern state form. But so too does protagonism apparently have its own limits. This sobering reality was already suggested by the debates between Negri and Dussel, in recognizing the need to develop and secure new modes of sociality to move beyond an immediate response to a crisis, or the fleeting opportunity of a political vacuum, and into a more concretized and sustainable mode of constituent power. The task, put differently, is to move constituent power from the extremes of political experience at the birth and death of constituted orders toward a more constant practice without also neutralizing its creativity, unpredictability, and uncompromising egalitarianism in the process—to find a constituent power and protagonism that is not merely the shadow of constituted order.

In his 2012 *Golpe de Timón* address, Chávez recognized that his government had done just the opposite. The Bolivarian Revolution had lost sight of its most powerful capacities, failing to foster the subjectivities that made his administration possible. It failed to, to use the preferred phrase of grassroots activists, help construct the communal state. Instead, the government engaged in a process of multiplying institutions, assigning tasks to proliferating administrators and eager business partners from elements of the private sector. In short, rather than fortifying practices of *cogestión*, it only succeeded in opening new spaces for the plunder of public resources and the abuse of power.

The iterated crises of 2012–2016 presented an opportunity for the government to reengage with constituent power and to follow the lead of protagonism. It did not do so.

This is of course only half of the equation. Protagonism did not come to define Venezuelan politics at the invitation of any head of state, and it has had to weather storms made by allies as much as by antagonists. Even in its most "progressive" iterations, constituted power can only at best hope to be a virtuous parasite; constituent power requires constant motion, constant protagonism if it can hope to resist neutralization by the state. To lose sight of this is to miss perhaps the most important lesson of the Bolivarian Revolution.

*   *   *

The constituent republic, postliberal politics, and the transformation of the Bolivarian Revolution from a constituent process to a constituted and autoreferential state each in their own way point back to Bolívar's lament. Ungovernability is both a source of immense potential and a challenge not only to obediential constituted power, but to constituent power itself. To plow the sea is to engage in the endless, collective, and immersive labor of constituent power. It is to construct a common that is in perpetual motion, propelled by egalitarian desire and the refusal to accept the separation, exclusion, and violences of the world. By 2016, the revolution may have ended, but the Bolivarian Revolution has illustrated that rebellion persists, that it will return, and that constituent power is its ceaseless and fickle motor.

Notes

❧

1. This and all other translations are the work of the author unless otherwise noted.
2. Caldera, importantly, was no stranger to Venezuelan politics. As the head of the center right COPEI, he was a founding member of the Puntofijo system. When the pacted order started to collapse in the 1990s, Caldera created a new political party, Convergencia (Convergence), in 1993.
3. This image, or some variation of it, could be seen throughout the Caracas metro throughout 2007. By the time of a later research trip to Venezuela in 2008, nearly a year after the failed campaign to reform the constitution (the second "motor"), the motif had been replaced by electioneering for candidates for the PSUV and various advertisements for beauty supplies featuring scantily clad female models.
4. China became an increasingly central partner for Venezuela during the Chávez years in an attempt to limit dependence on US markets. In addition to a market for its oil and a source of foreign investment, China provided Venezuela with cheap consumer goods, further lending the impression of a boom shared by all during the Chávez years. However, this newfound dependence on Chinese imports made it difficult to diversify the domestic industrial base.
5. The official name of Venezuela had been changed to "The Bolivarian Republic of Venezuela" with the approval by plebiscite of a new constitution in 1999.

Chapter 1

1. *Pueblo*—usually either translated as "the people" or left in the original Spanish—is a complex and contested term in Latin American political discourse. It carries with it a greater class inflection, usually associated with a notion of "the popular" than with the potentially neutral national identity that accompanies the English phrase "the (Venezuelan, English, Canadian, French, etc.) people." The *pueblo*, its theorizations, and implications for the Bolivarian Revolution will be explored in greater detail in chapter 3.
2. These early attempts to define the relationship between sovereignty, constituent power, and political community from seventeenth-century England

were in many ways preceded by other developments in the region in the earliest days of the modern world system, such as the Salamanca school of the Catholic Enlightenment in sixteenth-century Spain. In both cases, as in Jean Bodin's (1992) bifurcation of political authority between the "personal majesty" of the ruler and the "real sovereignty" of the people, thinkers attempted to strike a balance between notions of divine right and popular sovereignty—that is, between "natural" and "political" law (Loughlin 2014, 220). In the case of the Salamanca school, Francisco de Vitoria (1991) contended in *On Civil Power* that all civic power is both based in the community *and* in the divine will. The king's mandate is *popular* insofar as humans are *naturally* programmed as Aristotelian "political animals." Similar reasoning posits that the king receives his power from God, even though the office itself is created by the purely temporal commonwealth (11–13). Another key Salamanca theorist, Francisco de Suárez, reasoned that the sovereign people did not *delegate* their power to the king, but rather alienated it to him. The king, in turn, was above the law of the land as its secular origin but could be overthrown by the people if he breaks their trust (Morse 1989, 102–103). Suárez's schematization of civil power also incorporated another important secular aspect to its moral universe; for him, the justness or unjustness of any given law or person would be determined by its correspondence to the *common good*, which is both the basis and the goal of any human community (Perieira 2007). However, like their North Atlantic counterparts a century later, the thinkers of the Salamanca school's attempt to secularize and render immanent the basis of political authority—an absolute precondition for any conceptualization or praxis of constituent power (Kalyvas 2005, 229)—remained a specter at the extremes of political experience and a response to the crises in authority that accompanied the Reformation, colonization, and the spread of the secular Enlightenment.

3. See, for an early example, his *Libro Azul* (Chávez 2013).
4. Of course, El Libertador is not alone. The Misiones Bolivarianas—the social programs that target the health, educational, and cultural needs of the population along operational principles of *cogestión*—take their names from familiar and reconstructed figures from Venezuela's past: heroes of the independence wars like Ríbas, Sucre, and Miranda; more recent pan-American figures like Che Guevara; leaders of the indigenous resistance to Spanish colonialism like Guaicaipuro; and many more. These aspects of official discourse are also replicated and reworked by the rank and file of the revolution, who, following a long tradition of grassroots political and religious syncretism, reshape these figures into examples, protectors, and arguments as they navigate their daily lives (Kingsbury 2015; Salas de Lecuna 1987).
5. *Llanero*—one from the *llanos*, or the plains of southern Venezuela. The *llanos* have historically occupied a space in the national imaginary analogous to the "Wild West" in the United States—a vast territory on the fringes of civilized law and order, sparsely populated by ungovernable subjects.
6. Bolívar also included a fifth branch: a hereditary senate. Bolívar intended for

this institution to be made up of Liberators such as himself—revolutionary war heroes who had exhibited sufficient self-sacrifice and republican virtue to arbitrate among the inevitable interest groups and class conflict of the postcolony.

7. In the Decreto de Guerra a Muerte (Declaration of War to the Death) Bolívar makes no mention of abolishing slavery. Three years later he would do so in a special decree and would insist upon abolition for the rest of his life.

Chapter 2

1. These categories and their significance for the Bolivarian Revolution will be examined in greater depth in the following chapter.

2. Pérez was previously president from 1974 to 1979, a term which corresponded with a massive boom in international oil prices. The corresponding expansionary cycle in the Venezuelan economy failed to take for a number of reasons, most significantly corruption, a poorly executed and insincere "nationalization" of the oil industry in 1975, and a lack of political or social infrastructure to adequately reinvest the newfound wealth. He left office in 1979 under the cloud of corruption charges that cost his party the presidency.

3. The actual tally remains a point of politicized disagreement in Venezuela. Supporters of the government tend to favor the higher estimates of third-party investigators while opponents hew closer to the official count of just under three hundred.

4. It bears mentioning, however, that that candidate was Dr. Rafael Caldera, founder of COPEI, who read the political tea leaves and founded a new party—Convergencia por Venezuela (Convergence for Venezuela)—that promised a clean break from Puntofijo and, tellingly, an amnesty for the soldiers being held for the attempted coups of 1992.   In the offing, the latter was the much easier promise for Caldera to fulfill.

5. The neologism *buhoneroización* is based on the term *buhonero*, itself a Venezuela-ism for an informal worker, usually a merchant that operates on sidewalks and in ad hoc malls and plazas set up in the interstices of more conventional marketplaces.

6. For more on the securitization and spatial impacts of structural adjustment in the 1990s, see chapter 4.

7. There have been further instances of the PSUV expelling dissidents. Public figures from Marea Socialista, for example, have been expelled for criticizing the government's rapprochement with land owners and other traditional elites, long before the collective's public break with the PSUV (María 2014).

Chapter 3

1. Here Dussel is explicitly adapting Negri's distinction between the Latin terms *potentia* and *potestas* for his own purposes. Drawing on Spinoza's metaphysics, Negri uses *potentia* and *potestas* as analogues, respectively, to

constituent and constituted power as the foundational antinomies of bourgeois thought (Negri 1991, 215).

2. The original lyrics were also charged with revolutionary fervor. For example:
   "¡Abajo Cadenas! ¡Abajo Cadenas! Gritaba el señor, gritaba el señor, y el
   pobre en su choza libertad pidió" (Put down your chains . . . shouted the
   lord, and the poor in their huts demanded freedom). For the speech in full,
   see TeleSur (2009).

3. On the original formulation of *bricolage* and *bricoleurs* and their relationship
   to discourse, see Lévi-Strauss (1973, 15–33).

4. The CTV had long been considered by many to be the labor wing of AD. Its
   leadership, in particular, had since at least the 1970s dropped any pretense
   of working-class militancy in favor of a policy of shared management that
   saw the interests of workers and management (and thus of workers and the
   state) as common (Ellner 2008).

5. Subsequent investigations have implicated police sharpshooters from anti-
   Chavista parts of Caracas in the killings. To this day none of the intellectual
   masterminds of the coup or killings have been held accountable, though in
   2009 members of the opposition-controlled Caracas Metropolitan Police were
   sentenced for their roles in the shooting deaths of pro- and antigovernment
   forces at the Llaguno bridge in downtown Caracas.

6. 23 de Enero is a notoriously restive and left-leaning district named after a
   housing project in the east of Caracas. On the area's history, politics, and
   place in Venezuela's political imaginary, see especially Velasco (2015).

7. After the renaming of the country with the new constitution in 1999, many
   of Venezuela's official symbols were also changed. Among other changes,
   an eighth star was added to the flag. The opposition immediately raised
   protests that Chávez had overstepped his mandate and refused to use the
   new symbols; one can often divine the political allegiances of a particular
   neighborhood based on the flags displayed by its inhabitants and local
   government offices.

8. Beasley-Murray (2012) refers to this mobilization as a "pro-Chávez multitude"
   (294), which already suggests a degree of coherence and differentiation
   precluded by Negri's all-encompassing monism.

9. Obviously, this does not include members of the military who took part in the
   April 2002 coup, nor those who occupied eastern Caracas's Plaza Altamira
   in the fall of that year in open rebellion against the Chávez government.
   The composition of forces in the military is indeed an interesting question
   in Venezuela. While Chávez enjoyed wide support in the military and often
   played up his identity as a former officer, there remained in the barracks a
   degree of resistance to some of the changes proposed for the Fuerza Armada
   Nacional (National Armed Force, FAN). Perhaps the most significant tension
   has been around the very nature of the FAN as either a "traditional" and
   professional standing army or a "popular militia" of the armed and politicized
   public, an issue that was hotly debated in the lead-up to the (ultimately
   failed) constitutional referendum of December 2007. Finally, Chávez has been

criticized by many for including many former and current service members in his government and in the social programs of "Plan Bolívar 2000" both for the supposed "militarization" of Venezuelan society (a critique usually levied by the opposition and liberal observers) and for the fact that many of the ex-officers now make up a large part of the *derecha endogena* (internal right wing) of the Bolivarian Revolution (this latter critique issued by the left in Venezuela).

10. See, for a theorization and roadmap of the consejo's increased role in governance and politics in Venezuela, the Ministerio del Poder Popular para las Comunas y Movimientos Sociales (Popular Power Ministry for Communes and Social Movements) 2013–2016 Strategic Development Plan Comuna o Nada (Commune or Nothing) available at http://www.mpcomunas.gob.ve/plan-politico-estrategico-comuna-o-nada.

11. Cabello and Chacón were also participants—along with Chávez—in the attempted MBR-200 coup in 1992.

Chapter 4

1. I am extremely grateful to Theresa Enright for help in working through the thought of Henri Lefebvre for the purposes of this chapter. Any errors are of course entirely my own.

2. For a more detailed history of 23 de Enero and its uneven and restive development, see Bauchner (2009) and Velasco (2011, 2015).

3. In addition to a cabinet-level Ministry of Land Transportation, on March 16, 2014, the government announced the formation of Misión Transporte (Transportation Mission), one of the government's trademark *misiones bolivarianas* that promised to "revolutionize public transportation and to offer . . . inclusive, dignified, safe, high-quality, fair-priced forms of collective mobility" (Faoro 2014).

Chapter 5

1. "Adeco" refers to members of Acción Democrática. The MUD chose Jorge Ramos Allup, of AD, as its first speaker in the National Assembly. Ramos Allup has been a notoriously acerbic mainstay of Venezuelan politics since the Puntofijo era, who was described by former US ambassador William Brownfield as "crude, abrasive, arrogant, and thin-skinned" (Gollinger 2016). For the government and its supporters, the announcement of Ramos Allup as speaker of the AN was a clear signal of the MUD's desire to return Venezuela to the neoliberalizing Fourth Republic.

2. It is also worth noting that at the time elites in the Bolivian *media luna* (half-moon) departments of Santa Cruz, Pando, Beni, and Tarifa and in Ecuador in the Guayaquil region were also pursuing strategies of separation from the left-of-center governments in those countries (Eaton 2011).

3. First articulated in 1990, the Santiago Consensus ushered in what might

have been described as a "neostructural" adjustment to and correction for the full-throated, orthodox, neoliberalism championed by elites in Latin America and the North Atlantic in the 1980s (Leiva 2008). Neostructuralism purports to offer a more managed form of free market economics. Introduced by the United Nations' Economic Council on Latin America and the Caribbean (ECLAC), neostructuralism was presented as a paradigm capable of mitigating the negative social consequences of neoliberalism while prioritizing national and regional economic growth under the rules of capitalist globalization (Leiva 2008). Ironically, ECLAC had previously been most identified with its contributions to mid-twentieth-century dependency theory and import substitution industrialization (ISI). Rather than breaking from what ECLAC itself describes as the "savage capitalism" of neoliberalism, neostructuralism reinforces the export orientation of Latin American economies proscribed by neoliberal doctrine, a position it has not been revised since the 1990 publication of its report *Changing Production Patterns with Social Equity*.

4. Gil cites polls suggesting more than a third of the electorate self-identifies neither with the government nor the opposition; depending on when the survey is conducted, anywhere from 28 to 55 percent of those polled are *ni-nis*. He concludes, "Generally, [the *ni-ni*] is bigger than [Chavismo or the opposition], with the exception of those moments surrounding elections. This numerical superiority of the *ni-nis* means that the country isn't really as polarized" as is often suggested in both sympathetic and antagonistic portrayals of Bolivarian Venezuela (Gil Yepes 2011, 26).

5. The constitution stipulates that should a recall be convened more than halfway through the president's term, his or her vice president will serve out the remainder, meaning the PSUV would retain control of the executive branch until 2019. However, a referendum held prior to the midterm mark would trigger a new general election, from which the opposition clearly believe they have a better than good chance of emerging victorious.

Works Cited

Ackerman, Bruce. 1998. *We the People: Transformations*. Cambridge: Harvard University Press.

Acosta, Yamandú. 2008. *Filosofía Latinoamericana y Democracia en Clave de Derechos Humanos*. Montevideo: Editorial Nordan-Comunidad.

Agencia EFE—Servicio Internacional. 2014. "Sindicato de Metro presenta amparo contra Capriles y alcaldes opositores." *Agencia EFE—Servicio Internacional*. May 12, 2014.

Almandoz, Arturo. 1999. "Transfer of Urban Ideas: The Emergence of Venezuelan Urbanism in the Proposals for 1930s' Caracas." *International Planning Studies* 4(1): 79–94.

Alonso, Robert. n.d. "Sobre la Guarimba." http://www.venezuelanet.org/Sobre%20La%20Guarimba.htm. Accessed May 2, 2015.

Althusser, Louis. 2001a. *Lenin and Philosophy and Other Essays*. New York: Monthly Review.

Althusser, Louis. 2001b. *Machiavelli and Us*. New York: Verso.

Althusser, Louis. 2006. *The Philosophy of the Encounter: Later Writings, 1978–1987*. New York: Verso.

Amaya, Víctor. 2015. "Henrique Capriles: Maduro no quiere llegar a 2019." *Tal Cual Digital*. http://www.talcualdigital.com/Nota/121698/henrique-capriles-maduro-no-quiere-llegar-a-2019. December 23, 2015.

Angulo, Néstor. 2017. *Comuna: Construcción del Socialismo, desde Abajo y desde Adentro*. Caracas: El Perro y la Rana.

Appadurai, Arjun. 1996. *Modernity at Large: Cultural Dimensions of Globalization*. Minneapolis: University of Minnesota Press.

Araujo, Elizabeth, Fabricio Ojeda, Roberto Giusti, and Régulo Párraga. 1989. *El Día que Bajaron los Cerros*. Caracas: Editorial El Nacional.

Araujo, Orlando. 2010. *Venezuela Violenta*. Caracas: El Perro y la Rana.

Arditi, Benjamin. 2008. "Arguments about the Left Turns in Latin America: A Post-Liberal Politics?" *Latin American Research Review* 43(3): 59–81.

Arendt, Hannah. 1991. *On Revolution*. New York: Penguin.

Ari, Waskar. 2014. *Earth Politics: Religion, Decolonization, and Bolivia's Indigenous Intellectuals*. Durham: Duke University Press.

Azcargorta, Jesús, and Ivo Hernández. 2007. "PSUV: ¿Partido Hegemónico o Partido único?" *Temas de Coyuntura* 56: 7–23.

Azzellini, Dario. 2010. "Constituent Power in Motion: Ten Years of Transformation in Venezuela." *Socialism and Democracy* 24(2): 8–31.

Azzellini, Dario. 2015. *La Construcción de dos Lados: Poder Constituido y Poder Constituyente en Venezuela.* Caracas: El Perro y la Rana.

Azzellini, Dario, and Marina Sitrin. 2014. *They Can't Represent Us! Reinventing Democracy from Greece to Occupy.* New York: Verso.

Badiou, Alain. 2005. *Being and Event.* Trans. Oliver Feltham. New York: Continuum.

Badiou, Alain. 2007. *The Century.* Cambridge: Polity Press.

Badiou, Alain. 2010. "The Democratic Emblem." In Giorgio Agamben et al., *Democracy in What State?* New York: Columbia University Press, 6–15.

Badiou, Alain. 2009. *Theory of the Subject.* Trans. Bruno Bosteels. New York: Continuum.

Balakrishnan, Gopal. 2002. *The Enemy: An Intellectual Portrait of Carl Schmitt.* New York: Verso.

Balibar, Etienne, and Immanuel Wallerstein. 2011. *Race, Nation, Class: Ambiguous Identities.* New York: Verso.

Banko, Catalina. 2008. "De la Decentralización a la 'Nueva Geometría del Poder." *Revista Venezolana de Economía y Ciencias Sociales* 14(2): 167–84.

Bauchner, Joshua. 2009. "The City That Built Itself." *Triple Canopy.* http://www.canopycanopycanopy.com/contents/the_city_that_built_itself. Accessed April 1, 2013.

Bautista, Juliana. 2014. "Muchacho: Me desmarco y me deslindo de la violencia venga de donde venga." *El Nacional Online.* April 3, 2014. http://www.el-nacional.com/politica/Muchacho-desmarco-deslindo-violencia-venga_0_384561791.html. Accessed April 10, 2014

Bautista Urbaneja, Diego. 2013. *La Renta y el Reclamo: Ensayo Sobre Petróleo y Economía Política en Venezuela.* Caracas: Editorial Alfa.

Beasley-Murray, Jon. 2010. "Constituent Power and the Caracazo: The Exemplary Case of Venezuela." In *Latin America's Left Turns: Politics, Policies, and Trajectories of Change,* ed. Maxwell Cameron and Eric Hershberg. Boulder: Lynne Rienner, 217–244.

Beasley-Murray, Jon. 2012. *Posthegemony: Political Theory and Latin America.* Durham: Duke University Press.

Benhabib, Seyla. 2006. *Another Cosmopolitanism.* New York: Oxford University Press.

Beverly, John. 2011. *Latin Americanism after 9/11.* Durham: Duke University Press.

Biardeau, Javier. 2009. "Del Árbol de las tres raíces al 'Socialismo Bolivariano del Siglo XXI' ¿Una nueva narrativa ideológica de emancipación?" *Revista Venezolana de Economía y Ciencias Sociales* 15(1): 57–113.

Bodin, Jean. 1992. *On Sovereignty.* New York: Cambridge University Press.

Bolívar, Simón. 1985. *Doctrina del Libertador*. Caracas: Biblioteca Ayacucho.

Bolívar, Simón. 2003. *El Libertador: Writings of Simón Bolívar*. Ed. David Bushnell, trans. Frederick Hornoff. New York: Oxford University Press.

Borges, Trino. 2005. *Las rodriguerías de Samuel Robinson*. Mérida: Ediciones Mucuglifo.

Bosteels, Bruno. 2011. *Badiou and Politics*. Durham: Duke University Press.

Bray, Daniel, and Steven Slaughter. 2015. *Global Democratic Theory: A Critical Introduction*. Malden: Polity Press.

Briceño-León, Roberto. 2006. "Violence in Venezuela: Oil Rent and Political Crisis." *Ciência e Saude Coletiva* 11(2): 315–325.

Briceño-León, Roberto. 2012. "Three Phases of Homicidal Violence in Venezuela." *Ciência e Saude Coletiva* 17(12): 3233–3242.

Briggs, Ronald. 2010. *Tropes of Enlightenment in the Age of Bolívar: Simón Rodríguez and the American Essay at Revolution*. Nashville: Vanderbilt University Press.

Brown, Wendy. 2003. "Neoliberalism and the End of Liberal Democracy." *Theory & Event* 7(1): https://muse.jhu.edu/journals/theory_and_event/v007/7.1brown.html#NOTE2. Accessed June 20, 2003.

Brown, Wendy. 2006. "American Nightmare: Neoliberalism, Neoconservatism, and De-Democratization." *Political Theory* 34(6): 690–714.

Brown, Wendy. 2008. *Regulating Aversion: Tolerance in the Age of Identity and Empire*. Princeton: Princeton University Press.

Burnheim, John. 1985. *Is Democracy Possible? The Alternative to Electoral Politics*. Cambridge: Polity Press.

Buxton, Julia. 1999. "Degenerative Democracy." *Democratization* 6(1): 246–270.

Buxton, Julia. 2016. "Venezuela After Chávez." *New Left Review* 99: 3–25.

Caldeira, Teresa. 2001. *City of Walls: Crime, Segregation, and Citizenship in São Paulo*. Berkeley: University of California Press.

Cameron, Maxwell. 2002. "Democracy and the Separation of Powers: Threats, Dilemmas, and Opportunities in Latin America." *Canadian Journal of Latin American and Caribbean Studies* 27(53): 133–159.

Campbell, Tim. 2003. *The Quiet Revolution: Decentralization and the Rise of Political Participation in Latin American Cities*. Pittsburgh: University of Pittsburgh Press.

Canessa, Andrew. 2012. "New Indigenous Citizenship in Bolivia: Challenging the Liberal Model of the State and Its Subjects." *Latin American and Caribbean Ethnic Studies* 7(2): 201–221.

Cannon, Barry. 2014. "As Clear as MUD: Characteristics, Objectives, and Strategies of the Opposition in Bolivarian Venezuela." *Latin American Politics and Society* 56(4): 49–70.

Carrera Damas, Germán. 2008. "The Hidden Legacy of Simón Bolívar." In *Simón Bolívar: Essays on the Life and Legacy of the Liberator*, ed. D. Bushnell and L. Langley, 159–175. New York: Rowman & Littlefield.

Cartay, Rafael. 2003. *Fábrica de Ciudadanos: La Construcción de la Sensibilidad Urbana (Caracas 1870–1980)*. Caracas: Fundación Bigott.

Casarino, Cesare, and Antonio Negri. 2008. *In Praise of the Common*. Minneapolis: University of Minnesota Press.

Castañeda, Jorge. 2006. Latin America's Left Turn. *Foreign Affairs* 85(3): 28-43.

Castillo D'Imperio, Ocarina. 2003. *Los Años del Buldozer: Ideología y Política 1948–1958*. Caracas: Fondo Editorial Tropykos.

Chasteen, John. 2008. *Americanos: Latin America's Struggle for Independence*. New York: Oxford University Press.

Chávez, Hugo. 2005. *Understanding the Venezuelan Revolution: Hugo Chávez Talks to Marta Harnecker*. Trans. Chesa Boudin. New York: Monthly Review Press.

Chávez Frías, Hugo. 2007. *El Discurso de la Unidad*. Caracas: Ediciones Socialismo del Siglo XXI.

Chávez Frías, Hugo. 2012. *Golpe de Timón*. Caracas: Correo del Orinoco.

Chávez Frías, Hugo. 2013. *El Libro Azul*. Caracas: Correo del Orinoco.

Chávez Frías, Hugo. 2014. *Hugo Chávez: La Construcción del Socialismo del Siglo XXI. Discursos del Comandante Supremo ante la Asamblea Nacional 1999–2012 (Tomo 3: 2005–2008)*. Caracas: Fondo Editorial de la Asemblean Nacional 'Willian Lara.'

Cheresky, Isodoro. 2012. "Ciudadanía y Democracia Continua." In *Giros Culturales en la Marea Rosa de América Latina*, ed. Marc Zimmerman and Luis Ochoa Bilbao, 88–118. Houston: Editorial LACASA.

Christodoulidis, Emilios. 2007. "Against Substitution: The Constitutional Thinking of Dissensus." In *The Paradox of Constitutionalism: Constituent Power and Constitutional Form*, ed. Martin Loughlin and Neil Walker, 189–208. Oxford: Oxford University Press.

Ciccariello-Maher, George. 2007a. "Dual Power in the Venezuelan Revolution." *Monthly Review* 59(4): 42–56.

Ciccariello-Maher, George. 2007b. "Toward a Racial Geography of Caracas." *Qui Parle* 16(2): 39–71.

Ciccariello-Maher, George. 2013. *We Created Chávez: A People's History of the Venezuelan Revolution*. Durham: Duke University Press.

Ciccariello-Maher, George. 2014a. "Building the Commune: Insurgent Government, Communal State." *South Atlantic Quarterly* 113(4): 791–806.

Ciccariello-Maher, George. 2014b. "Venezuelan Jacobins." *Jacob Magazine Online*. March 13, 2014. https://www.jacobinmag.com/2014/03/venezuelan-jacobins. Accessed March 28, 2014.

Ciccariello-Maher, George. 2014c. "Collective Panic in Venezuela." *Jacobin Magazine Online*. June 18, 2014. https://www.jacobinmag.com/2014/06/collective-panic-in-venezuela/. Accessed June 20, 2014.

Colectivo Situaciones. 2002. *Notes for a New Social Protagonism*. Brooklyn: Autonomedia.

Colón-Ríos, Joel. 2011. "Carl Schmitt and Constituent Power in Latin

American Courts: The Cases of Venezuela and Colombia." *Constellations* 18(3): 365–388.

Colón-Ríos, Joel. 2012. *Weak Constitutionalism: Democratic Legitimacy and the Question of Constituent Power.* New York: Routledge.

Coronil, Fernando. 1997. *The Magical State: Nature, Money, and Modernity in Venezuela.* Chicago: University of Chicago Press.

Coronil, Fernando. 2011. "The Future in Question: History and Utopia in Latin America (1989–2010)." In *Business as Usual: The Roots of the Global Financial Meltdown*, ed. Craig Calhoun and Georgi Derluguian, 231–264. New York: New York University Press.

Coronil, Fernando, and Julie Skurski. 1999. "Dismembering and Remembering the Nation: The Semantics of Political Violence in Venezuela." *Comparative Studies in Society and History* 33(2): 288–337.

Corrales, Javier, and Michael Penfold. 2011. *Dragon in the Tropics: Hugo Chávez and the Political Economy of Revolution in Venezuela.* Washington, DC: Brookings Institute.

Correo del Orinoco. 2014. "Así marcharon trabajadores del Metro de Caracas contra los ataques fascistas." *Correo del Orinoco Online.* May 12, 2014. http://www.correodelorinoco.gob.ve/foto-dia/trabajadores-metro-caracas-piden-al-mp-investigar-ataques-fascistas-fotos/. Accessed June 20, 2015

Cristi, Renato. 1998. "Carl Schmitt on Sovereignty and Constituent Power." In *Law as Politics: Carl Schmitt's Critique of Liberalism*, ed. David Dyzenhaus, 179–195. Durham: Duke University Press.

Curato, Nicole. 2014. "Participation without Deliberation? The Crisis of Venezuelan Democracy." *Democratic Theory* 1(2): 113–121.

Dean, Jodi. 2012. *The Communist Horizon.* New York: Verso.

Dean, Jodi. 2016. *Crowds and Party.* New York: Verso.

Deleuze, Gilles. 1988. "A Philosophical Concept . . ." *Topoi* 7: 111–112.

Denis, Roland. 2005. *Los Fabricantes de la Rebelión: Movimento Popular, Chavismo, y Sociedad en los años noventa.* Caracas: Editorial Nuevo Sur.

Denis, Roland. 2013. "Definativamente llegamos al llegadero." April 7, 2013. http://www.aporrea.org/actualidad/a165356.html. Accessed April 23, 2014.

Denis, Roland. 2014. "Giordani: ¿Cuál Rendición de Cuentas?" http://www.aporrea.org/actualidad/a190090.html. Accessed June 25, 2014.

Diamond, Larry. 2002. "Elections without Democracy: Thinking about Hybrid Regimes." *Journal of Democracy* 13(2): 21–35.

Días, Trino, Luis Cipriano Rodríguez, and Silvio Villegas. 1996. *Venezuela: La República Subastrada: La Deuda Externa y sus Consequencias, 1830–1993.* Caracas: Los Heraldos Negros.

Diehl, Jackson. 1983. "Traffic-Bound Caracas Gets a Metro and a Sleek Solution to Urban Tangle." *Washington Post.* March 1, 1983. Final Edition, First Section: A16.

DiJohn, Jonathan. 2009. *From Windfall to Curse? Oil and Industrialization in Venezuela, 1920 to the Present.* University Park: Pennsylvania State University Press.

Drake, Paul. 2009. *Between Anarchy and Tyranny: A History of Democracy in Latin America*. Palo Alto: Stanford University Press.

Dryzek, John. 2009. "Democratization as Deliberative Capacity Building." *Comparative Political Studies* 49(11): 1379–1402.

Duno-Gottberg, Luis. 2011. "The Color of Mobs: Racial Politics, Ethnopopulism, and Representation in the Chávez Era." In *Venezuela's Bolivarian Democracy: Participation, Politics, and Culture under Chávez*, ed. David Smilde and Daniel Hellinger, 271–297. Durham: Duke University Press.

Duno-Gottberg, Luis. 2013. "'Mala conductas': Nuevos Sujetos de la Política Popular Venezolana." *Espacio Abierto: Cuaderno Venezolano de Sociologia* 22(2): 265–275.

Dussel, Enrique. 1995. "Eurocentrism and Modernity." In *The Postmodernism Debate in Latin America*, ed. John Beverly, José Oviedo, and Michael Aronna, 65–76. Durham: Duke University Press.

Dussel, Enrique. 2006. *20 Tesis de Política*. Mexico, DF: Siglo XXI.

Dussel, Enrique. 2007. *Política de la Liberación: Historia Mundial y Crítica*. Madrid: Editorial Trotta.

Dyzenhaus, David. 2007. "The Politics of the Question of Constituent Power." In *The Paradox of Constitutionalism: Constituent Power and Constitutional Form*, ed. Martin Loughlin and Neil Walker, 129–145. Oxford: Oxford University Press.

Dyzenhaus, David. 2012. "Constitutionalism in an Old Key: Legality and Constituent Power." *Global Constitutionalism* 1(2): 229–260.

Eaton, Kent. 2004. *Politics Beyond the Capital: The Design of Subnational Institutions in Latin America*. Stanford: Stanford University Press.

Eaton, Kent. 2011. "Conservative Autonomy Movements: Territorial Dimensions of Ideological Conflict in Bolivia and Ecuador." *Comparative Politics* 43(3): 291–310.

Elden, Stuart. 2007. "There Is a Politics of Space because Space Is Political: Henri Lefebvre and the Production of Space." *Radical Philosophy Review* 10(2): 101–116.

Ellner, Steve. 2008. *Rethinking Venezuelan Politics: Class, Conflict and the Chávez Phenomenon*. Boulder: Lynne Rienner.

Ellner, Steve (ed). 2014. *Latin America's Radical Left: Challenges and Complexities of Political Power in the Twenty-First Century*. New York: Rowman & Littlefield.

Ellner, Steve, and Miguel Tinker Salas. 2007. "The Venezuelan Exceptionalism Thesis: Separating Myth from Reality." In *Venezuela: Hugo Chávez and the Decline of an "Exceptional Democracy,"* ed. Steve Ellner and Miguel Tinker Salas, 3–15. New York: Rowman & Littlefield.

Escobar, Arturo. 2007. "Words and Knowledges Otherwise." *Cultural Studies* 21(2–3): 179–210.

Escobar, Arturo. 2010. "Latin America at a Crossroads: Alternative

Modernizations, Post-Liberalism, or Post-Development?" *Cultural Studies* 24(1): 1–65.

Evans, Nicmer. 2016. "PSUV y MUD Secuestraron Electoralmente el País." http://m.panorama.com.ve/opinion/Nicmer-Evans-Psuv-y-Mud-secuestraron-electoralmente-al-pais-20160412-0020.html. Accessed December 15, 2016.

Faddul, Venus. 2013. "Casa Comunal 'El Costurero' en Mérida es Rehabilitada por el Poder Popular Organizado." August 12, 2013. http://www.abrebrecha.com/299594_Casa-comunal-%E2%80%9CEl-costurero%E2%80%9D-en-M%C3%A9rida-es-rehabilitada-por-el-poder-popular-organizado.html. Accessed July 20, 2015.

Fajardo, Victor, and Miguel Lacabana. 1989. "Desequilibrio Externo y Políticas de Ajuste." In *Adios a la Bonanza? Crisis de la Distribución del ingreso en Venezuela*, ed. Hans-Peter Nissen and Bernard Mommer, 41–62. Caracas: Editorial Nueva Sociedad.

Faoro, Oriana. 2014. "Inicia 'Misión Transporte' con censo de transportistas en Caroní." *Correo del Caroní online*. July 9, 2014. http://www.correodelcaroni.com/index.php/cdad/item/16360-inicia-mision-transporte-con-censo-de-transportistas-en-caroni

Fariñas, Omar. 2009. "Hegemonía Bolivariana? Gramsci en la Venezuela Puntofijista y Contemporanea." *Context Latinoamericano* 11: 77–91.

Federici, Silvia. 2011. "Feminism and the Politics of the Commons." *The Commoner*. January 24, 2011. http://www.commoner.org.uk/?p=113. Accessed August 14, 2015.

Fernandes, Sujatha. 2007. "Barrio Women and Popular Politics in Chávez's Venezuela." *Latin American Politics and Society* 49(3): 97–127.

Fernandes, Sujatha. 2010. *Who Can Stop the Drums? Urban Social Movements in Chávez's Venezuela*. Durham: Duke University Press.

Ferrándiz Martín, Francisco. 1999. "El culto de María Lionza en Venezuela: Tiempos, Espacios, Cuerpos." *Alteridades* 9(18): 39–55.

Fisher, William, and Thomas Ponniah. 2003. *Another World Is Possible: Popular Alternatives to Globalization at the World Social Forum*. New York: Zed Books.

Foucault, Michel. 1991. "Governmentality." In *The Foucault Effect: Studies in Governmentality*, ed. Graham Burchell, Colin Gordon, and Peter Miller, 87–104. Chicago: University of Chicago Press.

Foucault, Michel. 2009. *Security, Territory, Population: Lectures at the Collège de France, 1977–1978*. New York: Picador.

Frank, Jason. 2010. *Constituent Moments: Enacting the People in Postrevolutionary America*. Durham: Duke University Press.

Gagnon, Jean-Paul, and Mark Chou. 2014. "Why Democratic Theory?" *Democratic Theory* 1(1): 1–8.

García Marco, Daniel. 2017. "'No votaría por la oposición. Y por Maduro, menos': El desencanto del barrio del 23 de Enero, el simbólico bastion del

Chavismo en Venezuela." *BBC Mundo*. April 22, 2017. http://www.bbc.com/mundo/noticias-america-latina-39677139. Accessed April 30, 2017.

García-Guadilla, María Pilar. 1997. "Crisis, Decentralización, y Gobernabilidad en el Área Metropolitana de Caracas." *América Latina Hoy* 15: 43–48.

García-Guadilla, María Pilar. 2011. "Urban Land Committees: Co-optation, Autonomy, and Protagonism." In *Venezuela's Bolivarian Democracy: Participation, Politics, and Culture under Chávez*, ed. David Smilde and Daniel Hellinger, 80–103. Durham: Duke University Press.

Garrido, Alberto. 2007. *Chávez con Uniforme*. Caracas: Ediciones Autor.

Gil Yepes, José Antonio. 2011. *Como Ganar o Perder las Elecciones Presidenciales de 2012 en Venezuela*. Caracas: Ediciones Libros Marcados.

Giordani, Jorge. 2014. "Testimonio y Responsibilidad ante la Historia." http://www.aporrea.org/ideologia/a190011.html. Accessed June 19, 2014.

O Globo. 2012. "Capriles Quer Seguir Modelo Econômico de Lula." February 12, 2012. http://oglobo.globo.com/mundo/capriles-quer-seguir-modelo-economico-de-lula-3964478. Accessed June 25, 2015.

Goldstein, Alyosha. 2014. "Colonialism, Constituent Power, and Popular Sovereignty." *J19: The Journal of 19th Century Americanists* 2(1): 148–153.

Goldstein, Ariel. 2012. "Capriles y el modelo Lula." *Pagina12*. June 14, 2012. http://www.pagina12.com.ar/diario/elmundo/4-196310-2012-06-14.html. Accessed June 25, 2015.

Gollinger, Eva. 2016. "Wikileaks Reveals What the US Really Thinks of Henry Ramos Allup." *TeleSur Online*. January 6, 2016. http://www.telesurtv.net/english/opinion/WikiLeaks-Reveal-What-the-US-Really-Thinks-of-Henry-Ramos-Allup-20160106-0049.html. Accessed January 10, 2016.

Gómez, Gonzalo. 2014a. "El I Congreso del PSUV Podría Ser el Último de la Revolución." www.aporrea.org. http://www.aporrea.org/ideologia/a185552.html. Accessed May 15, 2015.

Gómez, Gonzalo. 2014b. "10 Proposals for Venezuela's Maduro." *Socialist Worker*. June 24, 2014. https://socialistworker.org/2014/06/24/ten-proposals-for-maduro. Accessed May 15, 2015.

Gómez García, Alí. 2014. *Falsas, Maliciosas, y Escandalosas Reflexiones de un Ñángara*. Caracas: El Perro y La Rana.

González, Mike. 2014. "The Reckoning: The Future of the Venezuelan Revolution." *International Socialism* 143. http://isj.org.uk/the-reckoning-the-future-of-the-venezuelan-revolution/. Accessed May 15, 2015.

González, Silverio. 2005. *La Ciudad Venezolana: Una Interpretación de su Espacio y Sentido en la Convivencia Nacional*. Caracas: Fundación para la Cultural Urbana.

González-Vicente, Ruben. 2012. "The Political Economy of Sino-Peruvian Relations: A New Dependency?" *Journal of Current Chinese Affairs* 41(1): 97–131.

Goodale, Mark, and Nancy Postero (eds.). 2013. *Neoliberalism, Interrupted:*

Social Change and Contested Governance in Contemporary Latin America.
Palo Alto: Stanford University Press.

Gott, Richard. 2000. *In the Shadow of the Liberator: Hugo Chávez and the Transformation of Venezuela.* New York: Verso.

Gott, Richard. 2008a. "Venezuela under Chávez: The Originality of the 'Bolivarian' Project." *New Political Economy* 13(4): 475–490.

Gott, Richard. 2008b. *Guerrilla Movements in Latin America.* New York: Seagull Books.

Grohmann, Peter. 1996. *Macarao y Su Gente: Movimento Popular y Autogestión en los Barrios de Caracas.* Caracas: Editorial Nueva Sociedad.

Guattari, Fèlix, and Suely Rolnik. 2008. *Molecular Revolution in Brazil.* Trans. Karel Clapshow and Brian Holmes. Los Angeles: Semiotext(e).

Habermas, Jürgen. 1991. *The Structural Transformation of the Public Sphere: An Inquiry into a Category of Bourgeois Society.* Cambridge: MIT Press.

Hager, Carol. 2012. "Revisiting the Ungovernability Debate: Regional Governance and Sprawl in the USA and UK." *International Journal of Urban and Regional Research* 36(4): 817–830.

Hardt, Michael, and Antonio Negri. 1994. *Labor of Dionysus: A Critique of the State Form.* Minneapolis: University of Minnesota Press.

Hardt, Michael, and Antonio Negri. 2000. *Empire.* Cambridge: Harvard University Press.

Hardt, Michael, and Antonio Negri. 2004. *Multitude: War and Democracy in the Age of Empire.* New York: Penguin.

Hardt, Michael, and Antonio Negri. 2009. *Commonwealth.* Cambridge: Harvard University Press.

Hardt, Michael, and Paolo Virno. 1996. *Radical Thought in Italy: A Potential Politics.* Minneapolis: University of Minnesota Press.

Harnecker, Marta. 2005. *Haciendo Camino al Andar: Experiencias de Ocho Gobiernos Locales de América Latina.* Caracas: Monte Ávila Editores.

Harvey, David. 2005. *A Brief History of Neoliberalism.* New York: Oxford University Press.

Harvey, David. 2008. "The Right to the City." *New Left Review* 53: 23–40.

Harvey, David, and Cuz Potter. 2009. "The Right to the Just City." In *Searching for the Just City: Debates in Urban Theory and Practice*, ed. Peter Marcuse, James Connolly, Johannes Novy, Ingrid Olivo, Cuz Potter, and Justin Steil, 40–51. New York: Routledge.

Hawkins, Kirk. 2003. "Populism in Venezuela: The Rise of Chavismo." *Third World Quarterly* 24(6): 1137–1160.

Hawkins, Kirk. 2016. "Responding to Radical Populism: Chavismo in Venezuela." *Democratization* 23(2): 242–262.

Hawkins, Kirk, and David Hansen. 2006. "Dependent Civil Society: The Círculos Bolivarianos in Venezuela." *Latin American Research Review* 41(1): 102–132.

Hellinger, Daniel. 2011. *Comparative Politics of Latin America: Democracy at Last?* New York: Routledge.

Herrera Salas, Jesús María. 2005. "Ethnicity and Racism: The Political Economy of Racism in Venezuela." *Latin American Perspectives* 32(2): 72–91.

Hirsch, Alexander. 2011. "Fugitive Reconciliation: The Agonistics of Respect, Resentment, and Responsibility in Post-Conflict Society." *Contemporary Political Theory* 10(12): 166–189.

Hobbes, Thomas. 2000. *Leviathan.* New York: Cambridge University Press.

Hobsbawm, Eric. 1995. *Age of Extremes: The Short Twentieth Century, 1914–1991.* London: Abacus Books.

Holloway, John. 2002. *Change the World Without Taking Power: The Meaning of Revolution Today.* London: Pluto Press.

Humphrey, Michael. 2014. "Violence and Urban Governance in Neoliberal Cities in Latin America." *ARENA Journal* 41/42: 236–259.

Humphrey, Michael, and Estela Valverde. 2014. "Hope and Fear in Venezuelan Democracy: Violence, Citizen Insecurity, and Competing Neoliberal and Socialist Urban Imaginaries." In *Democracy, Revolution, and Geopolitics in Latin America: Venezuela and the International Politics of Discontent*, ed. Luis Fernando Angosto-Ferrández, 147–156. New York: Routledge.

Iturriza, Reinaldo. 2006. *27 de Febrero de 1989: Interpretaciones y Estrategias.* Caracas: El Perro y la Rana.

Jaume, Lucien. 2007. "Constituent Power in France The Revolution and its Consequences." In *The Paradox of Constitutionalism: Constituent Power and Constitutional Form*, ed. Martin Loughlin and Neil Walker, 67–85. Oxford: Oxford University Press.

Jefferson, Thomas. 2007. *Michael Hardt Presents Thomas Jefferson.* Ed. Michael Hardt. New York: Verso.

Jenkins, Rhys. 2012. "Latin American and China—a New Dependency?" *Third World Quarterly* 33(7): 1337–1358.

Jorge, Carlos. 2005. *Un Nuevo Poder: Estudio Filosófico de las ideas morales y políticas de Simón Rodríguez.* Caracas: Ediciones Rectorado.

Kalyvas, Andreas. 2005. "Popular Sovereignty, Democracy, and Constituent Power." *Constellations* 12(2): 223–244.

Kalyvas, Andreas, and Ira Katznelson. 2008. *Liberal Beginnings: Making a Republic for Moderns.* Cambridge: Cambridge University Press.

Kapcia, Antoni. 2008. *Cuba in Revolution: A History since the Fifties.* London: Reaktion Books.

Karl, Terry. 1997. *The Paradox of Plenty: Oil Booms and Petrostates.* Berkeley: University of California Press.

Karl, Terry. 1999. "The Perils of the Petro-State: Reflections on the Paradox of Plenty." *Journal of International Affairs* 53(1): 31–48.

Kelsen, Hans. 1945. *General Theory of Law and State.* Trans. Anders Weberg. New York: Russell and Russell Press.

Kingsbury, Donald. 2013. Between Multitude and Pueblo: Venezuela's Bolivarian Revolution and the Government of Ungovernability." *New Political Science* 34(4): 567–585.

Kingsbury, Donald. 2015. "Bolívar as Precursor: Contested Mythology, Social Movements, and Twenty-First Century Socialism in Bolivarian Venezuela." *Canadian Journal of Latin American and Caribbean Studies* 40(3): 255–257.

Kingsbury, Donald. 2016a. "Oil's Colonial Residues: Geopolitics, Identity, and Resistance in Venezuela." *Bulletin of Latin American Research* 35(4): 423–436.

Kingsbury, Donald. 2016b. "From Populism to Protagonism (and Back?) in Bolivarian Venezuela: Rethinking Ernesto Laclau's *On Populist Reason*." *Journal of Latin American Cultural Studies* 25(4): 495–515.

Kohan, Walter. 2015. *The Inventive Schoolmaster: Simón Rodríguez*. Trans. Vicki Jones and Jason Thomas Wozniak. Rotterdam: Sense Publishers.

Kozloff, Nicholas. 2007. *Hugo Chávez: Oil, Politics, and the Challenge to the US*. New York: Palgrave.

Kutiyski, Yordan, and André Krouwel. 2014. "Narrowing the Gap: Explaining the Increasing Competitiveness of the Venezuelan Opposition." *Latin American Politics and Society* 56(4): 72–97.

Lacabana, Miguel, and Carmen Cariola. 2003. "Globalization and Metropolitan Expansion: Residential Strategies and Livelihoods in Caracas and Its Periphery." *Environment and Urbanization* 15(1): 65–74.

Laclau, Ernesto. 2005. *On Populist Reason*. New York: Verso.

Laclau, Ernesto. 2006. "La Deriva Populista y la centroizuierda latinoamericana." *Nueva Sociedad* 205: 56–61.

Laclau, Ernesto, and Chantal Mouffe. 1985. *Hegemony and Socialist Strategy: Towards a Radical Democratic Politics*. New York: Verso.

Lajoie, Steffen. 2010. "Organizing, Power, and Political Support in Caracas, Venezuela." In *Cities for All: Proposals and Experiences towards the Right to the City*, ed. Ana Sugranyes and Charlotte Mathivet, 227–232. Santiago, Chile: Habitat International Coalition.

Lander, Edgardo. 2007. "El Partido Único y el Debate sobre el Socialismo del Siglo XXI." *Tareas* 26: 31–38.

Lander, Edgardo. 2008. "El Referéndum sobre la Reforma Constitucional al el Proceso Politico en Venezuela entra en una Encrucijada Crítica." *Revista Venezolana de Economía y Ciencias Sociales* 14(2): 133–166.

Lefort, Claude. 1986. *The Political Forms of Modern Society: Bureaucracy, Democracy, Totalitarianism*. Ed. John Thompson. Cambridge: MIT Press.

Leiva, Fernando. 2008. *Latin American Neostructuralism: The Contradictions of Post-Neoliberal Development*. Minneapolis: University of Minnesota Press.

León, Ibis. 2016. "López Maya: La Protesta en la era del Chavismo recuerda a la Etapa Pos-Caracazo." http://efectococuyo.com/politica/lopez-maya-la-protesta-en-la-era-del-chavismo-recuerda-a-la-etapa-pos-caracazo. Accessed July 20, 2016.

Levine, Daniel. 1973. *Conflict and Political Change in Venezuela*. Princeton: Princeton University Press.

Lévi-Strauss, Claude. 1973. *The Savage Mind*. Chicago: University of Chicago Press.

Levitsky, Stephen, and Lucan Way. 2002. "The Rise of Competitive Authoritarianism." *Journal of Democracy* 13(2): 51–65.

Linárez, Pedro Pablo. 2006. *La Lucha Armada en Venezuela: Apuntes sobre Guerra de GuerrillasVenezolanos en el Contexto de la Guerra Fría (1959–1979) y el Rescate de los Desaparecidos*. Caracas: Ediciones Universidad Bolivariana de Venezuela.

Locke, John. 1998. *Two Treatises of Government*. New York: Cambridge University Press.

Lombardi, John. 2008. "History and Our Heroes." In *Simón Bolívar: Essays on the Life and Legacy of the Liberator*, ed. D. Bushnell and L. Langley, 176–187. New York: Rowman & Littlefield.

López, Edgar. 2013. "Sabino Romero, el Irreductible." March 5, 2013. http://www.el-nacional.com/regiones/Sabino-Romero-irreductible_0_148186152.html. Accessed March 7, 2013.

López Calero, Iván. 2017. *Ezequiel Zamora y la Rebelión Popular de 1846–1847*. Caracas: El Perro y la Rana.

López Maya, Margarita. 2003. "The Venezuelan *Caracazo* of 1989: Popular Protest and Institutional Weakness." *The Journal of Latin American Studies* 35: 117–137.

López Maya, Margarita. 2005. *Del Viernes Negro al Referendo Revocatorio*. Caracas: Ediciones Alfa.

López Maya, Margarita. 2006. "Venezuela 2001–2004: Actores y estrategias en la luch hegemónica." In *Sujetos sociales y nuevas formas de protesta en la historia reciente de América Latina*, ed. Gerardo Caetano, 23–48. Buenos Aires: CLASCO.

López Maya, Margarita. 2011. *Democracia Participativa en Venezuela (1999–2010): Origenes, Leyes, Percepciones, y Desafíos*. Caracas: Universidad Católica Andrés Bello.

Loughlin, Martin. 2007. "Constituent Power Subverted: From English Constitutional Argument to British Constitutional Practice." In *The Paradox of Constitutionalism: Constituent Power and Constitutional Form*, ed. Martin Loughlin and Neil Walker, 27–48. Oxford: Oxford University Press.

Loughlin, Martin. 2014. "The Concept of Constituent Power." *European Journal of Political Theory* 13(2): 218–237.

Lugo-Galicia, Hernán. 2006. "'Operadores Políticos' se Engargarán de la I Fase del Partido Socialista Unido." *El Nacional*. December 17, 2006. Accessed May 10, 2015.

Lugo-Galicia, Hernán. 2007a. "Bareto: El PSUV tiene que ser flexible y no un MVR electoral." *El Nacional*. January 27, 2007. Accessed May 10, 2015.

Lugo-Galicia, Hernán. 2007b. "Partidos Chavistas Esperean Ser Invitados a Miraflores." *El Nacional.* February 16, 2007. Accessed May 10, 2015.

Lummis, C. Douglas. 1997. *Radical Democracy.* Ithaca: Cornell University Press.

Lynch, John. 1992. *Caudillos in Spanish America, 1800–1850.* New York: Oxford University Press.

Lynch, John. 2006. *Bolívar: A Life.* New Haven: Yale University Press.

Macpherson, C. B. 1977. *The Life and Times of Liberal Democracy.* New York: Oxford University Press.

Madera, Héctor. 2010. "Urban Land Committees, Venezuela." In *Cities for All: Proposals and Experiences towards the Right to the City*, ed. Ana Sugranyes and Charlotte Mathivet, 223–226. Santiago, Chile: Habitat International Coalition.

Maduro Moros, Nicolás. 2013. "Pórtico a el Libro Azul." In Hugo Chávez Frías, *El Libro Azul.* Caracas: Ediciones Correo del Orinoco.

Mainwaring, Scott. 2006. "The Crisis of Representation in the Andes." *Journal of Democracy* 17(3): 13–27.

Mainwaring, Scott, and Matthew Shugart. 1997. *Presidentialism and Democracy in Latin America.* New York: Cambridge University Press.

Marcano, Cristina, and Alberto Barrera Tyszka. 2005. *Hugo Chávez sin Uniforme: Una Historia Personal.* Buenos Aires: Debate.

Marcano Requena, Frank. 1979. *El Metro de Caracas: Una Estrategia Inmobiliaria.* Caracas: Facultad de Arquitectura y Urbanismo, Universidad Central de Venezuela.

Marcuse, Peter. 2009. "From Critical Urban Theory to the Right to the City." *City* (13)2: 185–197.

Marcuse, Peter. 2012. "Whose Right(s) to What City?" In *Cities for People, Not for Profit: Critical Urban Theory and the Right to the City*, ed. Neil Brenner, Peter Marcuse, and Margit Mayer, 24–41. New York: Routledge.

María, Eva. 2014. "Where Is the PSUV Headed?" *Socialist Worker.* August 14, 2014. https://socialistworker.org/2014/08/14/where-is-the-psuv-headed. Accessed May 15, 2015.

Marín, Carlos. 2011. *Dos Islas, un Abismo: AD a MIR (1948–1960).* Caracas: Fundación Celarg.

Márquez, Humberto. 2009. "Venezuela: Condena a Policías por Crímenes del Golpe de 2002." http://www.ipsnoticias.net/2009/04/venezuela-condena-a-policias-por-crimenes-del-golpe-de-2002/. Accessed July 21, 2014.

Martinez, Carlos, Michael Fox, and Jojo Farrell. 2010. *Venezuela Speaks! Voices from the Grassroots.* Oakland: PM Press.

Marx, Karl. 1988. *The Eighteenth Brumaire of Louis Bonaparte.* New York: International.

Mayer, Margit. 2009. "'The Right to the City' in the Context of Shifting Mottos of Urban Social Movements." *City* 13(2–3): 362–374.

McCann, Eugene. 2002. "Space, Citizenship, and the Right to the City: A Brief Overview." *GeoJournal* 58: 77–70.

McFarlane, Colin. 2009. Translocal Assemblages: Space, Power and Social Movements. *Geoforum* 40: 561–567.

McGuirk, Justin. 2014. *Radical Cities: Across Latin America in Search of a New Architecture*. New York: Verso.

Metro de Caracas, C.A. 1979. *El Metro de Caracas: Planificación, Proyecto, Construcción, Programación*. Caracas: Metro de Caracas, C.A.

Metro de Caracas, C.A. 1982. *El Metro de Caracas y su historia, La Gran Solución para Caracas, Tomo X*. Caracas: Metro de Caracas, C.A.

Metro de Caracas, C.A. 2007. *Un Metro en Revolución*. Caracas: Altolitho.

Meza, Alfredo, and Maolis Castro. 2016. "El Chavismo Impide el Desarrollo de la Marcha de la Oposición." *El País Online*. May 12, 2016. http://internacional.elpais.com/internacional/2016/05/11/america/1462985214_142746.html. Accessed August 22, 2016.

Mignolo, Walter. 2005. *The Idea of Latin America*. Malden: Blackwell.

Miller, Nicola. 2006. "The 'Immortal' Educator: Race, Gender, and Citizenship in Simón Rodríguez's Programme for Popular Education." *Hispanic Research Journal* 7(1): 11–20.

Millet, Richard, Jennifer Holmes, and Orland Pérez. 2009. *Latin American Democracy: Emerging Reality or Endangered Species?* New York: Routledge.

Ministerio del Poder Popular para la Comunicación y la Información. 2008. *Decálogo de las Leyes Habilitantes*. Caracas: Ministerio del Poder Popular para la Comunicación y la Información.

Mitchell, Don. 2003. *The Right to the City*. New York: Guilford Press.

Möllers, Christoph. 2007. "'We Are (Afraid of) the People': Constituent Power in German Constitutionalism." In *The Paradox of Constitutionalism: Constituent Power and Constitutional Form*, ed. Martin Loughlin and Neil Walker, 87–105. Oxford: Oxford University Press.

Mommer, Bernard. 2003. "Subversive Oil." In *Venezuelan Politics in the Chávez Era: Class, Polarization, and Conflict*, ed. Steve Ellner and Daniel Hellinger, 131–146. Boulder: Lynne Rienner.

Montesquieu, Charles. 1989. *The Spirit of the Laws*. New York: Cambridge University Press.

Moraña, Mabel, Enrique Dussel, and Carlos Jáuregui (eds.). 2008. *Coloniality at Large: Latin America and the Postcolonial Debate*. Durham: Duke University Press.

Morse, Richard. 1989. *New World Soundings: Culture and Ideology in the Americas*. Baltimore: Johns Hopkins University Press.

Motta, Sara. 2013. "'We are the ones we have been waiting for': The Feminization of Resistance in Venezuela." *Latin American Perspectives* 191(40): 35–54.

Mouffe, Chantal. 1992. "Democratic Politics Today." In *Dimensions of Radical Democracy: Pluralism, Citizenship, Community*, ed. Chantal Mouffe, 1–16. New York: Verso.

Mouffe, Chantal. 1999. "Deliberative Democracy or Agonistic Pluralism?" *Social Research* 66(3): 745.

Mouffe, Chantal. 2005. *On the Political.* New York: Routledge.

Müller, Luis García. 2001. *La Guerra Federal en Barinas: 1859–1863.* Barinas: Ediciones de la Universidad Ezequiel Zamora.

El Mundo (Venezuela). 2014. "TSJ Declaró Procedente Destitución de María Corina Machado." June 1, 2014. http://www.elmundo.com.ve/noticias/ actualidad/noticias/tsj-declaro-procedente-destitucion-de-maria-corina. aspx. Accessed June 12, 2014.

El Nacional. 2011. "Caracas tiene el metro cuadrado más costoso de America del Sur." *El Nacional.* November 29, 2012. Accessed July 6, 2014.

El Nacional. 2016. "Capriles: Quienes Antes Hablaban de Democracia Participativa Hoy No Quieren Elecciones." *El Nacional Web.* June 29, 2016. http://www.el-nacional.com/politica/Capriles-hablaban- democracia-participativa-elecciones_0_875312620.html. Accessed July 19, 2016.

Navarro, Hector. 2014. "Former Minister Navarro Launches Criticisms of the PSUV." https://venezuelanalysis.com/news/10790. Accessed May 17, 2015.

Navarro, Hector. 2015. "Hector Navarro: I'm Encouraging a Rebellion at the Bases of the PSUV." https://venezuelanalysis.com/analysis/11209. Accessed March 22, 2015.

Negri, Antonio. 1991. *The Savage Anomaly: The Power of Spinoza's Metaphysics and Politics.* Trans. Michael Hardt. Minneapolis: University of Minnesota Press.

Negri, Antonio. 1992. *Insurgencies: Constituent Power and the Modern State.* Minneapolis: University of Minnesota Press.

Negri, Antonio. 1996. "Constituent Republic." In *Radical Thought in Italy: A Potential Public,* ed. Michael Hardt and Paolo Virno, 213–224. Minneapolis: University of Minnesota Press.

Negri, Antonio. 2007. *Political Descartes: Reason, Ideology, and the Bourgeois Project.* New York: Verso.

Neuhouser, Kevin. 1992. "Democratic Stability in Venezuela: Elite Consensus or Class Compromise?" *American Sociological Review* 57(1): 117–135.

Neuman, William. 2014. "Slum Dwellers in Caracas Ask, What Protests?" *New York Times.* February 28, 2014. New York Edition: A1.

Noticias24. 2010. "Para Hugo Chávez, 'Ser Escuálido es una Enfermedad . . . y de las Graves." *Noticias24 online.* April 16, 2010. http://www.noticias24. com/actualidad/noticia/151577/ser-escualido-es-una- enfermedad/. Accessed June 20, 2015.

Noticias24. 2014. "Vándalos causan destrozos en Plaza Altamira: queman otra vez la caseta de Metrobús." *Noticias24 online.* May 6, 2014. http://www. noticias24.com/venezuela/noticia/237511/presuntos-encapuchados- incendian-caseta-del-metrobus-en-altamira/. Accessed February 10, 2015.

Noticiero Digital. 2012. "Chávez: A ese Cáncer lo Declaramos Escuálido y como tal será Tratado." *Noticiero Digital.* http://www.noticierodigital.com/2012/02/

chavez-a-ese-cancer-lo-declaramos-escualido-y-como-tal-sera-tratado/.
Accessed June 20, 2015.

Noticiero Digital. 2014. "Encapuchados asaltan estación de metro del Parque del Este, denucia El Troudi." May 27, 2014. http://www.noticierodigital.
com/2014/05/encapuchados-asaltan-estacion-de-metro-del-parque-del-este-denuncia-el-troudi/. Accessed February 10, 2015.

Ocaña Ortiz, Rosa Virginia. 2005. "Coordinación entre los gobiernos municipales y el gobierno metropolitano en materia de transporte urbano: Caracas." *Provincia* 13: 141–151.

Ocaña Ortiz, Rosa Virginia, and Inés Guardia Rolando. 2005. "El Transporte Urbano en Venezuela: Estudio de las Políticas Públicas y el Nuevo Rol del Estado (1991–2000)." *Provincia* 14: 159–182.

Ocaña Ortiz, Rosa Virginia, and Joheni Urdaneta. 2005. "Participación de los Municipios en la formación de la Política Nacional de Transporte Urbano en Venezuela." *Revista Venezolana de Gerencia* 10(30): 196–210.

O'Flynn, Ian, and Nicole Curato. 2015. "Deliberative Democratization: A Framework for Systemic Analysis." *Policy Studies* 36(3): 298–313.

Ojeda, Fabricio. 1970. *La Guerra del Pueblo*. Caracas: Edición Domingo Fuentes.

Padrino, Ender Ramírez. 2014. "El Troudi: Más de 200 usarios del Metro resultaron afectados por las manifestaciones." *El Nacional Online*. February 17, 2014. http://www.el-nacional.com/politica/Troudi-Metro-resultaron-afectados-manifestaciones_0_357564320.html. Accessed February 10, 2015.

Padrón Toro, Antonio. 1990. *Historia de un Boleto: El Metro de Caracas*. Caracas: APT Producciones.

Partido Socialista Unido de Venezuela (PSUV). 2014. *III Congreso, Partido Socialista Unido de Venezuela: ¡Por el legado del Comandante Supremo Hugo Chávez la militancia entra en Debate!* Caracas: PSUV.

Pereira, José. 2007. *Suárez: Between Scholasticism and Modernity*. Milwaukee: Marquette University Press.

Pili Hernández, Mary. 2007. "El PSUV no puede ser otro polo patriótico." *El Nacional*. March 8, 2007. Accessed May 12, 2015.

Portes, Alejandro, and Bryan Roberts. 2005. "The Free-Market City: Latin American Urbanization in the Years of the Neoliberal Experiment." *Studies in Comparative International Development* 40(1): 43–82.

Presidencia de la República Bolivariana de Venezuela. 2017. Gaceta Oficial de la República Bolivariana de Venezuela Extraordinario, Numero 6, 295.

Purcell, Mark. 2014. "Possible Worlds: Henry Lefebvre and Right to the City." *Journal of Urban Affairs* 36(1): 141–154.

Quijano, Aníbal. 1981. *Reencuentro y Debate: Una Introducción a Mariátegui*. Lima: Mosca Azul Editores.

Quijano, Aníbal. 2014. "Colonialidad de Poder y Clasificación Social." In *Aníbal Quijano: Cuestiones y Horizontes*. Ed. Danilo Assis Clímaco, 285–330. Buenos Aires: CLACSO.

Raby, Diana. 2006. *Democracy and Revolution: Latin America and Socialism Today.* New York: Pluto Press.

Radhakrishnan, Rajagopalan. 2006. "When Is Democracy Political?" *boundary 2* 33(2): 103–122.

Ramos Rodríguez, Froilán. 2010. "La inmigración en la administración de Pérez Jiménez (1952–1958)." *CONHISREMI, Revista Universitaria Arbitraa de Investigación y Diálogo Académico* 6(3): 29–43.

Rancière, Jacques. 1999. *Disagreement: Politics and Philosophy.* Minneapolis: University of Minnesota Press.

Rancière, Jacques. 2001. "Ten Theses on Politics." *Theory & Event* 5(3): http://www.colorado.edu/humanities/ferris/Courses/1968/Ranciere/Ten%20Theses/Ranciere_Ten%20Theses%20on%20Politics_Theory%20and%20Event5.3_2001.pdf. Accessed August 10, 2016.

Rancière, Jacques. 2004. *Disagreement: Politics and Philosophy.* Minneapolis: University of Minnesota Press.

Robinson, Max. 2005. *La Raíz Robinsoniana de la Revolución Bolivariana en Venezuela.* Caracas: Instituto Municipal de Publicaciones, Alcadía de Caracas.

Robinson, William. 2007. "Promoting Polyarchy in Latin America: The Oxymoron of 'Market Democracy.'" In *Latin America After Neoliberalism: Turning the Tide in the 21st Century?*, ed. Eric Hershberg and Fred Rosen, 96–119. New York: The New Press.

Rodríguez, Simón. 1916. *Defensa de Bolívar.* Caracas: Ediciones de la Imprenta Bolívar.

Rodríguez, Simón. 1990. *Sociedades Americanas.* Ed. Oscar Rodríguez Ortiz. Caracas: Biblioteca Ayacucho.

Rodríguez, Simón. 2004. *Inventamos o Erramos.* Caracas: Bilioteca Básica de Autores Venezolanos.

Rodríguez O, Jaime. 1998. *The Independence of Spanish America.* Cambridge: Cambridge University Press.

Rodríguez Rojas, Pedro. 2014. "¿José Tomás Boves: Trano o Líder Popular?" May 12, 2014. http://www.aporrea.org/ideologia/a199336.html. Accessed August 14, 2015.

Roediger, David. 1999. *The Wages of Whiteness: Race and the Making of the American Working Class.* New York: Verso.

Rojas, Daniel. 2008. *Simbiosis de los Simones: Socialismo desde el Alba.* Maracay: Fundación Aldeas.

Rothker, Susana. 2002. "Cities Written by Violence." In *Citizens of Fear: Urban Violence in Latin America*, ed. Susana Rothker, 7–22. New Brunswick: Rutgers University Press.

Rumbo Propio. 2006. "Nuestra Forma de Pensar." http://web.archive.org/web/20081009142942/http://www.rumbopropio.org.ve/rumbopropio/index.php. Accessed April 25, 2015.

Sader, Emir. 2011. *The New Mole: Paths of the Latin American Left*. New York: Verso.

Salas, Ricardo. 2005. *Pensamiento Crítico Latinoamericano: Conceptos Fundamentales*. Santiago de Chile: Ediciones Universidad Católica Silva Henríquez.

Salas de Lecuna, Yolanda. 1987. *Bolívar y la Historia en la Conciencia Popular*. Caracas: Universidad Simón Bolívar, Instituto de Altos Estudios de América Latina.

Sánchez Otero, Germán. 2012. *La Nube Negra: Golpe Petrolera en Venezuela*. Caracas: PDVSA.

Sanjuán, Ana María. 2002. "Democracy, Citizenship, and Violence in Venezuela." In *Citizens of Fear: Urban Violence in Latin America*, ed. Susana Rothker, 87–101. New Brunswick: Rutgers University Press.

Sanoja Obediente, Mario. 2011. *Historia Sociocultural de la Economía Venezolano*. Caracas: Banco Central de Venezuela.

Schild, Veronica. 2013. "Care and Punishment in Latin America: The Gendered Neoliberalism of the Chilean State." In *Neoliberalism, Interrupted: Social Change and Contested Governance in Contemporary Latin America*, ed. Mark Goodale and Nancy Grey Postero, 169–194. Palo Alto: Stanford University Press.

Schmitt, Carl. 1996. *The Concept of the Political*. Trans. G. Schwab. Chicago: University of Chicago Press.

Schmitt, Carl. 2004. *Legality and Legitimacy*. Trans. J. Seitzer. Durham: Duke University Press.

Schmitt, Carl. 2007. "The Age of Neutralizations and Depoliticization." In *The Concept of the Political, Expanded Edition*, ed. Tracy B. Strong, 80–96. Chicago: University of Chicago Press.

Schmitt, Carl. 2008. *Constitutional Theory*. Durham: Duke University Press.

Schmitt, Carl. 2013. *Dictatorship: From the Origin of the Modern Concept of Sovereignty to the Proletarian Class Struggle*. Ed. Michael Hoelzl and Graham Ward. Malden: Polity.

Schweber, Howard. 2007. *The Language of Liberal Constitutionalism*. Cambridge: Cambridge University Press.

Scott, James. 1998. *Seeing Like a State: How Certain Schemes to Improve the Human Condition Have Failed*. New Haven: Yale University Press.

Serrera, Ramón María. 1994. "Sociedad Estamental y Sistema Colonial." In *De los Imperios a las Naciones*, ed. Antonio Annino, Luís Castro Leiva, and François-Xavier Guerra, 45–74. Madrid: IberCaja.

Sieyès, Emmanuel. 2003. *Political Writings*. New York: Cambridge University Press.

Silva, René, and Víctor Uribe. 2014. "Spanish American Royalism in the Age of Revolution." *Latin American Research Review* 49(1): 270–281.

Sitrin, Marina. 2006. *Horizontalism: Voices of Popular Power in Argentina*. Oakland: AK Press.

Smith, William. 2007. "Multiculturalism, Identity, and the Articulation of Citizenship: The 'Indian Question' Now." *Latin American Research Review* 42(1): 238–251.

Smolansky, David. 2014. "Alcade de El Hatillo pide a vecinos protestas con 'impacto Positive.'" *El Universal Online*. February 24, 2014. http://www. eluniversal.com/caracas/140224/alcalde-de-el-hatillo-pide-a-vecinos-protestas-con-impacto-positivo. Accessed May 12, 2014.

de Sousa Santos, Boaventura (ed). 2007. *Another Knowledge Is Possible: Beyond Western Epistemologies*. New York: Verso.

de Sousa Santos, Boaventura. 2010. *Refundación del Estado en América Latina: Perspectivas desde una Epistemología del Sur*. Buenos Aires: Antropofagia.

Spång, Mikael. 2014. *Constituent Power and Constitutional Order: Above, Within, and Beside the Constitution*. New York: Palgrave Macmillan.

Spronk, Susan, and Jeffery Webber. 2011. "The Bolivarian Process in Venezuela: A Left Forum, with George Ciccariello-Maher, Roland Denis, Steve Ellner, Sujatha Fernandes, Michael Lebowitz, Sara Motta, and Thomas Purcell." *Historical Materialism* 19(1): 233–270.

Steinsleger, José. 2007. "Venezuela y el Separatismo Zuliano." April 11, 2007. http://www.jornada.unam.mx/2007/04/11/index. php?section=opinion&article=020a2pol. April 25, 2015.

Stoler, Ann Laura. 1995. *Race and the Education of Desire: Foucault's History of Sexuality and the Colonial Order of Things*. Durham: Duke University Press.

Sunkara, Bhaskar. 2012. "Hugo Chávez as Postmodern Perón." *Dissent* 59: 22–24.

Swyngedouw, Erik. 2009. "The Antinomies of the Post-Political City: In Search of a Democratic Politics of Environmental Production." *International Journal of Urban and Regional Research* 33(3): 601–620.

Taussig, Michael. 1997. *The Magic of the State*. New York: Routledge.

TeleSur. 2009. "Venezuela conmemora 20 aniversario de El Caracazo." http://www.telesurtv.net/noticias/secciones/nota/43829-NN/venezuela-conmemoro-20-aniversario-de-el-caracazo/2009. Accessed February 30, 2009.

TeleSur. 2014. "Conozca qué son las 'guarimbas' en Venezuela y quiénes están detrás." March 12, 2014. http://www.telesurtv.net/news/Conozca-que-son-las-guarimbas-en-Venezuela-y-quienes-estan-detras-20140312-0050.html. Accessed March 30, 2014.

Tinker Salas, Miguel. 2009. *The Enduring Legacy: Oil, Culture, and Society in Venezuela*. Durham: Duke University Press.

Tinker Salas, Miguel. 2014. "What Is Happening in Venezuela?" *CEPR Americas Blog*. March 4, 2014. http://www.cepr.net/blogs/the-americas-blog/what-is-happening-in-venezuela/. Accessed March 10, 2014.

Tinoco Guerra, Antonio. 2010. "Arturo Uslar Prieti y el Antipositivismo en Venezuela." *Utopía y Praxis Latinoamericana* 15(48): 97–105.

Tucker, Aviezer. 2008. "Pre-Emptive Democracy: Oligarchic Tendencies in Deliberative Democracy." *Political Studies* 56: 127–147.

Urdaneta, Joheni. 2012. "El Transporte Público Urbano en Venezuela: Hacia la inclusión Social?" *Revista de Ciencias Sociales* 18(3): 449–461.

Urueña Cervera, Jaime. 2007. *Bolívar Republicano: Fundamentos Ideológicos e Históricos de su Pensamiento Político*. Bogotá: Ediciones Aurora.

Uslar-Pietri, Arturo. 1954. "Prólogo." *Escritos de Simón Rodríguez, Tomo 1*, ed. Pedro Grases. Caracas: Imprenta Nacional.

Valencia, Cristobal. 2015. *We Are the State! Barrio Activism in Venezuela's Bolivarian Revolution*. Tucson: University of Arizona Press.

Vallenilla Lanz, Laureano. 1980. "Disagregación e integración (la influencia de los viejos conceptos)." In *Pensamiento Positivista Latinoamericano*, ed. Leopoldo Zea, 364–392. Caracas: Biblioteca Ayacucho.

Velasco, Alejandro. 2011. "'We Are Still Rebels': The Challenge of Popular History in Bolivarian Venezuela." In *Venezuela's Bolivarian Democracy: Participation, Politics, and Culture under Chávez*, ed. David Smilde and Daniel Hellinger, 157–185. Durham: Duke University Press.

Velasco, Alejandro. 2015. *Barrio Rising: Urban Popular Politics and the Making of Modern Venezuela*. Berkeley: University of California Press.

Venezolana de Televisión. 2014. "Con actividades culturales y intrega de volantes trabajadores de Metro iniciaron jornada de paz." *VTV Online*. April 2, 2014. http://www.vtv.gob.ve/articulos/2014/04/02/con-actividades-culturales-y-entrega-de-volantes-trabajadores-metro-iniciaron-jornada-por-la-paz-4079.html. Accessed October 1, 2015.

Venezolana de Televisión. 2016a. "Maduro: Frente a Parlamento Adeco-Burgués, Congreso de la Patria." April 11, 2016. http://www.vtv.gob.ve/articulos/2016/04/11/maduro-frente-a-parlamento-adeco-burgues-congreso-de-la-patria-5596.html. Accessed May 1, 2016.

Venezolano de Televisión. 2016b. "Investigaciones Determinan Vinculación de PoliChacao con Asesinato de Ricardo Durán." http://www.vtv.gob.ve/articulos/2016/06/20/investigaciones-determinan-vinculacion-de-polichacao-con-asesinato-de-ricardo-duran-video-1289.html. Accessed May 1, 2016.

Vielma, Franco. 2016. "¿Quién es el enemigo de los autores de la guerra económica?" http://misionverdad.com/la-guerra-en-venezuela/quien-es-el-enemigo-de-los-autores-de-la-guerra-economica. Accessed May 22, 2016.

Virilio, Paul. 1986. *Speed and Politics*. Los Angeles: Semiotext(e).

Virilio, Paul, and Sylvère Lotringer. 1997. *Pure War*. Los Angeles: Semiotext(e).

Virno, Paolo. 1996. "Virtuosity and Revolution: The Political Theory of Exodus." In *Radical Thought in Italy: A Potential Public*, ed. Michael Hardt and Paolo Virno, 189–212. Minneapolis: University of Minnesota Press.

Virno, Paolo. 2004. *A Grammar of the Multitude*. New York: Semiotext(e).

Virno, Paolo. 2006. "Paolo Virno: Una Visión de los Movimientos Sociales, desde el Autonomismo Italiano—Entrevista con Verónica Gago." *Paginaı2.* September 25, 2006. http://www.paginaı2.com.ar/diario/ dialogos/21-73518-2006-09-25.html. Accessed October 20, 2006.

de Vitoria, Francisco. 1991. *Political Writings.* Trans. A. Pagden and J. Lawrence. New York: Cambridge University Press.

Von Vocano, Diego. 2012. *The Color of Citizenship: Race, Modernity, and Latin America.* New York: Oxford University Press.

Wallerstein, Immanuel. 2003. "Citizens All? Citizens Some! The Making of the Citizen." *Comparative Studies in Society and History* 45(4): 650–679.

Weisbrot, Mark, Rebecca Ray, and Luis Sandoval. 2009. *The Chávez Administration at 10 Years: The Economy and Social Indicators.* Washington, DC: Center for Economic and Policy Research.

Wilpert, Gregory. 2003. "Collision in Venezuela." *New Left Review* 21: 101–116.

Wilpert, Gregory. 2007a. *Changing Venezuela by Taking Power: The History and Policies of the Chávez Government.* New York: Verso.

Wilpert, Gregory. 2007b. "Making Sense of Venezuela's Constitutional Reform." https://venezuelanalysis.com/analysis/2943. Accessed January 10, 2015.

Wolin, Sheldon. 2004. *Politics and Vision.* Princeton: Princeton University Press.

Wollstonecraft, Mary. 1995. *A Vindication of the Rights of Women* and *A Vindication of the Rights of Man.* New York: Cambridge University Press.

World Bank. 2016. "Governance for Growth with Equity in Latin America." *Cuentas Claras, Montevideo, Uruguay.* http://www.worldbank.org/en/ events/2016/01/29/conferencia-regional-cuentas-claras. Accessed June 10, 2016.

Wright, Steven. 2002. *Storming Heaven: Class Composition and Struggle in Italian Autonomist Marxism.* London: Pluto Press.

Wright, Thomas. 2001. *Latin America in the Age of the Cuban Revolution, Revised Edition.* London: Praeger Books.

Yashar, Deborah. 1999. "Democracy, Indigenous Movements, and the Postliberal Challenge in Latin America." *World Politics* 52(1): 76–104.

Young, Iris Marion. 2001. "Activist Challenges to Deliberative Democracy." *Political Theory* 29(5): 670–690.

YVKE Mundial. 2014. "Minister El Troudi: Acciones contra Trabajador del Metro Fueron Ejecutadas por un Comando Terrorista." *Aporrea.org.* http:// www.aporrea.org/actualidad/n250379.html. Accessed March 10, 2016.

Zamora, Antonio. 2006. *Memorias de la Guerrilla Venezolana.* Caracas: El Perro y la Rana.

Žižek, Slavoj. 2008. *In Defense of Lost Causes.* New York: Verso.

Žižek, Slavoj, 2011. *Living in the End Times.* New York: Verso.

Zubillaga, Verónica. 2013. "Menos Desigualdad Más Violencia La Paradoja de Caracas." *Nueva Sociedad* 243: 104–118.

Index

www.ingramcontent.com/pod-product-compliance
Lightning Source LLC
Chambersburg PA
CBHW020349270326
41926CB00007B/365